Praise for *Fearless Leadership*
by Loretta Malandro, Ph.D.

"This is not another theoretical business book. It is a book about fearless leadership in action—the spirit, resiliency, quick alignment, and the ability of teams to generate possibilities and results despite tough economic conditions. The process Loretta describes in this book works—if you have the courage to lead in a new way."

Jim Gowans,
President and CEO,
De Beers Canada

"The most difficult leadership challenge is changing behaviors. For companies to be different, leaders must lead differently. Loretta is the best at helping make these concepts real and actionable."

David M. Thomas,
former Chairman and CEO, IMS Health,
and former Senior VP, IBM

"Successful leaders take a hard stand about paying for performance, and do not fall into the trap of paying for effort. Loretta tells leaders exactly how to accomplish this by creating an environment where people take personal accountability, collaborate, and hold each other accountable for consistent exceptional results."

Raj Gupta,
Chairman and CEO,
Rohm and Haas Company

"Once again Dr. Malandro hits the bull's-eye. This book articulates a powerful strategy for leaders who aspire to be more than ordinary by building a high performance culture that produces consistent extraordinary results. I know it works. With her help, I have been there and have reveled in the success."

Frank Patalano,
former Chief Operating Officer,
Zurich North America

"Loretta's book is a powerful road map for anyone committed to being a transformational leader. It provides clear, actionable steps that drive organizational growth and long-term success."

Raj Rawal,
Senior Vice President and Chief Information Officer,
Burger King Corporation

"*Fearless Leadership* is an exciting and valuable book that will profoundly influence global leaders at a time when a new approach is urgently needed. This book is a compelling call to action that every leader must read."

John J. Ryan,
President and CEO,
Rabo AgriFinance

"This groundbreaking book is the first to clearly identify the behavioral barriers to change that every leader faces and provides a powerful solution that every leader can apply. Based on the business results we have achieved, I can tell you unequivocally that the process Loretta describes in this book works."

J. LaMont Keen,
President and CEO,
Idaho Power

"Loretta knows how to build a management team that will give any company a clear competitive advantage. She has described it all in this new book. A book that is sure to make it to the 'must read' list of business books in 2009 and beyond."

Frank Proto,
Chairman of the Board,
Agrium Inc.

"This insightful book clearly identifies how behavior sabotages personal and organizational success, and what to do about it. The powerful solution provided by Malandro— 100% Accountability—is exactly what every company needs, especially today."

Greg Stewart, P.Ag.,
President and CEO,
Farm Credit Canada

"At a time of unprecedented challenges to complicated academic and research institutions and when complacency from past successes collides with the harshness of today's environment, new leadership solutions are required. This thought provoking book provides leaders with new perspectives and skills that can be of immediate impact."

Michael A. Friedman, MD,
President and CEO,
City of Hope

FEARLESS

LEADERSHIP

How to Overcome Behavioral Blind Spots and Transform Your Organization

LORETTA MALANDRO, Ph.D.

New York   Chicago   San Francisco   Lisbon   London
Madrid   Mexico City   Milan   New Delhi
San Juan   Seoul   Singapore   Sydney   Toronto

Copyright © 2009 by The McGraw-Hill Companies, Inc. All rights reserved. Printed in the United States of America. Except as permitted under the United States Copyright Act of 1976, no part of this publication may be reproduced or distributed in any form or by any means, or stored in a database or retrieval system, without the prior written permission of the publisher.

The following are trademarks of Malandro Communication Inc.: 100% *Accountability* and *100%-zero Accountability*.

1 2 3 4 5 6 7 8 9 0   DOC/DOC   0 1 5 4 3 2 1 0 9

ISBN   978-0-07-162464-0
MHID 0-07-162464-3

McGraw-Hill books are available at special quantity discounts to use as premiums and sales promotions, or for use in corporate training programs. To contact a representative, please e-mail us at bulksales@mcgraw-hill.com.

This book is printed on acid-free paper.

Library of Congress Cataloging-in-Publication Data

Malandro, Loretta A.
   Fearless leadership : how to overcome behavioral blind spots and transform your organization / by Loretta Malandro.
      p. cm.
   ISBN 0-07-162464-3 (alk. paper)
   1. Leadership. 2. Organizational change. I. Title.

HD57.7.M346 2010
658.4'092—dc22   2009011284

Contents

Introduction   v

PART I: **Identifying Blind Spots and What Triggers Them**   1

Chapter 1: What It Means to Be a Fearless Leader   3

Chapter 2: The Blind Spots That Derail Leaders   33

Chapter 3: The Need to Be Right   63

Chapter 4: Victim Mentality and Playing Small   89

PART II: **Taking a Stand and Transforming Your Organization**   115

Chapter 5: Changing Your Direction and Taking a Bold Stand   117

Chapter 6: Standing for the Success of Each Other   145

Chapter 7: Honoring and Fulfilling Commitments   173

Chapter 8: Talking Straight Responsibly   199

Chapter 9: Aligning Emotionally and Intellectually   219

Chapter 10: Holding Each Other Accountable   247

Chapter 11: 100% Accountability: A New Canvas on Which to Paint the Future   267

About the Author and Malandro Communication   281

Acknowledgments   283

Index   285

Introduction

I was having a cup of coffee with a CEO of a global company when he said, "I'm a big fan of leadership books. I love learning all the latest concepts like synergism, emotional intelligence, team learning, and dialogue. But I have absolutely no idea how to apply them." This wasn't the first time I had heard this comment. Several months prior, I was speaking to a group of executives from the energy industry. The CEO of a major utility company came up after my presentation and said, "I like your explanation of how to build a high performance organization in such a no-nonsense manner. I know what I want, but I don't know how to get there. Would you help me?"

It took one more encounter for the message to hit home. I was working with a senior leader who had at least a half dozen leadership books on his desk. He said, "According to these books, I need to develop my attunement, orchestrate a massive cascade, harmonize individual energies, and be a pathfinder. All I want is an aligned team. How the heck do I do this?"

The message snapped into place: CEOs, executives, and leaders wanted to know how to take intellectual abstraction and turn it into practical action that could be integrated into the fabric of their organizations.

Although every organization is unique and there is no one-size-fits-all approach, it was clear to me that leaders needed a comprehensive road map for how to engage and align people to work together effectively to achieve enterprise objectives. These leaders viewed transforming their organization as an urgent priority. They wanted a method that would accomplish this transformation during their tenure in office, not a long, arduous, intergenerational process.

Our organization, Malandro Communication, had developed and perfected a methodology that was now in its maturity stage (approaching 30 years) and had successfully helped hundreds of organizations worldwide across all industries get to where they wanted to go, fast. From years of experience, we had gathered irrefutable data and case examples of how organizational change is unsustainable without behavioral change. The knowledge and expertise in this book were developed from working with thousands of executives and leaders in diverse industries—from Fortune 500 to midsize companies in Asia, Australia, Canada, Europe, South Africa, South America, and the United States.

When executives and leaders call on us, they are either frustrated with the slow pace of change or completely unhinged by the fact that change isn't happening at all. They tell us that they have tried everything but still have unaligned leaders, disengaged employees, silos, and unhealthy competition. These leaders are unwilling to settle for less; they know exactly what they want: the shortest and most effective route to mobilize people to deliver unprecedented business results.

Our group identified and documented common blind spots of leaders and teams that derailed major initiatives, process and system changes, careers, and long-term organizational success. What became evident was the courage required of leaders to successfully transform their organizations. These fearless leaders confronted their blind spots, turned values into explicit behavioral standards, provided people with the tools to learn and apply new behaviors, and integrated them into how business was conducted on a daily basis. This is *fearless leadership*: taking a bold stand, acting decisively, and engaging with others in an extraordinary way.

This book is for leaders who are unwilling to tolerate anything less than aligned and highly engaged people. It is for leaders who want to take their team, group, or organization to the next level of performance. It is for leaders who are frustrated with complacency, the slow rate of change, and recurring breakdowns between people and groups.

This book will make a difference for you if any (or all) of the following is true:

- You want to develop your leadership effectiveness to engage and align people and mobilize them to action.
- You want to successfully navigate your company through large-scale change.

- You want to optimize organizational efficiency and effectiveness, and you know much more can be achieved.
- You are frustrated with the slow pace of organizational change and the lack of sustainability: nothing seems to stick.
- You have noticed that your level of enthusiasm and passion are not what they used to be, and this is unacceptable to you.
- You are frustrated by ineffective teamwork, unproductive meetings, lack of collaboration, and a negative work environment.
- You are concerned about the low level of employee engagement in spite of numerous attempts to raise it.
- You want to build a team, business, or organization that is best of breed.

Perhaps you have encountered a roadblock or hit an impasse in your personal leadership effectiveness. Nothing has changed in your commitment and you continue to put in long hours, but something is missing—something is holding you back. Your mind may be wandering to the land of "what if?" "What if I change my job, change my organization, change profession, change location, change career, change my boss, change companies?" You have been asking every "what if" question except one:

What if you discover that behavioral blind spots are the barrier and change that first?

That's why I've written this book—to help you with that very question, *before* you change anything else. *Fearless Leadership* provides you with a proven methodology for expanding your capacity to achieve maximum effectiveness in any circumstance. This book is for leaders who have the inner strength and courage to demand the highest level of accountability and integrity from themselves and others. This is leadership in its truest sense.

I have spent my career surrounded by fearless leaders, and I cannot imagine a world without them. They have inspired and moved me. Over the years we have worked with courageous leaders to take on the most daunting challenges, and have triumphed. We have helped them expand their effectiveness and accelerate long-term organizational success with the methodology described in this book: 100% Accountability™. This methodology engages people to turn fundamental values into a uniform behavioral framework that raises the level of performance and results.

After receiving my Ph.D. in communication theory and research from Florida State University, I served as a professor at Florida State and Arizona State universities. In 1980, I started my company, and one of my early clients recommended me to an executive at IBM, where I was asked to develop and deliver leadership programs at their corporate headquarters in Armonk, New York. IBM leaders grew my company as they asked for more services worldwide. Word spread and my organization grew, which led to our working with leaders in many prestigious corporations and institutions.

In this book, I share the solutions we have discovered through working with thousands of leaders and executives. Part I focuses on identifying the behavioral barriers that prevent leadership and organizational transformation—blind spots—and what triggers them. Part II reveals how to master a methodology for transforming yourself and your organization, and unleashing the power of people to deliver exceptional results.

Throughout the book, I've included case examples based on our work with many different organizations—though of course, the companies and individuals have been given fictitious names. Some examples are composites to better illustrate a specific point. In addition to these real-life examples, which bring these problems and solutions to life, I've included questionnaires, guidelines, and tools to help you master an extraordinary way of engaging with others.

Finally, each chapter ends with a section on *leadership exploration* and *leadership action* because this book is not meant to be a theoretical, interesting-to-read, put-on-your-shelf book; it's intended to propel you, your team, and your organization into action.

My commitment to you is that our exploration together catapults you into a new era of leadership. It is my objective to provide you with a compelling call to be a fearless leader who plays big and expands the capacity of people and the organization to survive and succeed. Let's get started.

PART

I

IDENTIFYING BLIND SPOTS AND WHAT TRIGGERS THEM

Before you can solve the problems that prevent your company or team from achieving optimal performance, you need to fully understand the underlying behavioral issues that block sustainable organizational change, efficiency, and effectiveness. The four chapters in Part I of this book help you do exactly that.

Chapter 1 starts off with what fearless leadership is and how applying it can help an organization overcome unproductive behaviors that undermine change and prevent a robust capacity in the organization.

Chapter 2 explores the 10 most common blind spots of leaders and how they sabotage success, leadership alignment, and teamwork and at a significant cost to the organization.

Chapter 3 focuses on the all-too-common "need to be right" whereby leaders defend their personal views or positions, build silos, engage in unhealthy competition, and lose sight of their Number 1 accountability: to achieve enterprise objectives in partnership with others.

Finally, Chapter 4 looks at how victim mentality and conspiring against others lock in a cycle of unproductive behaviors that strangle an organization's ability to be agile, nimble, and resilient, especially in challenging times.

There is good news in all of this. Once you understand what triggers automatic and unproductive behaviors, you can master the methodology taught in Part II for transforming them into *extraordinary* behaviors that propel your organization into high performance.

Chapter
1
What It Means to Be a Fearless Leader

The price of greatness is responsibility.

—WINSTON CHURCHILL (1874–1965)

We need fearless leaders. Not one, but many. In times of chaos and uncertainty, as well as in good times, we need leaders who take a bold stand, act decisively, and engage with others in an extraordinary way.

You have two choices in front of you. One path is comfortable, safe, and familiar; the goal is to improve something you are already doing or fine-tune your blueprint for success. People are content with your decision to make incremental changes because it only requires modest effort from them.

The second choice compels you to move in a new direction and create a new reality. Even though this new direction requires additional effort, people are inspired by your courage to take a bold stand and act decisively. They willingly give you their energy, enthusiasm, and emotional commitment. This second choice requires *fearless leadership*—the courage to risk what is safe and comfortable to achieve a much higher level of success.

You have the power to shape the future. This is not in question. But do you have the courage to take a bold stand and transform the capacity and capability of people and the organization to achieve much more?

Fearless leadership is not a concept; it is an action. It is defined by the choices you make, how you take accountability for results and people, and how you interact with others.

> **Fearless Leadership**
> The courage to take a bold stand, act decisively, and engage with others in an extraordinary way.

It does not matter what you do or where you are in the organization. Title, position, status, and hierarchy do not characterize fearless leadership; it is defined by behavior, attitude, and results. You have the power to transform what you and others can create and achieve together. What you need is a powerful process for how people work together to make change happen fast and keep it going through good times and difficult challenges. This book provides you with a road map for transforming your leadership effectiveness, your team, and your organization.

In this chapter, we begin with the question, "What is holding us back?" which must be answered on two levels: what is holding *you* back, and what is holding your team or organization back?

Together we explore

- The promise and results of fearless leadership
- How changing behavior can change what an organization can achieve
- Why the organization doesn't change until the leaders do
- How a clear vision is blocked by vague behavioral standards
- The critical difference between gaining commitment versus unleashing commitment
- How fearless leadership is defined by extraordinary behavior, attitude, and results

You have a choice about the future—how you engage with others, how you contribute to the organization, and how you shape and influence change. The choice in front of you now is, "Are you willing to face the enemy head on and confront anything that is in the way of your optimal effectiveness and the organization's success?"

THE PROMISE AND RESULTS OF FEARLESS LEADERSHIP

Your business success as a leader is measured by the speed at which you produce results and bring new realities into existence. Fearless leadership provides you with the methodology and tools to unite and mobilize people to work together effectively in a way that drives change throughout the organization.

The promise of fearless leadership is fast individual and organizational transformation. It takes only one person to start the process. You have the ability to influence change and dramatically increase engagement, alignment, and business results. As a fearless leader, you have

- The capacity to eliminate barriers that block your leadership effectiveness
- The courage to take a stand and act decisively with renewed confidence and passion
- The freedom to choose a new level of participation and engagement
- The methodology and tools to transform individuals, teams, and organizations

Fearless leadership provides you with a methodology for breaking the cycle of unproductive and automatic behavior, and it teaches you and others how to engage in an extraordinary way. The first part of the book is designed to help you understand and identify blind spots and talk about them in a constructive way so you can overcome them. The second part helps you drive business results by creating a powerful context for organizational change, taking a bold leadership stand, and building trust and aligned action.

Building a high performance organization and positive work environment does not need to be a slow and laborious process. In traditional change processes, people are often the unwilling recipients of imposed change, which muddles the reaction and produces ineffective results. However, with fearless leadership, people choose to engage emotionally as well as intellectually, which alters organizational capability. The result: your most disbelieving and cynical people become the champions of change.

Organizations move rapidly from an ad hoc management approach to building a standard process and foundation for a world-class company.

People, strategy, and operations come together in a simple, fast, and effective manner as everyone applies a shared methodology for working together as committed partners.

It all sounds too good to be true. If fearless leadership is fast and easy to achieve, you may be thinking, then why isn't *everyone* using it? There is a caveat: to transform your organization, you must have the courage to examine your behavior and lead the way. If you want a recipe for how to fix others, this is it: fix yourself first, and others will respond to your commitment and follow suit.

THE NUMBER 1 LEADERSHIP QUESTION: "WHAT IS HOLDING US BACK?"

"Nothing is changing fast enough," said a frustrated CEO. "We have good people, good values, and a strong strategy, but change around here is painfully slow or just doesn't happen."

Frustrated with the slow pace of change, executives ask, "What is holding us back?" Employees, discouraged with countless ineffective change efforts, ask, "Why is this time any different?" People are not aligned, initiatives are derailed, and the organization does not transform.

The traditional formula for organizational success—good people, good values, and good strategy—is woefully inadequate to meet today's challenges. Although the traditional formula remains a necessary foundation for success, leaders who play a big-stakes game know they need to go beyond the formula. They understand that a complex and changing environment requires a new way of thinking and behaving. They anticipate challenges, continually envision what is needed, and ask the tough questions:

- "What is holding us back?"
- "What is preventing us from achieving a new level of performance?"
- "What is stopping our organization from moving faster, being more innovative, agile, and effective?"
- "What is stopping us from engaging our people to work more effectively together?"
- "What is blocking us from taking charge of our future and accomplishing what others believe is impossible?"

Here is the problem: How people behave and work together determines the success or failure of major change initiatives. Yet when leaders answer the question, "What is holding us back?" most focus exclusively on organizational change and fail to address the need for behavioral change.

The majority of leaders do not recognize the significant role that behavior plays in achieving the business results they want. The reality is that competent individuals do not spontaneously come together as a high performance team. A constructive and empowering work environment does not suddenly appear because the organization has been restructured. People do not routinely work effectively together because it is the right thing to do. Leaders do not align just because the organization has an aggressive strategy, clear vision, and strong values.

When people are emotionally disconnected from the organization and its leaders, they behave in counterproductive ways. They work in silos, fight for resources, and comply with directives but are uninspired.

Vision, mission, and values alone are insufficient for producing sustainable behavioral change. What most organizations are missing is a uniform process for people to align, collaborate, and work together across organizational boundaries. Without a standardized process, unproductive behavioral norms evolve by default. New rules of engagement are required to transform core values into an enduring behavioral framework that unites people to deliver exceptional results.

Although productive behavior is learned, unproductive behavior is automatic. People react instinctively to protect their interests, which results in unhealthy competition, defending turf, and divisiveness.

You already have a behavioral norm in your organization, but you may not be happy with the one you have. If you are experiencing recurring problems, a lackluster environment, low employee engagement, lack of leadership alignment, or ineffective and slow change, then the likelihood is high that the issue is behavioral. In the example below, Karl, the CEO of a global mining organization, failed to recognize a serious behavioral problem—the animosity between business units that was undermining the enterprise. Instead, he misdiagnosed the problem and fixated on organizational and structural change.

The Futile Endeavor of Trying to Manage People Issues with Business Solutions

Karl was comfortable troubleshooting business problems but uncomfortable managing people issues. Instead of dealing with behavioral issues head on, he focused on structural and organizational changes.

What Happened. After two years of infighting and undermining between business units, Karl asked his senior group what the Board had asked him: "What are you going to do about this?" Karl and his team argued and blamed each other, and they finally decided that the problem between business units could be fixed by restructuring a major division and replacing two managing directors. Not once did they examine, "How is our *behavior* as the senior team contributing to this problem?"

The Impact. A costly restructuring effort missed the point entirely; the real issue was the lack of leadership alignment and partnership. Leaders throughout the organization were discouraged and resigned; they felt that their input was not heard, valued, or considered.

In the end, senior leaders focused on organizational change but neglected to alter their behavior and transform how leaders worked together. Twelve months later, employee engagement scores hit an all time low and identified the lack of trust in leadership as the primary reason for the pessimistic and negative work environment. Top talent left the company for brighter prospects while Karl and his team remained mired in the same behavioral issues between business units.

Lesson Learned. Business solutions do not solve behavioral issues. Lack of leadership alignment and the absence of collaboration can be resolved only by confronting the underlying behavioral issues that perpetuate the problem.

You cannot transform an organization without transforming leadership behavior. Lasting behavioral change does not occur with traditional organizational change efforts. But change how leaders behave and you alter what the organization can achieve.

Behavior Drives Results

Business results are in direct proportion to how people work together. When leaders are not aligned and employees are not engaged, even the most brilliant business strategy will not succeed. How people behave and relate to the organization, coworkers, and leaders determines what is achieved. Unproductive behavior takes up your time, frustrates everyone in its path, and prevents the company from achieving its goals.

> Nothing works when people are not working together.

You cannot change how people behave with mandates, slogans, or programs-of-the-month. No amount of cajoling, persuading, or threatening will alter what people do. People will continue to behave in the same way; they will just take it underground where you cannot see it. The grapevine is the strongest communication network in companies that do not have an open and safe environment.

A culture of accountability is the hallmark of world-class organizations. These companies place a significant emphasis on how to maximize the value and contributions of people. They are distinguished by their unrelenting drive to create an environment in which people can perform at their best. Take a look at the top 10 attributes of the world's most successful companies shown below. As you read the list, identify which features apply to your organization and which attributes you need to develop.

You may clearly see the need for engaging and aligning people, but you may be looking for change in all the wrong places. Misdiagnosing people issues leads to (1) costly and ineffective business solutions—process and system changes—that do not resolve the underlying issues, and (2) an inconsistent leadership approach that lacks standardization and uniformity about how people are expected to behave.

Let's return to the question, "What is holding leaders and organizations back?" Transformation begins when leaders *choose* to change their behavior. The frequently misunderstood barrier to change is *behavioral blind spots*—automatic and unproductive behavior that blocks leadership effectiveness, organizational change, and business results.

The Top 10 Differences for the World's Most Admired Companies

1. **More effective at building clarity.** They are better at implementing strategy and simplifying complex organization structures.
2. **Have a stronger culture of accountability.** They excel at driving strategic accountability right down through the organization.
3. **Pay more attention to customers and growth.** They place greater focus on customer loyalty and long-term growth in performance measures.
4. **Are better at working across the organization and operating globally.** They place much more importance on leaders' working cross-organizationally, are more effective at it, and get more value from it.
5. **Have a stronger focus on innovation and resilience.** They are more effective at creating a culture of innovation and building resilience into the organization.
6. **Are better at climate management.** They more clearly understand the culture and more actively manage the climate of the organization.
7. **Have a stronger focus on people.** They are more effective at managing employee engagement and stronger commitment to internal development.
8. **Have a stronger focus on succession planning.** They apply a broader and more consistent approach to talent management.
9. **Have stronger leadership and focus on the top team.** Leaders are significantly better at self-management, empathy, teamwork, and collaboration.
10. **Are better at rewarding and giving recognition to attract and retain talent.** They have a stronger focus on total reward for and recognition of top performance.

Source: Adapted from a presentation by David Sissons, Vice President of Hay Group, Toronto, Canada, June 5, 2008.

THE LEADERSHIP IMPASSE: BLIND TO BLIND SPOTS

Blind spots include an entire array of ineffective and damaging behaviors such as conspiring against others, exhibiting an "I know" attitude, blaming people and circumstances, or treating commitments casually. In Chapter 2, we explore the 10 most common blind spots that derail leaders. For now, it is important to understand that both individuals and teams have blind spots that limit their effectiveness. Before you become hopeful that your company has escaped this malady, let me assure you that everyone has blind spots, even you. No one is immune, from CEOs to staff; blind spots abound in organizations of all sizes, geographic locations, and industries.

> **Behavioral Blind Spots**
> Unproductive behavior that undermines business results and working relationships.

Behavioral blind spots are similar to the blind spots we encounter when driving a vehicle. When driving, there are areas of the road that you cannot see while looking forward or through either rearview or side mirrors. Without other aids or adjustments of mirrors, blind spots can cause a serious accident. Most of us have experienced a time when we narrowly missed an alarming accident. As you begin to pull into a lane, you hear the blast of a horn from an angry driver just in time to avert a collision. Your heartbeat jumps, adrenalin pumps, and you quickly pull back into your lane. If you have had this experience, you will recognize the similarities between vehicular blind spots and behavioral blind spots:

1. They both have potential for causing serious damage.
2. They occur spontaneously and automatically.
3. There is no intention to hurt or injure another.

However, there is one significant difference between vehicular blind spots and behavioral blind spots: most people do not know that behavioral blind spots exist. Leaders who are blind to their blind spots have no way of avoiding repetitive breakdowns or having a negative impact on others. Self-awareness is essential in fearless leadership; without understanding how they impact others, leaders cannot alter their effectiveness and ability to influence others.

The challenge with blind spots is that you can readily see them in others, but you cannot see them in yourself. When you are blind to blind spots, you are left with poor choices such as working around people, tolerating ineffectiveness, and putting up with recurring problems.

The fastest way to cause morale to plummet is to deny that blind spots exist or ignore them and hope they go away. Either way, people become resigned when leaders do not take accountability for their impact on others. Then the inevitable happens: people give up believing that real change can take place.

When leaders are blind to their blind spots, they unintentionally create havoc in the organization, as revealed in the story below.

One Leader's Unrewarding Search for "New Dogs"

Aileen, the CEO of an international insurance company, saw the need for transformational change but she constantly focused on the deficiencies of others and ignored her role in leading change.

What Happened. Disgusted with the lack of leadership alignment, she threatened her senior team: *"If something doesn't change around here, I'm going to get new dogs to pull the sled."* Aileen's warning did not change behavior in a positive direction.

Exasperated, she fired her COO, reassigned an executive to another department, and brought in replacements. But even with "new dogs," the same problems remained. After the honeymoon period, leaders were still not aligned and execution continued to suffer.

The Impact. Aileen's new dog solution failed because there was still an *old dog* leading the pack: her. Her unwillingness to examine her impact as a leader was crippling to the group. Three other executives left the company, and Aileen struggled with a team that was not aligned but merely tolerated her leadership. Employees, disgruntled with mixed messages, divided into camps and backed the leader of their choice. The company lost major contracts, experienced a high turnover, and was unable to retain top talent. The senior group went from bad to worse, and in the end, the Board asked Aileen to resign.

Lesson Learned. Transformation starts with the leaders; if the leaders focus on changing others, they will fail. The fastest way to produce broad-based change is for leaders to alter their behavior, demonstrate accountability, and model what they expect from others.

When you cannot see a problem or do not believe there is a problem, nothing can be addressed. You will continue to do what you have always done, and when your behavior is unproductive, others will compensate by working around or avoiding you.

When leaders are unwilling to acknowledge and address their blind spots, the new dog solution of changing others becomes the easiest and most obvious thing to do. Here is the problem with this approach: people become resigned when leaders are unwilling to take accountability for their blind spots. When the leaders are rigid and inflexible, people adopt the belief that nothing can change.

Because team members have no way to communicate or address the leaders' blind spots in a safe environment, they do not speak up. The result: people shrink the game, reduce their focus to their area of responsibility, and performance suffers. They let leaders fend for themselves, and they emotionally withdraw from the team.

Before bringing in new dogs, leaders should stop and address the blind spots that keep their teams from performing at their optimal levels. If leaders ignore that step, even their most highly effective teams with talented people can become resigned, resulting in unproductive, automatic behavior.

One of the powerful tools you will learn in the chapters that follow is to identify how your behavior impacts your coworkers and team. By recognizing and overcoming your blind spots, you will learn how to increase your ability to unite and inspire others. When teams authentically confront their blind spots—individually and collectively—they openly discuss and resolve difficult issues, and resignation disappears. A cohesive, enthusiastic, and committed team emerges.

> **Change how people behave and you change what the organization can achieve.**

Blind spots are automatic, mechanical, and unconscious behaviors. They occur spontaneously and habitually, and they get worse in times of stress and anxiety. Unless you understand the hold that the automatic behavior has on you and others, you cannot alter it. Fearless leadership brings a clear distinction between automatic behavior and extraordinary behavior, which is covered in Chapter 5, "Changing Your Direction and Taking a Bold Stand."

To better grasp automatic behavior, it is important to understand that there is a positive intention behind most unproductive behavior. People, as a rule, do not intend to hurt, damage, or undermine others.

The question I have for you is, are you willing to examine your blind spots? We begin this process in earnest in Chapter 2. Keep in mind that (1) everyone has blind spots, and (2) blind spots are not bad, wrong, or malicious. They are automatic behaviors that each person experiences but no one talks about.

You Get What You Tolerate

What happens when companies ignore unproductive behavior? Our group worked with the CEO of a major business consulting company, who was experiencing challenges with his senior team. It became evident that there was one person in the group who was a lightning rod—we'll call him Doug. The rest of the group felt that the CEO let Doug get away with everything. Doug was condescending and made sarcastic comments such as "What's on your alleged mind?" He was personal in his insults. But because he was one of the top producers in the company, the CEO tolerated his behavior, and Doug was not held accountable for his impact. This sent a message to the organization that behavioral standards were applied inconsistently and arbitrarily.

It is not uncommon to see people spar with each other in meetings and nobody does anything to stop it. Even though it prolongs the meeting and makes the group unproductive, team members do not even acknowledge the problem. They simply allow the behavior and tension to continue. They are resigned and believe: "There's nothing we can do, and we are not accountable for how people behave."

> **The Unspoken Organizational Norm**
> Unproductive behavior is banned in principle but tolerated in practice.

In every organization, you can find a lack of teamwork, ineffective working relationships, and leaders who are not aligned. In a business-as-usual environment, low behavioral standards are tolerated, and people avoid unpleasant or uncomfortable conversations.

When was the last time you had a difficult conversation with an individual or put an issue on the table that made everyone uncomfortable? The more important question is, "What important conversations have you been postponing or unwilling to have?"

Because people are uncomfortable discussing behavior, they avoid the real issues and allow problems to fester. Most people do not know how to talk about behavior and blind spots in a positive manner, so they don't. Their belief is they have less chance of damaging the relationship by *not* talking about sensitive issues. When leaders do not deal with behavior in a consistent and effective manner, a new organizational norm emerges; unproductive behavior is banned in principle but tolerated in practice.

Without knowing it, you may be endorsing a behavioral standard that is undermining your leadership effectiveness and eating away at organizational performance. Leaders become so accustomed to unproductive behavior that they silently endorse it. When the real issues are not addressed and leaders are unwilling to confront their blind spots, people slow down or halt the progress of initiatives and change efforts.

Let's begin by examining the organizational norm that exists by default on your team or in your company. Answering the questions in Exhibit 1-1 will help you examine the behaviors you are tolerating in yourself and others.

Putting up with inconsistent and low standards of behavior impedes your effectiveness and thwarts organizational change. If you are tolerating something, chances are you are either unaware that you have accepted subpar behavior, or you are resigned that you cannot influence the change that is needed in your organization.

Directions: Using the scale below, complete the following assessment individually and with your team.

Scale:

1—Have not observed	**2**—Rarely	**3**—Some of the time
4—Frequently	**5**—Consistently	

Behaviors	Your Assessment	Team Assessment
1. Do you feel there are unresolved issues and problems that surface again and again?		
2. Are there unresolved conflicts between individuals on your team?		
3. Are there unresolved conflicts between your team and other groups in the organization?		
4. Is the work environment disempowering (unconstructive, uninspiring, pessimistic, or negative)?		
5. Do you align in meetings but conspire against others outside of meetings?		
6. Do you tolerate unproductive behavior in meetings?		
7. Does your organization ignore unproductive behavior or address it inconsistently?		
8. Do you talk behind each other's back instead of talking directly to each other?		
9. Do you trust the senior leaders?		
10. Do you trust the team leader and/or other immediate leaders?		
11. Do you trust the team members, and do they trust you?		
12. Do you hold others accountable for delivering on commitments?		
13. Do you blame, point the finger at, or complain about others or circumstances?		
14. Do you protect and defend your area (silo) to the exclusion of doing what is best for the enterprise as a whole?		
15. Do you have an unspoken truce with others to not hold each other accountable (that is, not to call each other out)?		

EXHIBIT 1-1: *Identifying Unproductive Behavior*

THE ORGANIZATION DOESN'T CHANGE UNTIL THE LEADERS DO

There is a sequence that must be followed in order to transform an organization. It is straightforward: leaders must go first. Leadership transformation is the precursor for organizational change. Leaders must take accountability for their blind spots, demonstrate how to work in committed partnerships, and build an environment where people are passionately focused on the enterprise mission.

> Leadership transformation is the precursor to organizational transformation.

As we discussed earlier, changing the organization does not guarantee a change in behavior. Changing behavior, however, decisively alters the organization. All eyes are on leaders, and when they change their behavior, everyone notices as they did in the case of Andre, the senior vice president of a business unit in a global information services company. After a powerful session with his senior team, Andre delivered the following webcast to his employees:

"A year ago I felt very concerned about our ability to effectively execute our strategic objectives. I had decided that there were not enough people 'in the game'—people who were fully committed and ready to do what it takes to produce our business outcomes. I felt as if I were the only one who was engaged, and I felt alone.

"I felt our senior team meetings did not lead us to productive action. We debated, argued, and defended our points of view. Several weeks ago, we participated in a leadership session with our consulting partners, and I discovered, much to my surprise, that I was not in the game. Instead, I was in the stands judging and evaluating others rather than partnering and supporting. My attention was on what others needed to do or change. What I learned was that leadership starts with me—what I need to do and change.

"What we need is to be an organization that works in partnership to capitalize on the diverse talents and contributions of our people.

What I need is to take accountability for my leadership. I learned several lessons that I want to share with you:

Lesson 1. *Nothing is ever accomplished alone; it is only accomplished through partnership.*

Lesson 2. *All action occurs in the game. The only thing that happens in the stands is that you get to be right about your point of view.*

Lesson 3. *I am not perfect and I need coaching.*

"I have a lot to learn, and I am up for the challenge. I need your partnership and support. Will you join me in learning how to work together as committed partners?"

Andre's webcast is a demonstration of courage. The moment he took accountability for his blind spots, others enthusiastically came on board. The response he received from his message was overwhelming. People asked, "How can I get involved?" "How can I learn these new skills?" and "What can I do to help the leaders and the organization transform?"

You cannot alter the direction of your organization without fearless leadership. People are counting on you. They need you to take the first step and demonstrate your unshakable resolve to transform yourself and the organization. Even the most skeptical are receptive to a courageous leader who takes a stand, acts decisively, and engages with others in an extraordinary way.

There are two factors that are instrumental to understanding transformation: (1) the importance of clear and explicit behavioral standards and (2) the distinction between gaining commitment versus unleashing commitment.

Clear Business Vision Blocked by Vague Behavioral Standards

Interestingly, most leaders provide clear and explicit *business* expectations but fail to provide the same when it comes to *behavior*.

I have two questions for you:

1. Do you clearly articulate explicit *behavioral* expectations?

2. Do you provide individuals and teams with the resources and tools to learn, standardize, and integrate new behaviors?

I am not referring to a list of competencies, strengths, or values. I am referring to a precise and clear list of behaviors that individuals and teams can learn. Most organizations do not have uniform, consistent, and standard behaviors, and they do not provide people with a means to learn new skills. When stress and uncertainty are high, people need a stable set of rules that define how they engage. Shared behaviors unite and inspire people. They allow everyone to be powerful and resourceful in addressing and resolving issues and in advancing the business agenda. In this dynamic culture, people are committed to the success of each other and do not allow unproductive behaviors to undermine business results.

The following are common, but inaccurate, assumptions that leaders make:

"Our company values describe our behavioral expectations."
Wrong. Company values provide important guiding concepts and principles; however, they do *not* delineate behavior. People need *shared behavioral standards* to translate your company's values into action that can be applied in day-to-day business interactions — *and you need to lead the way by telling them explicitly what those standards are.*

"Good behavior only requires common sense." *Wrong.*
Interacting effectively with others, especially where cultural differences are involved, is a learned behavior. And you, as a fearless leader, need to teach that behavior by your actions. For example, people need to see how you and senior leaders recover from mistakes, so they know they can do the same. They need you to model the behavior you expect of them.

"Telling people I expect them to work together is enough."
Wrong. Top-down messages about teamwork and collaboration do not, by themselves, change behavior. People need explicit behavioral expectations — what each company calls good or acceptable behavior. They need to learn, experience, and practice the new behaviors and make them part of the fabric of the organization.

"According to internal surveys, my team already has trust and
alignment." *Wrong*. Without third-party confidential surveys, *do
not trust the data*. Regardless of how effective you are as a leader,
people tell you only what you want to hear. They will not risk their
job, career, or good standing with you and others to give you candid
and honest feedback—especially when the feedback is on how *you*
need to improve your leadership. People need a safe environment
and process for talking about blind spots and other tough issues.
They need you to foster an open and constructive environment.

If any of the above assumptions apply to your organization, then this
book will help you. Establishing clear behavioral expectations is only the
first step in providing a framework for organizational effectiveness. You will
learn specific behaviors with precise guidelines and skills. These transformational behaviors achieve two objectives: (1) accelerate the accomplishment of business objectives, and (2) produce immediate business results.

Gaining Commitment or Unleashing Commitment

Most organizations do not lack committed people; what they have are
highly frustrated committed people. My guess is you have exactly this: people who want your organization to succeed and want to take pride in their
accomplishments.

A complaint is nothing more than a frustrated commitment. When people are resigned and discouraged, they complain, blame, and engage in
unhealthy competition. This unproductive behavior does not mean they
lack commitment. In fact, the opposite is true. People exert their energy
only when they care. When they do not care, they simply withdraw, emotionally and/or physically.

> Most organizations do not lack committed people; what they have
> are highly *frustrated* committed people.

If you are serious about organizational transformation, you must answer
a fundamental question: "Do you want to gain commitment from people,
or unleash the commitment they already have?" If your answer is to gain
commitment, you are starting with the assumption that it does not exist.

Your focus will be on what is missing, what you do not have, and what is defective, inadequate, or insufficient. Therefore, your solutions will also focus on "fixing" people, systems, and processes.

When your purpose is to unleash the commitment of people, you bring compassion and heartfelt understanding. You seek to understand how people have become resigned, and you gain an appreciation for the depth of their caring and commitment. You grasp that people truly want to give you the best they have but they do not know how to do this.

The automatic response to people when they are resigned is "You shouldn't feel this way" or "You need to get over this." But when you understand that resignation is a frustrated commitment, you can appreciate and care for people in a new way. When others know that you understand their disappointment and struggle, they give you their emotional commitment. With this, you can create a powerful and inspiring platform to help people renew their confidence and enthusiasm.

Unleashing the commitment of people sets the framework for transformation. Leaders who have the view that people are inadequate, insufficient, or not committed commonly display emotions of disappointment, anger, and frustration. It is hard for anyone to be inspired by these emotions, including the leaders.

If you start with the belief that you already have committed people, you will avoid the common pitfall of acting as if something is missing. When you unleash the commitment of people, you have everything you need. The power of your change effort comes from believing in people and helping them feel reenergized, emotionally connected, and passionate about shaping the future.

To build a positive platform for change, your focus must shift from fixing people to empowering them. To do that, people need to know you believe in them. The only way to convey your belief in them is to communicate with them authentically. They will view anything less than that as dishonest or false, and you will lose credibility and trust.

You are ready to pursue fearless leadership if you believe

- People have an inner need to do their best.
- People want to have a purpose, not just a job.
- People want to be fully engaged.

- People give their effort and enthusiasm when they are inspired.
- People produce extraordinary results when they work together as a winning team.

FEARLESS LEADERSHIP IS DEFINED BY BEHAVIOR, ATTITUDE, AND RESULTS

Leaders are often categorized as being results oriented or people oriented. Fearless leaders excel at both. They have the ability to connect with people and mobilize them to action that delivers exceptional business results.

The extraordinary way in which fearless leaders work together is what allows aligned, cohesive, and seamless teams to emerge. A high performance team requires fearless leaders. These teams are distinguished from business-as-usual groups by their behavior, attitude, and results.

Let's work with an accurate description of teams versus groups. Business-as-usual groups are not really teams at all; they are "bands of individuals" because they lack the solidarity, camaraderie, and cohesion of high performance teams. In traditional groups, members deny they have blind spots and cover up their mistakes in an effort to look good and be right. Group members lack trust and respect for one another and are often divisive and adversarial. Many business-as-usual groups appear polite and affable, but this is a pretense that masks unresolved bitterness between individuals. One client described her "polite group" as follows: "No one drives the debate or pushes issues forcefully enough, and we don't give each other the real, hard feedback. I'm exhausted at the end of each long meeting."

> **What cannot be addressed, cannot be resolved.**
> Unresolved issues sap everyone's energy.

Business-as-usual groups are indirect, underhanded, and conspire against each other and the organization. Although this may sound harsh, it is an accurate description of how traditional groups behave. This is not malicious behavior; it is automatic behavior.

Often people are unaware of their impact on others. And even those people who are aware often lack the skill set to address unproductive behavior in a productive way.

A pivotal difference between high performance teams and business-as-usual groups is that high performance teams identify, confront, and overcome blind spots. By having a method for talking about blind spots and building committed partnerships, these teams quickly resolve issues and keep the team performing at an optimal level.

Here is what characterizes high performance teams:

- Team members openly coach each other on blind spots and quickly correct unproductive behavior and resolve issues.
- Each member takes personal accountability for his or her impact on others.
- Team members collaborate with all other members to achieve strategic business objectives.
- Each member checks his or her ego at the door and sets aside personal agendas to achieve a greater mission—that of enterprise success.
- Each member commits to the success of all others and eliminates blame and silos.
- Team members hold each other accountable for high standards of behavior.

Do you take a stand and act decisively even when it is uncomfortable? If not, I want you to know that you can learn how to achieve this and increase your leadership effectiveness. Taking a stand requires you to go against the common advice of "blend in, don't stand out, and let others put themselves on the line."

Fearless leaders have the courage to take a stand even when there is no agreement or support from others. One stand you must take in leading others is to define uniform behavioral standards and teach people how to work together in committed partnerships. You will learn more about this in detail in Chapter 5.

Fearless leaders instill passion by building committed partnerships with employees, customers, communities, and other key stakeholders. The attitude of the entire organization shifts as a positive and constructive environment is created. People make the personal choice to be fearless leaders not because they have to but because they want to. They are exhilarated when they discover they have the power to influence and shape the future.

Victim and entitlement mentality is replaced by ownership, and people speak up and take accountability for enterprise results. There is an endless buzz of greatness that motivates people to do more than they believed was possible. It takes only one leader to confront resignation and transform others.

In a business-as-usual environment, you will hear, "I'm burdened, I'm pressured, I have too much to do and not enough time," and "If others would get their act together, I could do my job." This attitude adds a heaviness and weight to the organization and stifles leaders who are committed to aggressive goals. In a business-as-usual culture, complacency prevails, and everything is dragged down by a pessimistic view of circumstances and people.

Fearless leaders produce exceptional results by interrupting the cycle of automatic and unproductive behavior. They end suspicion, turf wars, and victim mentality and do not allow leaders to work in isolation. They build an organization where performance, innovation, productivity, and employee engagement soar. Lewis, a CEO of a financial organization, recognized the need for organizational change even though the company reported solid earnings.

When a Leader Is Not Willing to Settle for "Good Enough"

The company had good business results in spite of leaders and employees engaging in counterproductive behavior. Lewis saw opportunities for growth and was not content to allow people to be complacent. Over several years, the company brought in four different consulting groups to address the lack of leadership alignment and low employee engagement. But his leaders continued to "chew up the consulting groups and spit them out," as Lewis described it.

What Happened. We became Lewis's fifth consulting group. We worked with Lewis and his senior team in a leadership session during which he confronted his blind spots and inspired others to do the same. Addressing years of unresolved issues lifted a considerable weight off the team. By the end of the session, they were committed to each other and fully aligned.

The Impact. Word spread quickly about the senior team's new behavior, and people tested the senior leaders to make sure it would last. They found that leaders who were former adversaries now worked well together.

Lewis and his senior leadership team chose to transform the entire company starting with their leadership body of 200. Leaders and employees learned the same behaviors and methodology for working together in high performance teams and transformed the organization. The turnaround: profits increased tenfold, and the portfolio grew from $4.5 billion to over $15 billion. Product innovation soared with 60 percent of the business coming from new products. The company was publicly recognized as one of the top 10 employers in Canada, and employee engagement scores, measured by an outside third party, climbed from 69 percent to 85 percent.

Lesson Learned. It takes only one leader to start the process and build a high performance organization. Lewis did not wait for things to happen; he made things happen. His courage to transform the leadership body, then the organization, inspired everyone to learn and grow. The company transformed from "good enough" to becoming a world-class organization in which people today continue to produce unprecedented business results.

Fearless leaders like Lewis create a powerful context for change and unleash people's courage. They create an environment in which people take 100% accountability for business results and their impact on others. In this uncommon atmosphere, people work together as committed partners and stand for the success of each other. They coach each other on blind spots, turn automatic behavior into extraordinary behavior, and rapidly resolve challenges.

IT ONLY TAKES ONE PERSON TO CHANGE

You do not need to wait for others to change or hope that the organization will wake up and transform. You have the power to influence change, and fearless leadership provides you with the methodology.

But before you sign up for fearless leadership, you need to know that it is not for everyone; it is only for people who want to play big. It is for leaders who want to accomplish extraordinary results, achieve high aspirations, and who are willing to take accountability and act instead of sitting on the sidelines. It is a choice to be greater, live by your highest ideals, and take charge of the future.

When individuals and teams choose to alter how they work with one another, change is fast and permanent, and excitement is contagious. People experience profound personal breakthroughs and reach a higher level of personal effectiveness, fulfillment, and accomplishment. This makes fearless leadership self-replenishing and invigorating. Soon others are asking, "How can I get involved?" This is change at its best. It emerges from people who are on fire at all levels in your organization and want to lead the organization to greatness.

The Decision to Be a Fearless Leader Is Yours and Yours Alone

Fearless leadership is not another change initiative that can be mandated by an organization and top leaders. You do not need approval, agreement, or permission from anyone. This is your decision; you are in charge. This is something you can influence. Regardless of where you are in your organization, you can powerfully lead and shape the future. Here is the caveat: fearless leadership works *only* if you are willing to apply this methodology to yourself first before asking others to embrace it.

You may be a senior leader or an individual contributor; it does not matter. Change starts wherever you are. I often hear people say, "If senior leaders are not willing to do this, then it won't work." Certainly, it is more powerful and expedient when senior leaders embrace any change and lead the way for others. However, countless organizations have been highly successful by leading transformational change from the middle of the organization, such as a business or staff unit, and driving it upward. All ways work. With fearless leadership you can start anywhere and go everywhere, so do not limit your creativity and thinking. Think big and generate ideas for how you can apply fearless leadership in your company.

As you take on fearless leadership, resignation will attempt to creep in at every step of the way. It may appear as a thought in your head such as

"Sounds good, but none of this will work in my company." When you notice yourself becoming resigned, stop and pay attention but do not give in to it. Remember that resignation is an automatic behavior, and as with every automatic behavior, you have a choice. Either you can allow your resignation to dictate what you can achieve, or you can choose to empower your commitment to make change happen.

To clear up any confusion, let me emphatically state: fearless leadership can work in any company. It can work wherever there is a fearless leader who has the courage to start the process and take a bold stand.

How to Use This Book

This book is designed to personally guide you through the obstacles, challenges, and breakthroughs needed to become a fearless leader. I have written it as though you and I are sitting together talking about what is possible for you and what limits you. I have designed this book to be used by individuals and teams to learn how to work together at a new level of effectiveness.

For teams, I recommend you read this book together. Begin by identifying a breakthrough you want to achieve as a group. It may be as straightforward as building trust and committed partnerships. Focus your team breakthrough on a specific business objective so you have a way to measure your progress and effectiveness. For example, identify a priority project or breakdown you want to address. Then identify how trust and committed partnerships will alter your success and the milestones that will demonstrate you are achieving exactly what you want. I also recommend you read the chapters sequentially.

Each chapter builds a step-by-step framework for understanding the methodology of transformation. As building-block chapters, each expands and integrates concepts from the prior one. At the end of each chapter, there are two sections: leadership exploration and leadership actions.

In the leadership exploration section, there are provocative questions to stimulate and push your thinking. Here I am asking you to examine what is occurring with you, your team, and your company in the same way a scientist would use a microscope to see what is not obvious. Do not use these questions as an opportunity to judge yourself, others, or the organization. Judging and criticizing are not useful; all they do is make you right and everyone else wrong. Our desired outcome is not to discover who is right; it is to discover how you can be more effective.

In the leadership action section, I ask you to implement the new high performance skills and tools you will be learning. By taking specific actions, you will have real-time experiences and success that will inspire you to do more. In working with a team, assign these actions as homework, and debrief the results you achieve (and roadblocks you encounter) at your next meeting. The power of fearless leadership is to apply these skills in the moment, especially when the team is uncomfortable discussing sensitive issues.

Your Personal Invitation to Be Extraordinary

Are you prepared to go the distance and play full out? Are you ready to take the lid off what is possible for you and others, even if you are experiencing feelings of doubt, skepticism, or resignation? If you are, I am inviting you to participate in an extraordinary game—a game in which you have choice, power, and freedom. The price of admission is your willingness and courage to explore

- Who you are as a leader (your stand and commitment)
- How you impact others
- Your effectiveness in rapidly moving people into aligned action
- Your ability to inspire and connect people to a grand vision and mission

To participate in fearless leadership you must throw yourself in the game. You cannot sit in the stands and watch others play. I am asking for your emotional and intellectual commitment. You must be an active participant who is willing to suspend assumptions and beliefs that limit you. You must be willing to change your direction and try a new way to achieve an extraordinary level of leadership effectiveness.

My invitation to you is to produce a breakthrough in who you are as a leader. I am defining a *breakthrough* as a sudden discovery that hits you in a moment and jostles your mind, shaking up an old order in order to allow room for a new one. This "ah-ha" moment gives you a panoramic perspective you did not have before. I want you to have one ah-ha after another that dramatically expands your ability, choice, and freedom to create new realities. I must warn you, I have no tolerance for breakthroughs that lead only to insight: insight is intellectually stimulating, but what I want from you are breakthroughs that lead to decisive action.

Breakthrough
A sudden discovery that dramatically expands what can be achieved.

Each step of the way, I am going to ask you to make a series of choices. Each choice you elect to make progressively expands your power and freedom to transform. Bring your skepticism, doubt, and disbelief along with your frustration, disappointment, and discouragement. I want it all. Together, we will examine how resignation forms, how to break its grip, and how blind spots and automatic behaviors keep you stuck in an unfulfilling and unrewarding cycle.

Bring your enthusiasm, passion, and commitment. Decide now that anything is possible. Bring your courage to explore uncharted territory, and set aside your need to have all the answers. Trust that you will discover the answers each step of the way.

Bring your unshakable resolve to stay the course and never quit, even when you encounter breakdowns and roadblocks. As you build committed partnerships, you discover strength in partners who will stand shoulder to shoulder with you to overcome any challenge.

You are not alone, and you do not need to tolerate anything. By the end of this book, you will have the tools to take charge and make change happen. If you bring your courage, I will provide the rest. We need fearless leaders to restore our organizations and people to high levels of accountability and integrity. We need fearless leaders who are willing to take a stand and do what's right for right's sake.

Transforming Together

There are two truths I have learned about transformation: (1) you cannot seriously explore transformation without having it alter your behavior, and (2) you cannot do it alone.

You and I are taking this journey together. Although this is not my first book, it is by far the most emotionally and intellectually demanding. I am discovering that I cannot write about transformation without hearing the call to take accountability and transform my own behavior.

Without knowing it, you are already my partner in transformation. As we embark on this exploration together, I want you to know that I am taking this journey with you. Everything I ask you to do in this book, I am doing with you. Every time I ask you to confront something, I am confronting the same thing. I will ask of you only what I am personally willing to do. In fearless leadership, we must have the courage to lead the way for others.

What makes the difference for me, and I believe for you, are the committed partners who stand beside us. Transformation is not about being perfect or doing things perfectly. It is about the caring, compassion, and support we bring to each other when we stumble and the speed at which we recover. With committed partners, you can achieve a new and profound level of success.

LEADERSHIP EXPLORATION

Answer the following questions for yourself, your team, and the organization. Examine what unspoken behavioral norm you have been tolerating in yourself and with others.

Your Team

What unspoken norm for behavior is tolerated? For example, is it acceptable to not deliver commitments when promised, avoid uncomfortable conversations, be culturally insensitive, not take accountability for your impact on others, comply with decisions, gossip, blame individuals and groups, resist change initiatives, have unresolved issues between group members, defend turf, verbally attack others, or provide excuses and reasons for lack of business results?

What unproductive behaviors do you silently endorse? For example, do you accept excuses in place of results? Do you tolerate conflict between team members and conspiracies against others?

The Organization

What unspoken norm for behavior is tolerated? For example, is it acceptable to blame senior leaders, the organization, and other groups; discredit individuals; undermine business objectives and initiatives; focus on individual areas of responsibility rather than taking accountability for enterprise perspective; take credit rather than give credit to others; align intellectually but withhold emotional commitment; conspire against other people or groups; or be polite and indirect and avoid the real issue?

What unproductive behaviors do you silently endorse? For example, do you observe—but fail to take action—when you notice others' conspiring against people or groups or individuals' avoiding the real issues in meetings?

LEADERSHIP ACTION

Identify How You Relate to the Organization and Others

Are you resigned, hopeful, or fearless with (1) your team, (2) senior leaders, (3) the organization as a whole, (4) your ability to influence others, and (5) your ability to shape the future? Ask a colleague or your team to assess your behavior and compare responses. In fearless leadership, the perception of others is far more accurate than your own, especially when it comes to how you impact others and view yourself.

If you are resigned, you are working hard but without enthusiasm. Chances are you feel powerless to influence change and are shrinking the game and focusing only on your area of responsibility to the exclusion of the larger enterprise perspective.

If you are hopeful, you are watching and waiting for others to act first. You may be wishing that someone would step up and lead.

If you are fearless, you are taking a stand and taking action. However, you may not be getting the results you want. There is much more to learn in order to develop your effectiveness as a fearless leader.

Once you identify how you are relating to others and the organization (resigned, hopeful, or fearless), then examine how this shapes your actions and results. Honestly examine how your thinking and behavior prevent you from achieving the results you want. In fearless leadership, you must always examine your personal accountability instead of blaming others or the organization.

Permanence, perseverance, and persistence in spite of all obstacles, discouragements, and impossibilities: it is this that in all things distinguishes the strong soul from the weak.

—THOMAS CARLYLE (1795–1881)

Chapter
2
The Blind Spots
That Derail Leaders

Not everything that is faced can be changed.
But nothing can be changed until it is faced.

—JAMES BALDWIN (1924–1987)

Let's not kid ourselves. Blind spots are the root causes of some of the most severe breakdowns faced by leaders, organizations, and societies. Leaders who are unaware of how their behavior impacts others can create dire and unintended consequences. Blind spots corrupt decision making, reduce our scope of awareness, and lock in rigid and fixed viewpoints.

Everyone suffers when leaders are not awake to their blind spots. The work environment becomes lackluster and pessimistic. People spend more time talking about what is not working, than working. Productivity and performance drop. And mistakes and breakdowns are quietly covered up instead of openly discussed and resolved. No one takes accountability, but everyone freely hands out blame. An entire enterprise becomes focused on looking good instead of being effective.

Two things are clear:

1. Everyone has blind spots—unproductive behaviors that undermine effectiveness, limit results, and damage relationships.
2. You cannot see your own blind spots without the partnership and support of others, no matter how clever or discerning you are.

This chapter begins with how *unidentified* blind spots undermine leaders and business results. We will examine the 10 most common blind spots and how they not only limit one person's success but *everyone's* success. Your blind spots affect everyone you work with, whether you intend to impact others or not.

WHAT PREVENTS FEARLESS LEADERSHIP: UNIDENTIFIED BLIND SPOTS

Blind spots are automatic behaviors that people readily see in others yet avoid confronting in themselves. If I told you *what* blind spots you have, you would deny them, or you would argue, debate, and defend why you do what you do. At best, you might *intellectually* agree you have a blind spot or two.

But let me be clear: you have blind spots. It does not matter how successful you are. In fact, most successful leaders are unaware of two things: (1) the impact of their blind spots on others and (2) the degree to which others work around them and avoid confronting the real issues. What these leaders fail to realize is how their behavior works against them in achieving the very results they want.

For many of us, the very idea that we might have a blind spot—something we cannot see—is uncomfortable and threatening. Behavioral blind spots sound like character flaws, defects, or something that is wrong about us. Even the language we use—such as "I was blindsided by what happened"—reinforces our dislike of not being in total control. We are socialized to believe we should not have any glaring weaknesses, especially those that are concealed from our view.

Blind spots are not flaws, nor are they deliberate; they are unconscious behaviors. For example, Joe, a leader of a business unit, was known for his dual personality that went from being charming to having a sharp bite. After learning about a serious financial problem in his area, he cornered a direct report in the hallway, and while others watched, he ranted, "What were you thinking about—how could you allow this to happen?" By the end of his tirade, everyone within earshot had the energy drained out of them and walked away in a daze. Joe felt better having expressed his anger, but he was completely unaware of his detrimental impact on his direct report and everyone else. He was blind to his blind spots.

The real culprits are not the blind spots themselves; the offenders are *unidentified* and *mismanaged* blind spots. The automatic nature of blind spots—their ability to appear any time and anywhere—produces cycles of unproductive behaviors between individuals and groups that undermine change initiatives and business results. These cycles of unproductive behaviors also derail careers, sabotage success, and lead to ineffective decision making and execution. Although people can see the impact of unproductive behavior, they look the other way. It is an uncomfortable situation to deal with because people do not have a constructive method to resolve difficult situations or issues.

Without a clear and explicit standard of behavior, and a shared methodology to apply it in daily business transactions, unproductive behavioral norms form by default and degrade the culture and workplace environment. If leaders understood the degree to which blind spots undercut the results of their organizations, they would be screaming for solutions.

There is good news in all of this. You can defeat the cycle of automatic and unproductive behavior and build a culture of accountability. Fearless leadership *starts* with establishing uniform behavioral standards and learning how to confront and overcome blind spots.

THE 10 BLIND SPOTS THAT DERAIL LEADERS

For the past 30 years, our organization has worked closely with CEOs, executives, and their companies. Regardless of the industry—mining, agriculture, finance, technology—the same recurrent themes emerge. When leaders complain about stalled initiatives, inconsistent execution, or lack of leadership alignment, the primary source of the problem can be traced to the lack of a uniform standard of behavior that is consistently applied. Our consulting group documented common, repetitive behaviors we observed in over 30,000 leaders and executives.

In helping leaders learn how they could be more effective, we focused on areas they could influence and change: personal behaviors that were limiting their success and results. When we provided them with candid feedback from peers, direct reports, and the next level up, most said they had received this input before.

But when we identified their blind spots and the *emotional* impact they had on others, they did not recognize themselves. Up until this point, they had been able to intellectually justify and defend their behavior as "That's just who I am" and avoid seeing their emotional impact and how they left people feeling.

In learning about their specific blind spots, leaders were surprised that their actions had such a negative and crushing impact on others. When we probed deeper, we discovered the depth of their lack of awareness. The vast majority were oblivious and unaware of the impact of their unproductive behavior: they were committed, competent, and caring leaders who had no intention to damage people or undermine the organization. The overwhelming majority of leaders wanted to have a positive impact on others and experienced sincere remorse when they discovered they did not.

Our interviews focused on both intellectual perceptions and emotional impact on others. We researched how peers, direct reports, and superiors felt and compensated for behavioral blind spots of the leader in question. Below are examples of what others had to say:

- "I felt shut down and dismissed, so I withdrew and stopped speaking up."
- "I felt devalued and disrespected—I avoided any meeting that he would be in."
- "I lost my energy and enthusiasm and never got it back, so I do only what needs to be done."
- "I never felt included in decisions, so I went along with them, but secretly I did not support them."
- "I felt frustrated and discouraged. My boss doesn't have any time for me so I work around him and hope he will move on to another position soon."

It is one thing to understand blind spots at an intellectual level and another to recognize the emotional impact on others. What was most alarming from our research was how leaders unconsciously taught others poor behavior. For instance, leaders who consistently blamed others taught their people that it was appropriate to point the finger at other groups in the organization and avoid accountability. Poor behavior was informally taught by how leaders behaved and then it was copied by others. Unproductive behavior spread to entire groups and business units where people learned how to operate in silos, defend their interests, and engage in unhealthy competition. In all of this, the enterprise perspective was lost and performance suffered.

Many of our clients documented time and money that was lost due to people and groups not working effectively together. They identified significant and quantifiable losses in retention of talent, productivity, performance, and product innovation. They also used other indicators such as third-party measures of employee engagement and culture to examine the impact of leadership behavior. What they found was a direct path from how leaders behave to how the organization performs.

We wanted to provide our clients with an easy way to identify and transform unproductive behavior into extraordinary behavior in order to build a constructive performance culture. Our starting place was helping our clients understand and talk about blind spots openly so they could be resolved. We systematically identified the persistent and predictable blind spots that occur in leaders and teams. Exhibit 2-1 is a list of the 10 most common blind spots that derail leaders.

THE 10 BLIND SPOTS THAT DERAIL LEADERS

1. **Going it alone**

2. **Being insensitive to your impact on others**

3. **Having an "I know" attitude**

4. **Avoiding difficult conversations**

5. **Blaming others or circumstances**

6. **Treating commitments casually**

7. **Conspiring against others**

8. **Withholding emotional commitment**

9. **Not taking a stand**

10. **Tolerating "good enough"**

EXHIBIT 2-1: *The Blind Spots That Derail Leaders*

It is pointless to rely on *yourself* to accurately identify your blind spots. This is an area in which *your* point of view is irrelevant. It takes an outside perspective—such as that of your peers or direct reports—to let you know which blind spots you have. Others have a firsthand experience of your impact, while all you have is an intellectual assessment of how you *think* you come across.

If you are like most leaders, you may have the belief that although your behavior is not perfect, it certainly is not harmful. But before you jump to this conclusion, start by honestly examining where you have blind spots. It is only when you can clearly see your blind spots that you have access to dramatically increasing your effectiveness and transforming the organization. It starts by understanding the chasm that exists between what you intend and how you behave.

Included below are actual stories about talented leaders who were derailed by their ineffective behavior. For the purpose of this section, the focus of the stories is on the impact of the leader's blind spot on the work environment and business results. Although the final outcome of the leader is not provided in every story, it is important to note that there were two distinct outcomes: (1) leaders who did not learn from their mistakes and repeated the same behavior and had recurring problems, including losing an opportunity on the career ladder, and (2) leaders who learned from their mistakes and overcame their blind spots. As you read further in this book, you will learn more about fearless leaders who were courageous in confronting their blind spots and successfully transforming their organizations.

Blind Spot 1: Going It Alone

The Number 1 blind spot is *going it alone*. Leaders who are self-sufficient, independent, and resourceful often fall prey to this blind spot. When facing a tough challenge, they feel responsible and shoulder the burden by themselves. With an innate need to be strong and tough, leaders who go it alone endure whatever is necessary. They unintentionally exclude others from decision making—colleagues, friends, and even family—and withdraw their energy and support. Every degree of isolation in which the leader separates from others and the organization fragments the team and erodes momentum.

Symptoms of Going It Alone

- Rejecting offers of support and not asking for help
- Not talking about stress, pressure, or anxiety
- Isolating and withdrawing from others (not being accessible)
- Not including others in decision making
- Deflecting others' concerns by making vague statements such as "I have a lot on my mind"

Suraj, lead counsel for a global organization, was frustrated and discouraged and was under stress from business and personal concerns. His method of coping was to withdraw and isolate himself from his team and peers. His direct reports complained, "He forgets that he is only one person, and he charges ahead without including us. We try to help, but it's as if he's wearing a 'do not enter' sign." Suraj's withdrawal and isolation spanned a period of approximately eight months. At the height of Suraj's disengagement, he took a holiday, in spite of the fact that significant legal issues were percolating in his area.

A major case involving the company's liability hit a crisis point while Suraj was away. A decision needed to be made, but Suraj had critical information that he had not shared with anyone. Panic took over and leaders frantically attempted to reach him, but he was inaccessible. The CEO and several executives became involved, and it took an army of the company's top talent to avert disaster. By the time Suraj returned calls, the situation was under control, but his future was not. Suraj was completely disconnected from how his withdrawal and isolation had impacted others. Even upon his return, he was unaware of how his behavior had set off a four-bell alarm. The Board became involved and took a hard stand: they were unwilling to have an executive who was "missing in action."

The Impact of Going It Alone. When you go it alone, you create a high level of stress and frustration in others. While you are internally focused on what you need to do, others experience a high state of anxiety. From their perspective, you are "missing in action," and they take their attention off of business needs and focus on what is happening to you.

Because you are not focusing externally on others, your ability to pick up cues about their needs and reactions is greatly diminished. You miss how upset and frustrated those around you are. Consistent with the behavior of going it alone, you reject offers of help and support. This sends a message that says "back off." People try to reach you, but after a while they give up. In all of this, business results suffer: high levels of anxiety and uncertainty destabilize the team and organization.

When you exclude others, they fill in the blanks. Your behavior communicates, "I do not need you to think, take action, or lead. I am handling everything myself." (In Chapter 6, we discuss how to overcome the behavior of going it alone through building committed partnerships.)

Blind Spot 2: Being Insensitive to Your Impact on Others

Leaders who are insensitive to their impact on others do not have a clear understanding of how they come across. They miss completely how their choice of words, tone of voice, and nonverbal behavior sends a message of disapproval and dissatisfaction. Because they have a low threshold for picking up on the reactions of others, they make blunders they cannot see, therefore cannot correct.

When leaders are insensitive to their impact on others, one of two things is occurring: (1) they are unaware of their emotional impact or (2) they recognize their impact but do not care. In our years of experience, we have found that the great majority of leaders care a lot. If you have this blind spot, it is most likely rooted in your inability to read, understand, and respond appropriately to the cues of others, not in callous and coldhearted views.

In a group, insensitivity to others leads to team dysfunction. Individuals are self-absorbed and drive their personal agenda at the expense of others. A team will spend an inordinate amount of time arguing and posturing. Dissension takes over, and a few vocal members dominate the team while others disengage.

> **Symptoms of Being Insensitive to Your Impact on Others**
> - Not noticing, seeking out, or caring what others experience or feel
> - Expecting others to respond the same way you do, regardless of cultural differences
> - Not recognizing how your comments and behaviors provoke a negative response
> - Criticizing, devaluing input, and questioning the credibility of others
> - Minimizing others' reactions to your behavior such as "They'll get over it"

Synthia, a senior vice president of mergers and acquisitions, belittled and micromanaged others. Her coworkers were accustomed to the disapproval she showed in her face and tone of voice. Nothing was ever good enough for Synthia, and she constantly edited the memos and reports of others. Memos were not circulated until Synthia edited them to her perfection. "It's Synthia's way and only Synthia's way—which includes intimidation and manipulation," said a member of her management team.

People felt stupid and incompetent around Synthia. They also felt that she did not trust them to do their jobs. Everybody lost something in this debacle. Many people lost confidence, others lost their jobs because of Synthia's dissatisfaction with their work, and many left the company. Turnover soared in her area, and Synthia, insensitive again, simply said, "Poor performers don't last long with me."

Synthia was perpetually dissatisfied, and people were resigned that no matter what they did, they could never please her. She always focused on what people were doing wrong and seldom acknowledged what they were doing right. Her lack of sensitivity to how her behavior impacted others was the cause of significant business and leadership issues. No matter what she attempted to change in the organization, she was unsuccessful. The environment she had created was not conducive to change, and nothing took hold.

The Impact of Being Insensitive to Others. When you are insensitive to others, people avoid you and withdraw their trust. At best, they merely tolerate you. They keep their guard up to protect themselves from feeling devalued and unappreciated. A few may spar with you, but most will withdraw.

Your behavior damages the confidence of others, especially those who report to you. When you repeatedly focus on what is wrong and what is missing, you demonstrate your lack of trust in their ability. In turn, others begin to doubt themselves and stop trusting in themselves to make good decisions. Over time, people abdicate their accountabilities to you, and they shut down and shut you out. No one is willing to be used for target practice, and you will lose the support of your group.

If your insensitivity extends to cultural differences, people will feel misunderstood and not respected, and your behavior will lead to considerable antagonism. Because we act upon cultural influences instinctively, we are unaware of our most prevalent assumption: "Everyone is just like me." This assumption causes leaders to respond to people in the same manner. Cultural insensitivity impacts people at the deepest level of their beliefs and core values. This is particularly treacherous. People are often unforgiving when you trample on their traditions and way of life.

When you do not listen, you cultivate an unsafe environment where people become resigned and do not speak up. People pretend to listen, but they hold back because they know they have no real voice. (In Chapter 6, we discuss how to take accountability for your impact on others and restore the relationship.)

Blind Spot 3: Having an "I Know" Attitude

Leaders with an "I know" attitude have an answer for everything. Others perceive them as petty tyrants, solution machines, human bulldozers, and command and control autocrats. They leave others feeling exhausted, diminished, angry, and insignificant. They are high maintenance and a continual source of irritation.

An "I know" attitude is based on rigid and fixed views and the lack of intellectual curiosity. Leaders with this blind spot stifle innovation and change by constantly defending their beliefs and trying to prove they are right and everyone else is wrong. Their actions communicate, "I have all the answers and I don't need anyone to tell me what to do." For some, there is a sense of false bravado, overconfidence, and arrogance.

Symptoms of an "I Know" Attitude

- Not listening to others or diminishing what others have to say
- Making assumptions and judgments
- Acting as if you have all the answers
- Being rigid and inflexible in your viewpoints
- Refusing to explore alternative ideas and options

With the simplistic approach—I'm right and you're wrong—leaders with an "I know" attitude diminish the desire for others to contribute, learn, and grow. This was the case with Anthony, a business unit leader of a global manufacturing firm. Anthony was aggressive and hard-hitting, but one behavior stood out: "This guy is self-righteous about his point of view, and if you don't agree, he doesn't want to hear it," protested his peers.

For two months, Anthony's senior team worked on preparing a presentation for a potential client. They spent countless hours looking at innovative ways to meet the client's needs and were excited to present their proposal to Anthony. Always busy with something else, Anthony did not meet with his group until the day prior to the client meeting. In the meeting, when his group attempted to explain the client's challenges, Anthony interrupted and said, "I know all about this; it's been all over the trade journals." He proceeded to pontificate for 20 minutes on his thinly researched opinion of the client's strategy, and then he left the meeting.

Anthony's arrogance got him into trouble. He was unprepared for the client meeting and relied on his seat-of-the-pants behavior. The client was unimpressed, and Anthony and his team lost the account.

But his problems did not end there. Anthony liked to work with a core group—his inner circle—of three key people. They emulated Anthony and behaved in an arrogant "I know" style with others. To make themselves look good, Anthony and his lieutenants shot down ideas from others. Under Anthony's leadership, the business unit derailed and went from being highly successful to becoming a liability to the enterprise.

The Impact of Having an "I Know" Attitude. If you have an "I know" attitude, you are downright annoying to others, especially people who like to use their minds. Your attitude effectively shuts people down and displays a dangerous delusion: "There is only one reality and it is mine." No one likes to be around someone who is unwilling to consider new possibilities or explore new ideas. Even if you say the words, "I'm open to new ideas," your behavior belies your message.

Your "I know" attitude frustrates people to such a high degree that most would prefer working with anyone but you. What your behavior teaches people is they do not need to think. You have all the answers and solutions, so why should they use their energy to come up with new ideas that you will just shoot down.

You probably become annoyed when others do not bring new ideas and solutions. You may even complain that you are the only one doing all the thinking in your group. Yet you do not see how your behavior teaches others to stop thinking; after all, you already have the answer.

An "I know" attitude does not inspire high performance in others. Chances are you do not delegate effectively. Your need to control and manage everything ends up leaving people feeling unnecessary and superfluous. You, in turn, have an excessive workload. By not empowering and delegating to others, you must then carry the burden of work.

This blind spot costs the business the collective intelligence of others. (In Chapter 6, we discuss how to listen with positive intention and maximize the contributions of others.)

Blind Spot 4: Avoiding Difficult Conversations

Avoiding difficult and sensitive conversations is an everyday occurrence for one simple reason: such conversations are uncomfortable. People fear they will open Pandora's Box and be faced with their own embarrassment, a negative reaction from others, being labeled or judged, or the loss of a relationship. They sidestep difficult conversations because they do not feel confident in their ability to be emotionally honest and direct. Do you know how to tell a coworker to stop gossiping, or how to tell your boss that he is demotivating the group?

Symptoms of Avoiding Difficult Conversations

- Withholding how you think and feel
- Softening the message and not communicating your real concern
- Making it difficult for others to talk with you about sensitive issues
- Staying on the surface of issues and not allowing the conversation to go deeper
- Avoiding discussions that could evoke an emotional response

---

If you cannot talk about it, you cannot resolve it. When leaders avoid tough conversations, problems remain unresolved. Poor performance continues, less than acceptable products and services are produced, and morale plummets. Being polite and not wanting to hurt another's feelings are the common excuses used for not talking straight responsibly. When leaders soften the message, the other party walks away confused.

Gwen, a director of organizational development, was afraid of hurting people's feelings, and as a result, she was not completely honest, particularly when it came to delivering bad news. Two key people on her team were not performing up to standard, and in two years, she had not taken decisive action.

We had an opportunity to watch how Gwen handled a conversation with one of the key people in question: "This is a high-profile project, and I want to make sure others see the great work you and your team are doing. Perhaps there is something you need from me, or some way I can help you." Her direct report interpreted this message as an offer to help, not a statement about something he needed to address and correct. He responded to what he heard and said, "Thanks, Gwen. If we run into a challenge, you'll be the first person I call."

Mission not accomplished. Gwen did what many others do: she did *not* talk straight. Her unwillingness to be direct and responsible in her communication left her reports with inadequate information to address performance issues, and they had no opportunity to turn them around.

Gwen's lack of straight talk perpetuated the lack of results in her area. People were highly frustrated with how she allowed inconsistent standards of performance to continue being the status quo. For those who worked extremely hard, it was insulting and frustrating to see people who did not perform or deliver results remain in key positions. What Gwen thought was "being nice" was actually "being ineffective." Due to Gwen's lack of decisiveness and straight talk, the company was unsuccessful in launching a major initiative.

Change initiatives lose all credibility when the people leading them do not demonstrate the change they are attempting to bring into existence. Ironically, one of the core competencies identified for high-potential leaders was the willingness and ability to have difficult conversations. The lesson learned here is that whatever you want to change in others, you must model it first as the leader.

The Impact of Avoiding Difficult Conversations. If you avoid difficult conversations and are not direct with others, you are not doing anyone a favor. People are more troubled and disturbed when you do *not* talk straight than they are by the prospect of being hurt by what you have to say. How do you want others to communicate with you? Do you want people to beat around the bush and send an ambiguous and implied message, or do you want them to honestly tell you what is on their mind? If you chose the latter, then you need to apply the same rule to others and talk straight responsibly—with an emphasis on the word "responsibly."

When you avoid tough conversations, you leave people with an uneasy and unsettled feeling. Because they never know where you stand, they are wary and stop trusting you. They deal with a constant state of misdirected attention and fixate on you, at the expense of business needs. Your behavior is a primary contributor to high levels of underperformance.

Bottling things up, harboring resentments, and not responsibly expressing your concerns and feelings sends a message. Just because you are not using words, you are still communicating with your behavior. People interpret your actions and make up their own meaning. And you can expect people to make up the worst. (In Chapter 8, we discuss how to be emotionally honest and talk straight responsibly.)

Blind Spot 5: Blaming Others or Circumstances

Pointing the finger at others is much easier than taking accountability. Leaders deflect, rotate the discussion, and focus the spotlight on what is wrong with someone else. Blame is often used as an offensive tactic to avoid defending one's position. An easy way to escape being blamed is by attacking and blaming someone else.

Blame in an organization creates a volatile environment. Silos, warring groups, and factions choke off the emergence of collaboration and teamwork. Valuable time is spent attempting to resolve conflict in the proverbial battle of "he said, she said."

Symptoms of Blaming Others or Circumstances

- Always having a reason, excuse, or explanation ("Yeah, but . . .")
- Pointing the finger at others or circumstances to avoid accountability
- Constantly criticizing and complaining about others
- Being adversarial and opposing ideas and people
- Having divided loyalties and priorities and not working as a team

This was the case with Felipe, a recently promoted CEO in the energy industry. Because of his 25-year tenure with the organization and his position, few challenged him. He worked with a tight circle of people, and if you were on the outside, you were a potential threat and enemy. Felipe blamed and attacked those he did not view as his allies.

Once Felipe became the new CEO of the company, he promptly began blaming his predecessor, Paul. In a meeting of leaders, he said, "Paul created a lot of problems that we now need to solve." Felipe lost the trust of many by blaming his predecessor for problems, and what little support he had, dried up. People complied with what he wanted because they saw no other choice, but few were inspired to follow him.

Market conditions made the business successful during his tenure, but Felipe sabotaged what the business could have become under his leadership. The work environment was deplorable, people did not feel safe to speak up for fear of repercussions, and they did not want to become a target for Felipe's ready criticism and blame. Once known for their potent combination of specialized products and marketing talent, the company lost their top marketing people and along with it, their global leadership position.

The Impact of Blaming Others or Circumstances. Blaming others rubs people the wrong way, especially those who are responsible and accountable. It is perceived as petty and small and lacking integrity. If you are in a position of power, others will not verbally tell you how you impact them, but they demonstrate their loss of respect for you in their behavior. When you are unwilling to take accountability and display strength of character, fairness, and honesty, people will not support you.

You run another risk with this blind spot. Blaming others divides people into two camps—your allies and your enemies. People know which camp they are in, and they either fight or comply. Even your allies may withhold trust fearing they could easily be next on your list. You are left without the willing cooperation required to achieve authentic and sustainable alignment. Others give lip service but do exactly what they want.

Your behavior can polarize an entire organization and reinforce boundaries and divisions instead of collaboration and cooperation. While you may think you have the support of others, people know how to play the game, and they will blame you just as you blame them. They adopt an attitude of "this too shall pass" and wait for you to fail or move on. (In Chapter 6, we discuss how to take accountability for enterprise results and collaborative relationships.)

Blind Spot 6: Treating Commitments Casually

Casual commitments and promises happen all too often and destroy the credibility of leaders. When leaders make throwaway promises with no intention of keeping them, they are not believable. One of the worst offenders that prevent organizations from staying on track and achieving objectives are words *not* tied to solid action and a firm deadline. They cloud even the clearest objective and send people in different directions.

For example, you are much better off stating a clear no than implying a possible yes. You disappoint people when you promise something— big or small—that you do not deliver. When your words are inconsistent with your behavior, people believe what you do and dismiss your words. Little by little, your comments lose their power, and people discount what you say.

Symptoms of Treating Commitments Casually
- Not making and not keeping commitments
- Not fulfilling promises on time
- Always maintaining an "escape hatch" to avoid being held accountable
- Not providing a clear "I commit" or "I do not commit"
- Making informal promises without a clear intention to keep them

Angus, a leader in a technology company, was always quick to volunteer his help, such as offering to head up a project. But he did not keep his promises consistently—big or small—and developed a reputation as "I'll promise you anything Angus."

In working with Angus in a private leadership session, we counted 22 promises that he made and broke in less than 24 hours—from "I'll be back in 10 minutes" to "I'll complete this by tomorrow morning." We discovered that Angus did not want to be held accountable for his promises and treated his commitments casually with an "I'll try" attitude versus an "I will" mindset. He had an escape hatch every time he committed, and you could never fault him.

The problem with Angus's personal strategy of avoid commitment–avoid accountability was that no one trusted him and no one could count on him. He was not taken seriously by his peers, and he was passed over for career advancement numerous times. Until our work with him, he was unable to see how even his smallest repetitive behaviors impacted others. Angus learned that he had burned a lot of bridges. He also learned that every broken promise was added to a long list of offenses leaving people disgusted and unwilling to support him.

The Impact of Treating Commitments Casually. When people cannot trust your words, they judge you as unreliable. People notice when you break a promise. They notice everything from small promises such as "I'll call you tomorrow" to big promises such as "You'll have my report by Friday." It does not matter if promises are big or small. They are tallied in one giant ledger against which you are judged.

The biggest challenge you face is that when the ledger is imbalanced with broken commitments, people distrust *all* your commitments. Without the honor of your word, others protect themselves from your undependable behavior.

Your word matters; it is better to make fewer commitments and keep them than to make many commitments and break them. (In Chapter 7, we discuss how to honor and fulfill commitments and revoke them responsibly.)

Blind Spot 7: Conspiring Against Others

Conspiring against others runs rampant in most organizations via rumors, gossip, and watercooler conversations. People talk negatively about coworkers and diminish their credibility by casting doubt and suspicion and then attempt to get others to agree with them.

Sometimes these conspiracies are behind people's backs, and other times they are open warfare. For example, a conspiracy against a person can be demonstrated in meetings by nonverbal behaviors. To discredit the speaker, others may ignore the presentation, work on their computers, check cell phone messages, or just check out and not listen. Any nonverbal demonstration of disinterest, disagreement, or disapproval, whether intentional or unintentional, is a conspiracy against others.

Silent conspirators are deadly conspirators. The most common form of conspiring is by saying nothing at all. When you listen to others but do not correct an erroneous assumption or do not take a stand for a person, you are sanctioning their comments. Underground conversations and conspiracies contaminate an entire organization. They build internal barriers to partnership and collaboration.

Symptoms of Conspiring Against Others

- Speaking negatively about people or their ideas
- Discrediting and discounting others
- Silently agreeing with a negative point of view by not speaking up
- Displaying nonverbal cues of disapproval or disinterest
- Not talking directly to the appropriate person

When groups conspire against each other, they cost the organization significant time and money. This was the case between the research and marketing groups in a specialty chemical organization. The relationship between these two areas for the past 20 years could be described as strained, at best.

The marketing group introduced a new customer model to the corporate leadership team that directly impacted research. Given the long-standing rivalry between these two areas, it was not surprising that marketing did not fully include the research group in the development of the model, nor did they consult them in detail about how the new approach would change a number of their processes.

The research group began a volley of fire, which started by accusing marketing of undermining their work. Marketing folks returned fire and charged research with being myopic and inattentive to customer needs. E-mails went flying with dozens of recipients copied.

The conspiracy against each department grew into a full-fledged war with camps clearly divided. Although the corporate leadership team approved the new model for implementation, the collaboration needed between research and marketing to make it successful was unobtainable. Because neither group trusted the other, the brilliant new approach died after millions of dollars were invested and two years of time wasted.

Conspiracies between individuals and groups are the Number 1 saboteur of senior teams, business success, and change initiatives. What makes conspiracies against others so insidious is that they are underground where they cannot be readily seen. Rigid and fixed beliefs, false assumptions about others, and the lack of trust produce disastrous results. Because individuals and teams do not have a shared methodology to address issues, these issues then escalate and spread to other parts of the company.

The Impact of Conspiring Against Others. When you conspire against people or ideas—whether by participating or by silent endorsement—you are perceived as weak, deceitful, and dishonest. Others withdraw their trust, and your credibility takes a nosedive. The unasked question is, "If a leader talks negatively about someone else, what prevents him or her from talking about me?"

This blind spot is like breathing; it is invisible until we raise our level of awareness and focus our attention on it. You may not recognize how much you engage in conspiring against people and initiatives. Everyone does it, and it is easy to overlook. But if you add up every time you listened to a negative conversation about another person and said nothing, you will have a long list. Chances are you engaged in a conspiracy against a person or idea in the last 24 hours. (In Chapter 6, we discuss how to overcome the automatic behavior of *conspiring against others* through working in partnership.)

Blind Spot 8: Withholding Emotional Commitment

When we examine commitment, we must take into account two factors: intellectual and emotional engagement. The presence of intellectual commitment without emotional engagement results in compliance. But when an organization can capture both "hearts and minds"—emotional and intellectual commitment—people engage and focus their energy on implementing change.

Emotional commitment—being inspired and passionate—unleashes the discretionary effort of people. When economists use the term *discretionary income*, they refer to the portion of your income you can use after paying fixed and necessary expenses. Discretionary effort works in the same way. It is the portion of your effort and energy that you personally control and that cannot be mandated by the organization.

Symptoms of Withholding Emotional Commitment
- Complying and going along with the decision
- Resisting change and withholding support
- Withdrawing your passion and enthusiasm
- Not being moved by the passion and commitment of others
- Going through the motions—waiting to see if change is really going to happen

---

There are two manifestations of this blind spot. One is when leaders withhold their emotional commitment and do not authentically align. The second is when leaders *think* they have alignment from others, and all they have is intellectual commitment or compliance. Charlie, the CEO of a business operation in the oil services industry, ran into the latter problem.

Charlie supported a new model for shared services that would be implemented in North America first and then expanded to global operations. It appeared that everyone on his senior team was aligned until it came time to implement the model in their geographic area. As soon as leaders had to make the tough decisions in their areas and change what was going on, they resisted. The implementation came to a standstill as individual areas failed to adopt the new shared services model. Charlie became increasingly frustrated and irate, which did nothing to alter how his leaders behaved. He was furious and felt betrayed. The model, projected to save the company $18 million in the first year, did not get off the ground until several years later.

What Charlie did not recognize was the difference between intellectual commitment and emotional commitment. He assumed he had both from his leaders, but what he had was only one—intellectual commitment.

Blaming his leaders for the lack of authentic alignment was not an effective approach. Charlie needed to take accountability for the lack of alignment, learn how to identify the difference between emotional and intellectual alignment, and how to gain both.

The Impact of Withholding Emotional Commitment. When you claim to be aligned or supportive but withhold your emotional commitment, others perceive you as disengaged and disingenuous. People know when you are not fully on board. They see it in how you behave and how you speak. How can you be emotionally honest with others if you are not emotionally honest with yourself? When you withhold your energy and enthusiasm, others do the same.

You gain respect when you tell people the truth, such as "I am *not* completely on board. I have reservations." You must have the courage to tell the truth instead of covering up what you are really thinking.

Without full emotional and intellectual commitment, you will not be able to weather the storm and achieve the results you want. It is the strength of both emotional and intellectual commitment that allows you to effectively engage people in the face of challenging circumstances. (In Chapter 9, we explore how to gain authentic emotional and intellectual commitment.)

Blind Spot 9: Not Taking a Stand

Leaders who do not take a stand are indecisive, hold on to their views too long, and vacillate to the point that it drives everyone crazy. Teams spin in an endless cycle of no decision and no action, and eventually people give up. An indecisive leader cripples a group or organization by sapping the energy and drive of people.

Often, indecisive leaders make their case and ask others to respond. Then they think about the input and return to the team to revisit the same topic. The group, once again, walks through the tedious process of reexamining the same problem. This dreary and mind-numbing pattern frustrates people.

Vacillating on decisions is frequently based on the fear of not *looking good* by making a mistake or miscalculation. But the opposite is true. Not taking a stand or making a decision offers no immunity; people know what the leader is attempting to do.

Symptoms of Not Taking a Stand

- Decisions are not clear.
- Decisions are not made or take a long time.
- Decisions are often reversed.
- Meetings are unproductive and inefficient.
- Group members work around the leader and get decision-making authority from others.

Louise was a senior vice president in a utility company. She had been in the position a little less than a year, and people had already decided she was weak, ineffective, and indecisive. No one was able to get any work done or move ahead with projects because she hedged on giving the go-ahead.

Louise and her team faced an infrastructure overhaul problem that would require significant support from an outside supplier. Her team thoroughly researched the options and provided her with a strong recommendation, which she *said* she fully supported. But she held up the funds for the project and kept coming up with excuses for not releasing them. Her group was frustrated and discouraged, and the problems were multiplying.

Several months later, Louise went to the CEO and made a weak case for the investment. "My direct reports think we should contract an outside supplier to troubleshoot the technology problem we're having. But I'm not sure about this—it's a lot of money." Louise did not take a stand. Instead, she used an escape hatch to avoid potential criticism by putting the responsibility on her team for the decision. If the CEO thought the decision to move forward was the right one, she could easily rotate her position and say, "It is a lot of money, but I'll make sure we get the return needed." On the other hand, if the CEO thought it was too much money, she would escape blame because it was her team's idea, not hers.

The CEO was preoccupied with larger concerns and casually said, "If you don't see the need, don't move ahead."

Because she couldn't determine which way the wind was blowing, Louise continued to sit on the fence. The problem ballooned when it impacted a major client and seriously compromised the relationship. The CEO stepped in and fixed the situation, which once again sent the message: Louise will not make a decision. Louise was demoted to a lesser position with much less scope.

Covering up and avoiding making crucial decisions is a surefire recipe for leadership failure. When you are unwilling to take a stand and make a firm decision, you lose power as others step in and take charge. People do not have a problem with a leader saying "I don't know" or "I made a mistake" or even "I have not made a decision yet." But they do have a problem with a leader who lacks the strength to take an unrelenting stand and make a firm decision.

The Impact of Not Taking a Stand. People lose confidence and their desire to contribute when you are indecisive and unwilling to take a stand. They feel disconnected to business goals and the actions needed to achieve them. When you waver, they fill in the blanks and either make decisions on their own, or "wait and see" what will happen. In either case, you have uncoordinated action and the lack of cohesion and alignment. Without your stand, forward motion comes to a halt, and critical actions are delayed.

When you do not take a stand, people hedge their bets. They feel ineffective and unable to do what is needed. Although you may be able to tolerate a high level of ambivalence, most people cannot. What others want from you are clarity and timely decisions that allow them to successfully execute their accountabilities. (In Chapter 5, we explore how to take a bold stand and unite, mobilize, and inspire others to action.)

Blind Spot 10: Tolerating "Good Enough"

Most leaders do not recognize when they are tolerating or settling for less. One reason this occurs is the natural tendency to focus on an individual area of interest or expertise. The upshot is the leaders unintentionally marginalize important areas and stamp them as "good enough." The drawback is that leaders pour their efforts into initiatives of their choice and abdicate areas of less compelling interest to others. In accepting good as "good enough," leaders inadvertently settle for the status quo or incremental reforms. This automatic drift results in the lack of exploration of new ideas and initiatives outside a leader's comfort zone.

This explains why cultural transformation is widely misunderstood and why often the business value is discounted. It stands to reason that unless a leader has experience or competency in the science of human behavior, this area appears to be a quagmire with no end in sight. For many leaders, this uncharted territory looks risky and disconnected from the organization's strategic objectives. Tolerating "good enough" is an avoidance behavior that keeps leaders safely pursuing familiar paths, even when they are ineffective.

Symptoms of Tolerating "Good Enough"
- Avoiding the discomfort of uncharted territory
- Not willing to investigate or explore needed changes outside of one's comfort zone
- Sitting back and being content with things as they are
- Defending the status quo
- Accepting incremental improvement as "good enough"

Steve, a CEO with employees worldwide, had an investment banking background with an expertise in mergers and acquisitions. He acquired businesses quicker than they could be readily assimilated into the organization. Steve's director of human resources told him of a major cultural clash with a newly acquired firm. Steve retorted, "Just give them a copy of our values—that should clear up any confusion." His HR director argued vehemently that this would not work; it would not engage people or align them with the parent company objectives. Although Steve was interested in the success of the merger, he had absolutely no interest in leading cultural transformation. So he gave the job to his HR director.

A considerable amount of money and time was spent on merging the cultures of the two companies, but the success achieved was unsustainable. The lack of high-profile involvement and commitment of Steve and senior leaders from both companies eventually led to the unraveling of the culture and the merger.

The Impact of *Tolerating* "*Good Enough.*" People are discouraged when leaders apply personal preference to leadership initiatives and ignore critical needs of the business or delegate them. When you are unwilling to learn and explore areas outside of your knowledge base, experience, and comfort, you not only limit yourself, you also limit the organization.

People want leaders who demand excellence and high standards of behavior that are consistently applied. Your leadership is essential to chart a new course and to move the company to the next level of performance. If you give lip service to cultural transformation and behavioral standards, you sacrifice the unified support of people and lose the most powerful mechanism available for creating extraordinary teamwork and alignment. Nothing will accelerate your business targets as quickly and effectively as people who are passionately focused on giving you more than what you ask for.

When you tolerate "good enough" and fail to move outside your comfort zone, you hold people and the organization back. (In Chapter 10, we explore how to hold yourself and others accountable for business results and impact on people.)

CONFRONTING BLIND SPOTS: THE CORNERSTONE OF FEARLESS LEADERSHIP

Most organizations have workforces who are change fatigued and cynical. People are subjected to countless change initiatives; some result in modest improvements, others flounder, and many are abandoned. The toll of failed change efforts builds a higher wall to climb for each subsequent effort.

As a fearless leader, you must be willing to help individuals and teams talk openly about honest mistakes and learn from them. This is where blind spots play a key role. People do not have the confidence or tools for having conversations that can transform business results and relationships. They lack shared skill sets for clearly articulating behavioral issues and do not know how to correct them.

All too often, leaders attempt to transform the culture of their organization or group through intellectual methods. Consensus building, feel-good team activities, developing a list of cultural practices and drivers—these do not transform people or organizations.

What transforms organizations is the transition from an intellectual approach to a process that is based on emotional and intellectual alignment. You must have a way to connect people so they want to work in a committed partnership with you and others.

Your accountability is to raise the level of transparency, participation, and involvement of people. They will not engage unless they see you engaging both emotionally and intellectually. Speak openly about your blind spots to others, ask for their input and coaching, and enlist others in talking about *their* blind spots. Foster an environment where it is safe for people to put sensitive issues on the table, without fear of repercussions, so they can be resolved. For teams and organizations to achieve high performance, blind spots must become an open discussion that occurs naturally in business.

The human element in leadership is what inspires people. This was evidenced by the extraordinary behavior of a CEO, whom we will call Logan, who was going it alone. His courage to confront his blind spots and openly include others in what happened launched the start of a highly successful cultural transformation in his operation.

How a CEO's Courage to Confront His Blind Spots Launched a High Performance Culture

Logan, the CEO of a major business operation in a well-known company, was ready to resign and move on. He had been with his current organization for six years, taking on enormous and unprecedented engineering challenges that had left him exhausted and discouraged.

What Happened. Logan worked with our group, even though he was deeply resigned and believed nothing would change. Before we met, we talked with his peers, direct reports, and next level up. A universal theme emerged: Logan's behavior over the past six months had changed from his usual easygoing manner to being abrupt, shut down, and defensive. As he had become more withdrawn and inaccessible, the organization came to a virtual standstill with everyone tiptoeing around his unpredictable moods.

The Impact. When we asked Logan why he was so discouraged, he explained, "My boss and I are no longer on the same page." Logan had drawn the conclusion that his role was being diminished from building and growing an organization to simply maintaining it. As a result, he lost his spirit and drive. Although Logan and his boss talked regularly, Logan never raised his real concerns. Instead, they had business-as-usual conversations and discussed strategic issues.

In our work together, Logan became aware of his blind spot of going it alone and the emotional impact it had on others. He had a breakthrough about the extent to which he had been resigned and withholding his emotional commitment and not talking straight.

The Courage to Take a Stand and Act Decisively. He shot off an e-mail to his boss—one from the heart where he disclosed his resignation and took accountability for his lack of engagement—and asked to talk. Within an hour, his boss called him. This time Logan initiated a different conversation and talked about what had derailed him. His boss was unaware of his impact and listened carefully to what was needed to resolve what turned out to be a simple misunderstanding.

A week later, the CEO of the global enterprise flew to Logan's operation. Together they met with over 700 employees and included them in discussing the breakdown that had occurred and how they had realigned and restored their partnership. They took a stand for building a high performance organization based on committed partnerships and accountability, and they used this experience as an example for how any issue could be openly discussed and resolved.

People were visibly moved and inspired by the authenticity of the two courageous leaders. The environment transformed, and a new culture began to emerge. Logan is now in his eighth year with the organization producing strong results and leading a high performance organization.

Lesson Learned. Transparency is a cornerstone of fearless leadership. Instead of deliberately hiding actions, leaders deliberately reveal their actions. Secrecy disappears, and a higher level of trust, inclusion, and engagement occurs. Commitment increases dramatically when leaders talk openly and honestly.

THE COURAGE TO CONFRONT YOUR BLIND SPOTS

Fearless leadership starts with you. Intellectually understanding your blind spots is insufficient. You must be willing to understand your emotional impact on others so you can choose if this is what you want. In other words, you must take 100% accountability for how you come across without justifying, defending, or explaining. This is easy to understand but difficult to do because we all have the need to be right, as you will learn in Chapter 3.

It takes committed partners to create an environment of trust and results. Your committed partners are the people you count on to tell you when blind spots are limiting you, your coworkers, or team. This is information you need to have in order to transform an organization. The more people see you striving to learn and grow and be a better leader, the more they will follow in your steps.

Transformational change requires the willingness to risk what has worked in the past to introduce a new leadership era. Bring your fearless leadership—your steadfast resolve and courage to transform your organization.

LEADERSHIP EXPLORATION

Identify the Blind Spots That Derail You and Your Team

Answer the following questions, but do not rely only on your opinion. Your opinion about your blind spots is biased and invalid; what others say is the only true measure. Ask others to provide you with feedback and listen carefully to what they have to say.

What Are Your Top Three Blind Spots? Over the years, you have received considerable feedback about your effectiveness as a leader. Consider what you have heard, and identify the common theme such as "People say I don't listen." Now multiply what you have heard by a factor of 100. Most likely, the feedback has been softened and delivered in a polite and cautious manner to you. It is likely that you have not received the message others were trying to communicate. Or you may understand the intellectual message but not appreciate your emotional impact on others.

What Are the Top Three Blind Spots of Your Team? Consider how your team works together, and identify the top three blind spots. Ask other team members to do the same, and compare your perceptions. Remember that others may be cautious in expressing their genuine point of view, so treat this as a first step in discussions about blind spots. Until others know that it is safe to speak up and that they will not be judged, they will be hesitant.

LEADERSHIP ACTION

Be Courageous: Ask Your Team to Coach You on Your Blind Spots

Ask your group to participate in a discussion about how *you* can be a more effective leader (or partner) to them. Let the group know you want to share your blind spots, learn how you impact them, and hear their coaching. It is important that others know that you are *not* asking them to discuss their blind spots; the focus is strictly on you. Also, do not put others on the spot by asking them to defend or justify their views. Perceptions are real, and all points of view are valid.

If you are not ready to listen and be coached, do not attempt to lead this activity. This is a powerful conversation, and your fearless leadership is required. You will lose credibility if this is perceived as a meaningless exercise or if you explain or rationalize your behavior. Your accountability is to listen fully—without judging or reacting, create a safe and open environment, and take accountability for your impact.

Be prepared for the fact that people may be uncomfortable and unwilling to provide you with candid feedback. If this is the case, work is needed to establish trust and safety, which is covered in Part II of this book.
Follow the steps below for the discussion.

Step 1. Be courageous and share your blind spots. Provide specific examples and ask: "What blind spots do you see that I have missed?"

Step 2. Take accountability for your impact. Ask: "How do my blind spots impact you? Do you have to work around me, do you comply, do you withdraw your emotional commitment and energy? How does my behavior frustrate you?"

Step 3. Ask your group to coach you on how to be more effective. Ask: "What coaching do you have for me? What actions do I need to take to be a better partner and leader for you? How can I learn and grow in my effectiveness?"

Step 4. Acknowledge the group. Express your appreciation for the willingness of others to speak up and provide you with candid input.

Things do not change; we change.

—Henry David Thoreau
(1817–1862)

Chapter
3
The Need to Be Right

The need to be right all the time is the biggest bar to new ideas.
It is better to have enough ideas for some of them to be wrong
than to be always right by having no ideas at all.

—EDWARD DE BONO (1933–)

There is nothing wrong with the need to be right; it is instinctive and natural. The problem rests with our inability to recognize when we become stuck in unbending and unyielding views and do not know how to move beyond them.

The startling fact is not that we have the need to be right; it is how we allow our need to be right to drive our thinking and actions despite disastrous consequences. Leaders defend their views even when it sabotages their personal success, reduces their choices, and locks them into inferior options.

We fail to recognize a critical principle of behavior: *the need to be right is much stronger than the need to be effective*. You may be trading your effectiveness and relationships for the need to be right.

In this chapter, we explore why leaders loathe being wrong and how the need to be right triggers blind spots. You will learn the behaviors that keep you stuck in defending your views. We will also explore the mechanism of automatic listening and how the mind filters and distorts information. Understanding the consequences of the need to be right on decision making is critical and examined in this chapter. The chapter concludes with how fearless leadership reverses our automatic impulse to be right and places our focus where it belongs: on being effective.

> The need *to be right* is much stronger than the need *to be effective*.

WHY WE LOATHE BEING SEEN AS WRONG

For many leaders, the very thought of being publicly wrong or making a mistake implies a personal inadequacy. They become inflexible and stubborn in protecting their point of view and attack anyone or anything that is in their way. Leaders dig their heels in and make poor decisions to protect their public image and avoid losing face. The irony is they reap exactly what they are attempting to avoid because they lose credibility.

Needing to be right is reinforced by a prevalent belief that leaders are expected to have all the answers and that followers expect them to provide the solution. Do you need to have all the answers and be right? If your response is yes, then you may be unconsciously adopting an "I'm right–you're wrong" attitude. When you need to be right, you willfully impose your views on others—whether they want them or not—and turn the words *collaboration* and *teamwork* into meaningless buzz terms.

Odd as it may seem, the need to be right is normal; human beings are instinctively hardwired to protect themselves to survive at all costs. The mind functions in survival mode in which there is never enough of *anything*; therefore, we feel we must fight for *everything*. Our thinking is shaped from this perspective, and we come from a condition of insufficiency—"I am not enough" or "I don't have enough." Our need to be right results in competing with others and defending our point of view. Our underlying belief—one person cannot gain unless another one loses—sets up conflict from the start.

The need to be right increases when we experience stress, fear, and high levels of uncertainty. We fear being wrong when our survival is at stake, but we loathe being wrong when it makes us feel inadequate or insufficient.

You can trust the fact that you have areas in which you have an arrested point of view and have become fixed and rigid in your thinking. You may not recognize where this has occurred, but others see it. When you have a myopic outlook, you are left with no choice but to argue for your point of view.

The Need to Be Right
A fixed view that becomes "the truth" and prevents you from seeing other perspectives.

When your thinking becomes narrow and limited, the world shrinks to the same limitations. You are unable to see other viewpoints or entertain an alternative perspective. Information is selected based on what you believe, then distorted and twisted to match your views. The mind fills in the blanks by gathering evidence—not to test a theory but to lock in a conclusion.

The longer you hold onto an unbending view, the greater the price you pay in terms of effective relationships. This was the case with Barrett, the head of auditing in a major global accounting and consulting firm.

When a Leader Insists on Being Right in Spite of Consequences to His Career

Others described Barrett as follows: "He loathes being seen as wrong. If he doesn't know an answer to a question, he makes one up."

What Happened. There were serious problems in Barrett's area— he had a reputation for being argumentative and polarizing people. His boss suggested that Barrett participate in a leadership development process, but Barrett hedged in committing and said to others, "*I know what I'm doing and I have no interest in changing.*" It seemed to elude him that he could be part of the problem and that his boss's instinct might be correct.

As time progressed and Barrett took no action, there was a mutiny of his direct reports, and people were lobbying to get transferred out of his area. No one wanted to work with Barrett including his boss.

The Impact. Instead of firing Barrett, a new position was created, where Barrett became an in-house consultant without any direct reports. Even though he was marginalized and lost his place on the career ladder, Barrett held on to his need to be right and rationalized his downgrade to others: "*I'm the best at troubleshooting and that's why I asked for this new position.*"

Lesson Learned. Barrett's need to be right was stronger than his need to be effective. He unwittingly sacrificed his career to tenaciously hold onto his entrenched position.

Companies frequently resort to the easy solution of marginalizing a leader who does not work effectively with others. The leader in jeopardy is isolated, where there is no hope for permanent and positive change. Everyone knows what has happened but pretends the move is "for the good of the company."

Why do leaders despise being wrong? They fear losing credibility and the respect of others, and they can't bear feeling inadequate or embarrassed or experiencing shame.

The behavioral prognosis is not good: you will fight to be right regardless of the cost to your effectiveness.

THE DEADLY COMBINATION: THE NEED TO BE RIGHT AND BLIND SPOTS

The need to be right is designed to protect you from perceived threats and keep you out of harm's way. Blind spots are driven by the need to be right and are your first line of defense to help you cope with challenging situations. Think of blind spots as your "army of behaviors" that is cleverly designed to take the heat off of you and put it on others. They strategically divert attention and help you stay below the radar in a low-risk and fortified position.

Blind spots and the need to be right have a single, unifying purpose: they are designed to avoid accountability. They allow you to roam freely without being accountable for much of anything.

You probably consider yourself to be a highly accountable person. Most leaders tell us they are, and from a surface examination, they appear quite respectable and responsible. However, when we drill down to their automatic behaviors—their blind spots—leaders discover a whole new meaning to the word *accountability*.

What we call accountability today is another word for deflection. We have become so accustomed to accepting a low standard of behavior— one that I wager is significantly lower than your own personal values— that we no longer notice it.

Every day you witness this lack of accountability. Committed, but frustrated, people conspire against each other and company initiatives, and they withhold their contribution and support. We give and accept reasons, excuses, and justification in place of results. We pay for effort and not for performance. We tolerate vague and ambiguous promises, and we allow people to hedge instead of committing.

We have become so indoctrinated to these behaviors that we have allowed an implied code of "no-accountability" to emerge. We do not even notice the slippage between words and actions, and we miss the fact entirely that we have blind spots that are designed to avoid accountability.

Looked at in this perspective, you can begin to appreciate the insidious nature of automatic behaviors:

Going it alone allows you to be a victim and avoid being accountable for your resignation and unwillingness to confront and resolve issues.

Being insensitive to your impact on others lets you justify your behavior and avoid taking accountability for how it impacts people and business results.

Having an "I know" attitude gives you cover to attack and diminish others—after all, you're right.

By avoiding difficult situations, you place the burden on others to read between the lines and avoid taking accountability for being emotionally honest.

Blaming others or circumstances allows you to take the offensive and point the finger instead of taking accountability for how your behavior has contributed to the situation.

Treating your commitments casually gives you a convenient way to hedge and escape being held accountable for your word.

Conspiring against others or initiatives allows you to flagrantly demonstrate that you are not accountable for partnership, teamwork, or the success of the enterprise.

Withholding emotional commitment lets you pretend to be engaged while you avoid being accountable for fully committing.

Not taking a stand lets you slide and wiggle around issues because no one can tie you down.

Tolerating "good enough" gives you a license to play it safe by avoiding being accountable for exploring new solutions and ideas and taking bold action.

When the need to be right is dominant and becomes the General in charge, the blind spots become its foot soldiers and keep you stuck in playing small and playing safe. When you feel threatened—real or perceived—the need to survive and be right takes over. You unknowingly shrink the game, and people around you disengage and withdraw. Guarded and shielded leaders do not inspire others to greatness.

If you want to play big and ensure that your organization survives and moves to the next level of success, then protecting yourself from making mistakes or being wrong is an ineffective strategy. You must learn how to include your imperfections in how you unite and motivate others and to do what fearless leaders do: be transparent, authentic, and accountable.

TRADING RELATIONSHIPS AND EFFECTIVENESS FOR THE NEED TO BE RIGHT

When you trade effectiveness and relationships for the need to be right, everything becomes small: your thinking, how you relate to others and the organization, and your level of engagement. It happens in an instant. Something occurs and you react, and your thinking and perception contract. You may be unaware that your perception has altered and in its place, a fixed view has formed.

Without realizing it, you no longer see yourself as an owner or view the organization from the larger perspective. Your framework for how you think about your role and your company shrivels and prevents new possibilities from emerging. Finally, you become resigned and lose your vitality, and along with it, your sense of having a greater purpose. For high-achieving leaders, this is the greatest loss of all.

When the need to be right becomes more important than the need to be effective, you become internally focused and lose sight of what is really happening. Others may offer much-needed solutions that provide you with exactly what you need, but you don't hear them because of your inflexible position.

Once you are on the warpath of being right, you ride it all the way until you are "dead right." This is what happened with two business partners—Jake and Kris—in the story below.

Two Leaders Argue over the Need to Be Right, and Employees Become Frozen

Jake, the CEO of seven acquired companies, purchased the majority share in a software company owned by Kris. They agreed that Kris would continue as CEO of the company for a period of three years.

What Happened. Within the first year, Jake and Kris came to loggerheads. Shortly after acquiring Kris's company, Jake wanted to use it for collateral to get capital investments. Kris disagreed with this approach and wanted to operate with caution and avoid risk. Jake, who acquired businesses for a living, was entrepreneurial and was unconcerned about calculated exposure. His formula had worked brilliantly and his successful enterprises were proof. Both CEOs became rigid about their positions and had heated arguments. They became so concerned about being right that nothing else was in their line of sight.

The Impact. During the six-month war, employees became unproductive and the company began losing business. Employees did not know whom to trust or follow, and many highly talented people left the company. The ones who remained gave minimal effort, and a competitor took advantage of the situation and captured a significant portion of their market share.

The Result. Even though Jake knew he could impose his controlling interest and make the decision, he did not want to lose Kris as CEO of the software company. But the chasm between them grew, and Kris left the company. They both got to be right.

Lesson Learned. The irony of needing to be right is that you end up killing the very thing you were originally attempting to protect. The need to be right does not stop with a point of view—it becomes an entrenched and deeply rooted position that people hold onto in spite of consequences.

We trade our effectiveness and relationships for the need to be right. And we pay a high price in terms of consequences.

The Impact of Needing to Be Right

- **Business results and relationships are damaged, and an adversarial environment emerges.** Leaders defend, protect, and argue positions to the exclusion of the enterprise perspective.
- **Positional thinking dominates, and focus shrinks.** People focus on "who will win" instead of "how we can accomplish our mutual and higher goals." Some leaders fight for their position, and others comply to avoid conflict.
- **Unhealthy competition and a we-they environment emerge.** People debate about positions instead of exploring new solutions.
- **Conflict escalates, and the business unit or organization becomes divided.** People line up behind leaders and their positions, and camps materialize.

WHAT KEEPS US STUCK IN THE NEED TO BE RIGHT

When you become stuck in the need to be right, you have a compelling goal: to win and have your view prevail. Once your view becomes a defended position, perspective is lost. People begin to identify you not as "Joe" but as your "position." You feel the need to defend yourself and be right. Backing down and losing face is not an option because it comes at too high a price—the perceived loss of credibility. You lose sight of the original event that triggered your reaction and become trapped in the need to be right.

The factors that keep you fixated on the need to be right are

1. Believing your perception is the truth
2. Expecting others to judge you by your intention
3. Building a case
4. Not investigating other views
5. Engaging in either-or thinking

Believing Your Perception Is the Truth

As a leader, the most dangerous delusion is believing your perception is reality. It stops you from challenging assumptions, examining thinking, and questioning conclusions. The belief that "my reality is the truth" prevents committed partnerships from forming. It places the burden on others to understand you and lets you off the hook for understanding others.

In Robert Heinlein's book *Stranger in a Strange Land*, he talks about a "fair witness"—an individual who reports what is or is not true. His character Jubal asks Anne, a fair witness, to describe the color of a recently painted house on a hilltop. Anne replies: "It's white on this side." As a fair witness, she does not infer anything other than what she can actually observe. She will not report that the other side of the house is white unless she actually went there and looked, and even then, she would not assume that it had stayed white after she left.

> Your perception of reality is not the truth. It is an interpretation—one among many.

Unless you are a fair witness, you treat your perceptions as the truth, and not as your interpretation of reality. The world appears as you perceive it, and what you cannot see, you infer. In short, you do what all human beings do: you make up stories.

Expecting Others to Judge You by Your Intention

We place an enormous burden on others to understand us and read between the lines. We know why we do things and we expect others to appreciate our reasons. When there is a misunderstanding, we assume others saw the situation in the same way we did. We think that others should realize we have a positive intention and understand that we do not intend to hurt them. When we have a negative impact, we believe we should be able to say "That was not my intention" or "I'm sorry" with the expectation that everything will instantly clear up.

We operate with a double standard: we judge others by their behavior, but we expect them to judge us by our intentions. We quickly blame others when their behavior is imperfect, but when it comes to our behavior, we expect people to give us the benefit of the doubt and trust our intention.

> We judge others by their *behavior* but expect them to judge us by our *intention*.

We often hear leaders defend their intention when their behavior is damaging. They say things such as "I didn't intend to hurt him" or "I was just trying to help." Your impact remains the same regardless of what you intend. Although you may be trying to help someone, if that person feels micromanaged, that's all that matters. People don't stop to consider your intention; they judge you by your behavior in the same way you judge them.

When you need to be right about your "intention," it makes it impossible for you to take accountability for your impact. This was what happened with Valdez, the director of exploration in a mining company. His direct reports described him as "reacting with anger and not listening." When his team told him that his behavior caused them to stop talking, he felt unjustly judged. Rather than listening to the group, Valdez became defensive. The problem: he could not take accountability as long as he was defending his intention.

We worked with Valdez and his group, and a lightbulb went on when he saw that (1) no one was questioning his intention and (2) his intention did not alter his impact. He took accountability for his impact and apologized to the group, and most importantly, he altered his behavior. Valdez saw what we all must see: two domains exist simultaneously—positive intention and negative impact.

> Your positive intention does not alter your impact on others.

Where do you put your focus when others tell you how you land on them? Do you focus on defending your intention—"I didn't mean to do that"—or do you listen and take accountability? Until you stop defending your intention and take accountability for your impact, others do not feel heard or understood.

Building a Case

Building a case is collecting evidence to prove you are right and accumulating reasons, justifications, and explanations for what you believe. Your case—based on your perception of what is and is not possible—happens in an instant when you collapse facts with interpretation.

Serious problems occur in decision making and relationships when we misidentify facts and interpretation. A fact is a fair witness observation—what you can observe to be true. An interpretation is your inference about the observation. But even observations can be tricky, so you must be particularly rigorous in asking, "Is this a fact or simply my interpretation?"

Let's look at an example. You observe a colleague close an office door while she is having a conversation with one of your peers. You do not trust your colleague, and you interpret the closed door as a deliberate attempt to keep you from hearing a conspiracy against you. Your mind is filling in the blanks. You knock on the door and they stop talking. You now have proof and a case: they are conspiring against you. But let's separate the facts from the interpretation. The facts: the door was closed, and when you walked in, they stopped talking. Your interpretation: they are plotting against me and trying to undermine me.

Building a case is self-reinforcing. Once you have wrapped your mind around a point of view, you then argue and twist information to support the validity of your case. When you attempt to find the resolution to a problem inside a reduced framework, things can look pretty dismal. And just think, you did this all by yourself with no help from anyone.

Not Investigating Other Views

When you need to be right, you stop investigating other interpretations and perspectives. You have a "yeah, but" response for everything. In other words, "Yeah, I hear you, but that doesn't apply to my situation." A "yeah, but" response lets you make your situation unique and impenetrable so you can reject alternative views or solutions. Your only choice of action is to do the same things over and over again, with the same results.

Many leaders feel that investigating other views or perspectives makes them look bad; after all, they should have all the answers. If you are embarrassed by not knowing or by admitting you do not have all the answers, it is difficult to investigate any other option. Beyond this, you will find it impossible to dig yourself out of the hole of needing to be right. Asking for help and input from others expands your view. Without it, you only have one limited perspective: yours.

You must decide if you are going to play big or play small. If you are unwilling to explore other options, examine different approaches, and listen to others to learn what they see that you do not, you are left being right regardless of the consequences.

Engaging in Either-Or Thinking

Either-or thinking sets up an us-versus-them mentality. It keeps your thinking inside defined boundaries and barriers, and it limits the scope for solving problems. The smaller your frame of reference, the fewer the options. Examples of either-or thinking are

- Either I win and they lose or they win and I lose.
- Either option A is right or option B is right.
- Either you are right or I am right.

When you fall into either-or thinking, your focus shifts to "who is right" and "what is right." An either-or belief, where two or more views are mutually exclusive, places you in the position of having to destroy your original view in order to see another perspective. Explained another way: you must be wrong in order to move to another perspective.

You lose the freedom to explore when decisions are reduced to "I have to choose either this or that." If you are faced with an either-or choice, ask yourself, "Why do I have to choose inside this framework?" Why indeed. You do not have to limit your thinking to a restricted framework. You can create a third alternative called "both, and" where *both* options are valid, and *all* options are acceptable. Shades of gray are desirable; they actually help people move beyond black-and-white thinking and allow them to connect and build on ideas. When you abandon rigid and limiting thinking, you can easily switch from one perspective to another.

THE MECHANISM: THE CLOSED LOOP OF AUTOMATIC LISTENING

The mechanism that explains the need to be right and keeps it in place is automatic listening. Automatic listening is the process of unconsciously filtering and distorting information to support your views and beliefs. From start to finish, the entire process is designed to give validity to your interpretations. It ultimately shapes how you behave and the choices you make.

Before we explore how automatic listening works, let's look at how the mind deals with information. Think of the content of your mind as "stuff." This includes all beliefs, opinions, points of view, judgments, assessments, prejudices, delusions, and positions.

Our stuff is made up; it is invented. It is an interpretation of reality and not reality itself. It takes a lot of rigor to separate what we conjure up (our interpretation) from what is really happening (the facts).

Automatic listening starts in the mind as a "wonder about" such as "I wonder if I can trust Jack" or "I wonder if the company will really succeed." But early doubts pave the way for fixed thinking and harsh judgments. Since there is not enough time to do exhaustive research on every situation or person you encounter, you pay attention to trigger features—small aspects of a larger situation used to infer additional information. Trigger features are an automatic means of eliminating ambiguity, making a decision, or inferring a judgment.

> **Automatic Listening**
> Filtering and distorting what you hear to support what you believe

When you stop "wondering," you euphemistically say "I have made up my mind." It would be more accurate to say that "I have made up my story" because what you have done is invent your own interpretation of reality.

The automatic listening cycle is a closed loop. Once it has begun, all information and evidence are distorted to support your beliefs. In this way, the cycle is self-fulfilling—you get what you believe. Without intervening and breaking the cycle, it gains momentum and rigidity over time.

Automatic listening is not rational or logical, but it is processed and reshaped in a particular order of steps, as depicted in Exhibit 3-1.

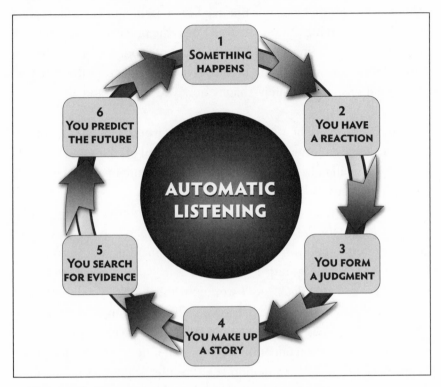

EXHIBIT 3-1: *The Closed Loop of Automatic Listening*

How Assumptions Become the Truth

Automatic listening starts the moment you notice a trigger feature— a single point of data—and make assumptions. In the mind, assumptions are treated as the truth, and they gather steam as you gather evidence.

Automatic listening happens in both directions: you form fixed views about others, and they form fixed views about you. Neither party is concerned with the intention of the other person; instead, both are busy gathering evidence to build their cases. The mind fills in the blanks based on how people behave, not what people intend.

This is what happened when employees formed an automatic point of view about Fred, the CEO of a health-care company.

How Small Behaviors of Leaders Can Lead to a "Tropical Storm"

Fred was known for being quick to anger and react. Unbeknownst to Fred, employees developed a system by which they classified his mood in the same way one would a tropical storm. Each morning, when Fred got on the elevator at the first floor, someone called in the warning before he got off at his sixteenth-floor office:

- Category 1: Mild winds—Fred is friendly and talkative.
- Category 2: Intermittent hot air—Fred mumbled hello but nothing else.
- Category 3: Strong storm surge—Fred is preoccupied and looks upset.
- Category 4: Warning, massive damage expected—Fred is making caustic and sarcastic remarks.

What Happened: The Interpretation. A Board meeting had just concluded, and many people speculated that the Board was not happy with Fred. The next day, Fred stepped into the elevator, frowned, grunted, and made several sarcastic remarks. This was enough for a Category 4 alert to be sent to the sixteenth floor advising everyone to run for cover.

The stories started spreading. People assumed that the Board meeting went badly and that they had asked Fred to submit his resignation. Work on the sixteenth floor came to a standstill. People canceled meetings with Fred and found excuses to avoid him.

What Really Happened: The Facts. The Board meeting had gone very well, and Fred's job was not in jeopardy. However, while driving to work, Fred was talking on his phone and accidentally curbed his right front tire resulting in a flat. He was late to work and annoyed at himself.

Lesson Learned. Our lack of awareness about automatic listening results in erroneous assumptions that impact daily interactions. It takes only one small behavior for assumptions to form and stories to spread. Once people fixate on a conclusion, they gather evidence to be right, and the closed loop begins to form.

Your behavior—regardless of what you intend—sends a message that others will interpret. The same process occurs inside your mind where you observe the behavior of others and use small trigger features to form assumptions and make judgments.

Let's examine each step of the automatic listening model in Exhibit 3-1 and see how assumptions are formed and locked in place.

1. **Something happens.** Automatic listening starts with an event, a situation, or a behavior. Your mind notices the trigger feature—a small aspect of a larger situation—and you begin to wonder. Wondering is the first stage of doubt and casts suspicion. In the case of Fred, a handful of employees noticed trigger features—frowning, grunting, and a sarcastic remark—and began wondering.

2. **You have a reaction.** Reactions take the form of emotions, such as concern, annoyance, or frustration. Instinctive responses happen quickly and automatically in the same way you have fight-or-flight reactions. People reacted to Fred's behavior with trepidation: *"Oh no, here he goes again— we need to protect ourselves."*

3. **You form a judgment.** The mind forms a judgment and infers meaning from the trigger features. The judgment of Fred was that he had a hair-trigger temper and was *"going to rip someone's head off."*

4. **You make up a story.** Once a judgment is formed, you make up a story that is consistent with your point of view. For example: *"Something happened at the Board meeting— Fred is in trouble"* or *"Fred is in a bad mood, and he's going to take it out on us."* The story may be simple or elaborate, but it fulfills its purpose, which is to explain the behavior or situation.

5. **You search for evidence.** Your mind then searches for past evidence to prove you are right. For example: *"Fred always acts this way when he is upset."* The mind references a past experience and provides weight for the inference. The story may be further embellished with past evidence: *"Last quarter Fred had a run-in with the Board, and he flew off the handle*

afterward with one of his direct reports." All of this speculation began with the interpretation of Fred's "elevator behavior."

6. **You predict the future.** The final step in the automatic listening loop is predicting the future. We anticipate future behavior to prepare and protect ourselves. For example: *"Fred's not going to last long—he'll be out of here by the end of next month."* Once you've made a future prediction, the loop is now complete, and you will continue to gather evidence.

The automatic listening loop described above is self-reinforcing and closed. Regardless of what happens, you have developed a story and an interpretation that locks in your point of view. You will be committed to being right about your view and will defend it. To add strength to your case, you will conspire with others, and you will cast doubt and suspicion on an individual or group. Your automatic listening prevents you from seeing any other interpretation, and your freedom to invent the future is gone.

How Exceptions Prove the Rule

This raises a question: what happens when Fred's behavior changes the next day, and he enters the elevator and greets everyone with a smile and a friendly "How are you?" Does the word spread that all bets are off and everything is all right with Fred and the Board? No, an exception in the automatic listening loop is *not* used to challenge the original assumption. Instead, the exception proves the rule.

Let's walk through what happens when Fred's behavior changes from frowning and grunting to smiling and chatting:

1. **Contrary evidence is presented (something happens).** Fred gets into the elevator on the first floor. He smiles and says, *"How are you today?"* and *"How's everything going in your area?"* He is friendly and talkative as he rides the elevator to the sixteenth floor.

2. **You have a reaction to the incongruent behavior.** You are disconcerted and uncomfortable. On one hand, it's nice to see Fred smiling. On the other, this makes you nervous because Fred's behavior is inconsistent with how he normally behaves. The mind thinks, *"He must be up to something."*

3. **You form a judgment about the "exception."** It doesn't make sense that Fred is friendly today and was abrupt and aloof yesterday. You add an interpretation to the facts and attempt to make meaning of this change in behavior. You may think, *"Fred is political so he's covering up the problem and putting on a good show."*

4. **You make up a story about the "exception."** You build a story that links and explains why Fred is behaving differently today. Your story is designed to ensure that the exception proves the rule. For example: *"Fred's slick; he's buying time with the Board situation. He's going to manipulate this so he comes out on top."*

5. **You search for past evidence about the "exception."** The search for past evidence is to prove that you are right, not discover something new. For example: *"Fred never reveals what is really going on so we need to watch him carefully."*

6. **You predict the future using the "exception" to be right.** You have now traveled full circle, and the mind predicts the future. You might think, *"All of this friendly behavior is just a show so Fred can get himself a great package when he leaves."*

By the end of the loop, the exception has proven the rule. Contradictory information, behavior, and actions are distorted to support your view. In automatic listening, you are guilty and will not be proven innocent, and there is no court of appeals.

The following example of two business groups in an insurance company illustrates how automatic listening can lead to costly problems.

Automatic Listening and Distrust between Two Groups Impacts Business Results

The New York claims office had decreased its referrals to the San Diego office by an estimated 50 percent. This was based on their automatic point of view, which was described as follows: *"We no longer have confidence that the San Diego office will adhere to our process."*

What Happened. There was a long history between these two offices, which fueled the belief that the San Diego office was not up to the task of handling significant cases. Substantial changes had been made in personnel in the West Coast office, such as bringing in a new managing attorney and removing a trial attorney who was not effective. But even with these changes, the New York office was unwilling to refer any significant cases until, as they said, "the San Diego group proved itself." By refusing to refer cases to the San Diego office, the New York office was able to be right about its point of view.

On the other side, the San Diego office had an automatic view about the New York group. They perceived them as "arrogant, belligerent, and stubborn" and gathered evidence for this view every time the New York group refused to send them cases.

The Impact. The lack of confidence and trust resulted in the New York office sending new litigation files to outside counsel, who charged substantially more than the West Coast office. Consulting fees went through the roof because internal resources were not used.

Lesson Learned. The need to be right always comes with a cost; in this case the cost was both a financial loss and inefficiency. When people do not have a way to talk about rigid views and work through conflict, they default to their automatic listening and automatic behavior.

THE CONSEQUENCES OF NEEDING TO BE RIGHT

> *I do not suppose that either of us knows anything really beautiful and good. I am better off than he is—for he knows nothing, and thinks that he knows. I neither know nor think that I know.*
>
> —SOCRATES (C. 469–399 BC)

Working with leaders who need to be right is like running into a brick wall. No matter how many times you hit the wall, it remains standing but you are left in bad shape. Although this may conjure up thoughts about others, do not forget that you are the "wall" for many. This leads to the following circumstances:

1. People work around you and not with you.
2. People abdicate accountability and let you do all the thinking.
3. Problems are not resolved effectively.
4. You lose the ability to adapt and recover quickly.

People Work *around* You, Not *with* You

People will not expend the enormous amount of energy required to go toe to toe with someone who is argumentative and unyielding. They do not want to waste their time, or more importantly, their energy in a no-win situation. If you already have a fixed view—and you look for what's wrong in other perspectives—people will avoid working with you. If you are in a higher-status position, others will not confront you because you hold all the power. Even though you may say, "I like strong people who challenge me," your behavior says, "You're target practice for me." People will believe your behavior before they trust your words.

Those who must work with you will run for cover and pull back the moment you come out with guns blazing. After experiencing your reaction and anger, people choose the most expedient and comfortable route, which is to work around you. They comply and give you lip service instead of having to go through one more conversation that leaves them drained.

People Abdicate Accountability and Let You Do All the Thinking

Others stop making decisions and contributing when you demonstrate the need to be right. They stop thinking and shut down conversations and options. When you are inside your automatic listening loop and searching for evidence to prove your point, you literally cannot hear what others are saying, and they know it. People do not have the skills to break the cycle so they don't try to change your mind. They let you do all the thinking since you're doing it anyway. Your mind takes the place of the group mind, and the message is, "Do not question or doubt me; just do as I say."

When you operate with an "I'm right" attitude, you are saying, "You're wrong." You are also communicating that you trust your thinking over the collective wisdom of the group. Even though you may have a great mind—perhaps a brilliant mind—it is still only one mind with its built-in limitations. When your opinions and views dominate, the organization goes on autopilot, and real thinking vanishes.

Problems Are Not Resolved Effectively

Solving problems within the framework of what you already know results in closed problem solving, which means that ideas are examined only within a defined and rigid structure. You get to be right, and you find evidence (and people) to support your beliefs. No new information can come in to alter your thinking, and you are left with the same solutions—just tweaked with new variations. In closed problem solving, the limitations of what you know define the boundaries of all possible solutions.

You get to be right and solve the same problems over and over again. The sidebar "Defending What You *Think* You Know" lists the ways in which we ensure that all thinking remains inside our closed loop of automatic listening. Inside this closed thinking, there is no room for exploration, dialogue, or inquiry into new possibilities.

Defending What You *Think* You Know

- "*I know there is not a problem.*" You defend the adequacy of the present and deny that a problem exists.
- "*I know how to solve the problem.*" You defend what you already know and stop investigating further.
- "*I know the right way to solve the problem.*" You restructure what you already know, and you call it a new solution when, in fact, it is the same information in a new order.

You Lose the Ability to Adapt and Recover Quickly

The law of requisite variety (sometimes known as Ashby's Law after William Ashby, who proposed it) states, "The variety in the control system must be equal to or larger than the variety of the perturbations in order to achieve control." The popular interpretation is, "The most flexible system or person is the most powerful one." When the complexity of the environment exceeds the capacity of leaders and organizations, the environment dominates and ultimately destroys both.

A leader or organization has requisite variety only when its responses meet or exceed the stimuli encountered in the environment. When you lose the ability to adapt and recover quickly, you lose power and the ability to influence change. The need to be right creates a rigid, inflexible structure where adaptation is not possible.

> Your need to be right exacts a high cost: your leadership effectiveness and your future.

EVERYTHING STARTS WHEN YOU TURN INSIGHT INTO ACTION

Personal transformation often occurs in times of crisis. Something happens that makes you suddenly realize that the cost of holding on to your need to be right has become too great. You pry your fingers off of your rigid view for no other reason than you are losing *everything* with your intractable position. This epiphany allows you to get outside of your point of view and see the validity of other perspectives. In an instant, what appeared to be an irreconcilable or hopeless situation suddenly shifts, and your mind is flooded with new thinking and possibilities.

You do not need to wait for a crisis to transform your organization. Fearless leadership provides you with the road map for gaining immediate access to transformation. When you can truly understand how others experience your behavior, without defending or judging, you then have the ability to produce a breakthrough in your leadership and team. Everything starts with your self-awareness. You cannot take charge without taking accountability, and you cannot take accountability without understanding how you avoid it.

As a fearless leader, you must learn how to bring compassion and understanding when you and others are stuck in your point of view. We must understand that the need to be right is automatic and learn how to recover quickly when it occurs.

Bring compassion for yourself and others when people become positional, rigid, or fixed in their views. If you can see this as a natural occurrence, rather than judging yourself or others as being wrong or inadequate, you can help people get out of the hole instead of pushing them further in.

With fearless leadership, you will have the tools to generate new resolutions for challenging problems through bringing a larger perspective, collaborating, and innovating. This requires a willingness on your part to let go of the need to be right and to expand your thinking. Unless this changes, the long-term prospect of increasing your leadership effectiveness is dim. The progression from how you think and what you believe to how you behave is key to understanding how to optimize performance—yours and others. Right now your automatic listening is mechanical and habitual. As you begin to recognize how you filter and distort what you hear, you will have access to a powerful method for intervening in this unconscious process. You will be able to make purposeful choices and take decisive action that significantly accelerates the outcome and results you want. The choice before you at this point is: are you willing to turn insight into action?

LEADERSHIP EXPLORATION

Answer the following questions for yourself. Then ask a coworker to provide his or her assessment about you. As always, trust the perspective of others above your own.

Do You Have the Need to Be Right?

1. Do you usually have the last word on a subject?
2. Do you interrupt and cut people off when they are talking?
3. Do you state your position repeatedly?
4. Do you dominate conversations or meetings by talking most of the time?
5. Do you make up your mind before asking others for input?
6. Do you ask for input and destroy it when it doesn't support your beliefs?

What Judgments—Automatic Listening—Have You Formed about People and Groups?

Identify an individual or group with whom you have challenges, and answer the following questions:

1. What is my judgment about the individual and group?
2. What evidence have I collected?
3. What story have I made up?

Example: I have a judgment that *"I can't trust Joe."* My evidence is that he does not follow through on what he promises, he talks behind my back, and others tell me that he makes negative comments about me. The story I have made up is that Joe is politically motivated, has a strong personal agenda, and doesn't care who he tramples in the process.

Which Is Your Greater Commitment: Needing to Be Right or Being Effective?

1. Where are you holding onto the need to be right in spite of undesirable consequences?
2. What price are you paying?
3. How are you avoiding being accountable?
4. What is stopping you from letting go of your need to be right and refocusing your attention on how you can be more effective?
5. What would you have to give up in order to let go of your need to be right?
6. What would you gain by expanding your thinking, investigating other viewpoints, and listening fully to others?

LEADERSHIP ACTION

Check Your Ego at the Door, and Examine How Your Need to Be Right Impacts Working Relationships and Business Results

Your need to be right will not disappear; it is an instinctive response. But you can begin recognizing when it surfaces, take accountability for your impact, and choose a more productive response. To raise your level of awareness about how your need to be right derails problem solving, prevents contributions from others, and limits collaboration, ask the following questions of a coworker or your team. Resist the temptation to drive your agenda and control the discussion, and listen to the answers without defending, explaining, or justifying.

1. Do I attempt to solve problems prematurely instead of fully listening to you? How does this impact our working relationship and business results?

2. Do you feel that I judge what you say and limit your contributions? How does this impact our working relationship and business results?

3. Do you feel that I listen for information to validate my existing beliefs and that I am not open to new ideas and other points of view? How does this impact our working relationship and business results?

4. What have you been trying to tell me that I haven't been listening to? How does this impact our working relationship and business results?

> *One doesn't discover new lands without consenting*
> *to lose sight of the shore for a very long time.*
>
> —ANDRE PAUL GUILLAUME GIDE (1869–1951)

Chapter
4
Victim Mentality and Playing Small

*People seem not to see that their opinion of the world
is also a confession of their character.*

—Ralph Waldo Emerson (1803–1882)

Do you play big and give everything you have at all times? Do you face challenging situations head-on and confront the real issue? When we ask this of leaders, the majority reply, "Absolutely. That's the only way I play—full-out or not at all."

Fearless leadership begins when you choose to *play big*—without limits to what is possible—despite difficult or challenging circumstances. When you play big, your behavior is consistent with your values and beliefs; you throw your hat in the ring and fully engage.

However, even with your zest and commitment, you will fall into automatic behaviors that keep you playing small. In this chapter, we add another automatic behavior—victim mentality—and how it contributes to resignation, shrinking the game, and building silos. This is pivotal in understanding why internal groups struggle and engage in warfare against each other. It brings together the need to be right, blind spots, and victim mentality in a way that illuminates the problem and introduces its solution.

We also discuss the imperative need to move beyond denial so new thinking and behavior can occur. Then we examine the importance of personal and organizational context and how it defines the difference between playing small and playing big.

DEFINING YOUR PERSONAL CONTEXT: PLAYING BIG OR PLAYING SMALL

The first step in transformation is to move beyond denial. Many leaders argue that there are no significant behavioral or cultural issues in their organization. Others deny that their behavior is a primary contributor to organizational performance.

When you are in denial, the problem will either not appear on your radar screen or it will appear as the fault of others or circumstances. With this limited view, you lose the ability to act, and you are left only with the ability to react. Denial not only impacts decision making, it slows the organization to a snail's pace. But when you acknowledge that there is a problem and you are part of the problem, you can take action.

If there is a gap between what you have and what you want, you can do something about it—that is, if you are willing to take accountability and change *your* behavior.

If you have a voice inside your head saying, "I like myself just the way I am and I'm not changing," tell it to pipe down. Your internal voice—the one that argues, defends, and justifies—keeps you stuck playing small. That's what your automatic behaviors are designed to do. But you have a choice: commit to playing big or remain stuck in old behaviors that hold you back.

If what you have read so far applies to everyone else but you, it is time to let go of your need to be right and investigate how you limit yourself and others. To be a fearless leader, your attention must shift to *your* locus of control—what *you* can do to powerfully influence change, how *you* can make significant choices, and how *you* can take decisive action.

In order to play big, you must (1) move beyond denial and (2) expand your personal context or framework for how you relate to yourself, others, and your company. Here's what is essential to understand:

1. You have a personal context—a framework of thinking and beliefs—that defines whether you play big or small and determines your capacity to succeed.

2. You vacillate between playing small and playing big depending on how you interpret a given situation.

3. Your personal context shrinks when you are unwilling to confront your blind spots, your need to be right, and your victim mentality.

Let's start by defining the broader term *context* and how it defines both the game and how it is played. Think of context as the whole — the framework surrounding a situation that provides the background and helps define meaning. Context helps you make sense out of a situation by reducing ambiguity and uncertainty and by providing clarity.

In the same way you can change how a picture looks by merely changing the frame, you can change what you and others focus on by altering the context. The context *is* the frame; it defines what people pay attention to and notice. When you alter the frame or context, you change the game.

As a leader, you provide organizational context every time you speak about the purpose of the organization and what you want to achieve. You set up this framework by answering questions such as "What is our company up to?" "Who do we want to be?" "What contribution do we want to make?" and "What are we up to creating and generating?"

> When leaders play small, the organization can *only* play small. When leaders play big, the organization can transform.

Similarly, your personal context is the framework for how *you* relate to the organization, other leaders, and colleagues. If your personal context is small — "I cannot influence change" — then your focus, choices, and possibilities are limited. When it is big — "I have the power to take action and influence change" — you dramatically expand what you notice and, as a result, what is possible. A small personal context limits you, while a big context gives you access to a new domain of thinking and the power to break down barriers and shape the future.

Taken together, organizational and personal context define the potential of the enterprise to excel by powerfully connecting people to its strategic objectives. Your challenge is to ensure that organizational and personal context converge so that people are emotionally engaged and act with urgency to achieve the mission of the organization.

The critical factor missed by most leaders is this: an organization cannot succeed in achieving a large, all-encompassing context when leaders have a small personal context. When leaders play small, the organization cannot expand beyond its current capacity. When leaders play big and engage with one another in an extraordinary way, they operate with a large personal framework. This is what allows the organization to transform and grow.

Exhibit 4-1 provides a snapshot of how your personal context—playing small or playing big—defines behavior and impacts business results.

Fearless leadership is a big game that powerfully connects personal and organizational context, and radically alters what leaders and companies can achieve.

EXHIBIT 4-1: *Playing Small versus Playing Big*

HOW RESIGNATION CREEPS IN AND SHRINKS THE GAME

Playing small occurs when resignation sets in and you believe that the status quo—people, circumstances, or the organization—is more fixed than it actually is. Even the most competent and hard-working leaders become resigned, although this is inconceivable to them. Resignation in strong leaders is difficult to see because they continue to demonstrate a high level of commitment and put in grueling hours. But it is what's going on inside of them that tells the real story.

When you become resigned, you reach an impasse where you are struck with sudden doubts. You may be feigning enthusiasm, managing your emotions instead of expressing them, or feeling yourself shut down and becoming defensive and closed. You know you are resigned when the mere absence of feeling discouraged is exhilarating.

If you are among those leaders who are brave troopers and shoulder the burden by themselves, you will find it difficult to believe that you can become resigned. There is an erroneous belief that "strong and tough leaders do not become resigned." This is inaccurate and fallacious. A high degree of leaders are resigned to the point that it impacts their effectiveness and the organization.

Let's set the record straight. Resignation is not quitting or giving up; it is not *showing* up. When you become resigned, you continue to work hard, but your personal context shrinks, the game becomes smaller, and you lose interest, heart, and enthusiasm. To the outside world, you are still highly committed, but *you* feel the difference. When you become resigned, you don't look for choices anymore because you don't believe they exist. You feel that the future is fixed, and in your resignation, you become oblivious to the prison you have created.

Resignation is not *giving* up; it is not *showing* up.

Resignation happens gradually. It may be a single event or a series of events that leads you to decide you cannot win, you cannot make a difference, your boss will never listen to you, or your company will never change. Although your decision is unconscious, your behavior changes to match your beliefs about what can or cannot be accomplished.

Teams or business units often share a resigned point of view that is unspoken but present in every conversation and decision. Team behavior can become pessimistic and downtrodden, and leaders miss the fact that the entire group is resigned. Once team members solidify their view and are resigned that nothing will change, the game shrinks and problem solving is reduced to the smaller framework. Resignation often shows up in the comments that team members make privately to each other, for example:

- "We can't get this done fast enough."
- "We aren't going to pull this off."
- "We don't have enough support or resources to make this work."
- "We'll never hit our numbers."

When leaders or teams do not recognize that they are resigned, they create the same behavior in others and resignation spreads. This is what happened when leaders in a technology company became resigned during companywide downsizing.

When Leaders Are Resigned, They Telegraph It in Their Behavior, and People Lose Confidence

Maureen, the director of product development, and her operation worked nonstop on new and promising consumer products. Although things were not going well due to downturns in the market, Maureen's group was delivering results.

What Happened. Gunnar, Maureen's boss, spoke to her group of 200 and delivered the following message: *"The market is volatile, and we're cutting back in all areas. All funding of new products is frozen, and we will downsize significantly in the next several months."*

The Impact. Gunnar's talk was short, to the point, and had unintended consequences. Although Maureen and her group were not surprised by the "content" of the message, they were stunned by the detached and cold manner in which it was delivered. They became despondent and resigned, and innovation collapsed.

Gunnar was unaware of two things: the fact that he was resigned and how his resignation impacted Maureen's group. Our group worked with Gunnar and drilled down to the real problem. Gunnar realized that he was uncomfortable talking about cutbacks and downsizing; all he wanted to do was get the presentation over with. What he failed to recognize was that he left the entire group—both those staying and those who would be leaving— devastated.

The Recovery. Gunnar went back to the product development group and took accountability for his impact. He said, *"The last time I spoke to you, I did not communicate well. I was uncomfortable talking about downsizing and cutbacks. What I want is your partnership to get through these tough times together so we can continue to build on the great results and performance that each of you has delivered."* The group, including those who were leaving, felt acknowledged for their contributions. They responded immediately and generated ideas and solutions to ensure that the company survived.

Lesson Learned. When leaders are resigned, it is evident in their speaking and behavior, and it cascades throughout the organization. People mirror the mood and behaviors of leaders: resignation breeds resignation.

As a leader, you set the course for everyone else. When you play small, no one can play big. Your resignation not only inhibits your ability to rise above circumstances, it stops everyone from being able to generate solutions in difficult situations. Everyone pays the price; the esprit de corps of the group is lost, and people resign and disengage.

You can create a larger context—a bigger game—in which people feel they can influence change and shape the future. But you cannot do this unless you ask yourself, "Where am I resigned?" Notice the question is not *if* you are resigned. I want you to examine where you have become discouraged or frustrated and where you have attempted to carry on in spite of these feelings. When you are resigned, you cannot expand your personal context. The leadership exploration section at the end of this chapter will help you identify resignation.

Chances are that you have some degree of resignation—we all do. Others notice your resignation by a change in your behavior. But resignation is pervasive throughout all organizations from the top to the bottom.

There are two messages in all of this. First, *don't give up on people.* Resignation masks anxiety and discouragement, and it makes even highly competent leaders appear detached or disengaged. Providing that competency is not the issue, it is always worth the investment of time and money to work with a leader in jeopardy to produce a breakthrough in his or her effectiveness.

Second, *don't give up on yourself.* You may be stoically accepting resignation and working hard despite feelings of discouragement and disillusionment. But as you are beginning to see, fearless leadership is not the absence of resignation or automatic behaviors. It is the courage to confront them to expand personal and organizational context.

THE VICTIM TRIANGLE AND HOW IT WORKS

Victim mentality and resignation go hand in hand. When you become resigned, you inadvertently adopt victim thinking and behaviors that lead to viewing others as the opponents. This subtle process happens below the surface of our awareness and agitates responsible leaders when they discover they have fallen prey to victim mentality.

If you are like most leaders, you won't like the word "victim" applied to you in any capacity. But that is exactly why it is used; the word rankles us and gets our attention. Leaders do not view themselves as victims; however, victim mentality can happen to anyone, anytime, anywhere. Even you.

Victim mentality is based on the view that there is an ever-present enemy, adversary, or opponent working against you. When you become resigned that something is not possible or that change is unachievable, victim mentality takes over. You feel powerless to alter what appears to be fixed, and you would rather deal with the consequences of your behavior instead of taking accountability.

The victim is not only bitter about the past; the victim is already disappointed with the future.

When you expect someone else to be the responsible agent for your future, you have crossed the line into the world of the victim. This state of dissatisfaction and disappointment comes with the feeling that nothing is ever right or good enough. Unmet expectations, disenchantment, and unfulfilled promises become the fodder of victim mentality. Because victims see others as adversaries, they feel as if outside agents or forces control their actions and their future.

Victim mentality can be summed up in one word: *should*. Victims believe things *should* be different; they *should* have more, or someone else *should* do something. There is always a *should* for the victim.

When you fall into the victim trap, and you do, the fundamental belief is that the problem is outside your locus of control and everyone and everything else is to blame. Recognizing when you fall into victim mentality is the key to transformation and fearless leadership. Remember that anything that can be confronted can be addressed.

The Victim, the Persecutor, and the Co-Conspirator

Victim mentality is based on three interdependent roles: the *persecutor* (the person or circumstance you are blaming), *co-conspirators* (people who agree with you and your point of view), and the *victim* who has been unjustly wronged. When you fall into the victim trap, you build a case, conspire with others, and collect evidence to demonstrate that you are right and others are wrong. The victim triangle shown in Exhibit 4-2 identifies these three roles: the victim, the co-conspirator, and the persecutor.

The Victim. Victims feel entitled and expect life and others to satisfy their needs. They believe they are the injured party and are suffering a great injustice and blame people and circumstances for getting in the way of what they *should* rightfully have.

Victims explain, justify, rationalize, and defend their point of view. From the victims' perspective, there is only one truth—theirs. When

EXHIBIT 4-2: *The Roles in the Victim Triangle*

you fall into victim mentality, you get to be right and totally power-less. By definition, victims do not take accountability and let others dictate their actions.

What keeps victims stuck is denial. They don't believe they are victims; in fact, most perceive themselves as highly responsible. The more fervently someone denies that they are a victim, the greater the likelihood that they are.

The Persecutor. Where there is a victim, there is always an enemy or persecutor. Victims feel forced into a bad situation or into doing something against their better judgment or will. The people who are perceived as inflicting pain are called the persecutors, the bullies, or tormentors. The persecutors can be individuals, groups, or circum-stances. This is important in the victim triangle because the perse-cutors fuel the victims' need to blame and fight against something or someone.

Persecutors become frustrated when they feel stonewalled and unable to resolve a problem. They are seldom aware they are perceived as the enemy and discover this only through the behavior of others.

The Co-conspirator. In order to maintain victim mentality, victims must have a band of followers who believe that the victims are right. Victims are skilled at building camps and silos in which people conspire against others and complain about groups, senior management, and the company. Victims seek co-conspirators who already agree with their views or can easily be persuaded.

Co-conspirators enable and rescue the victims by buying into the victims' interpretation of what happened. If you're a co-conspirator, you share the feeling that the victim is being unfairly treated. Your anger and frustration are directed *against* something or someone, and like the victim, you blame others and perpetuate the problem.

In Chapter 2, we discussed the blind spot of conspiring against others. In the victim triangle, co-conspirators take this behavior to a new level. They engage in unproductive behaviors that occur in a variety of settings including meetings, hallway conversations, and one-on-one interactions as described in the sidebar "Examples of Conspiring Against Others."

Let's be clear about the role of a co-conspirator: if you listen to a conspiracy, hear a conspiracy, or know of a conspiracy and do not take a stand or action to intervene, *you are a co-conspirator*. A silent co-conspirator is as guilty as a vocal one.

The roles constantly change in the victim triangle, and you may find yourself in any one of the three roles in different situations. For example, you may be in the victim role with your boss and in the role of the persecutor with a direct report. Because the roles in the victim triangle are unconscious and not clearly identified, a swirl of emotions and undermining behaviors occur.

There is a fourth role that takes you outside of the victim triangle: the role of a fearless leader. The victim triangle is sustained by being right and not taking accountability, but when you add fearless leadership, the cycle is broken and victim mentality cannot endure.

Examples of Conspiring Against Others

1. **Sabotaging a group or person by innuendo.** Suggestive comments cast doubt: *"How can you possibly claim these figures are accurate when your last report had major errors?"* Questioning someone's honesty, integrity, or credibility is enough to create reservations and misgivings in others.

2. **Inferring a malicious intent.** An aggressive and offensive position is often used. For example, *"You're obviously trying to make us look bad. So don't try to pin this problem on us—you missed the deadline."*

3. **Spreading gossip and rumors.** Making assumptions and allowing them to run rampant launches the grapevine and enlists others in the conspiracy. For example, *"I heard that the company is going to downsize by 30 percent. You better start looking for another job."*

4. **Silently agreeing.** Silence is an action; it is the act of withholding a stand or commitment. Every time you silently agree with a point of view, you endorse it.

5. **Sending a conspiratorial nonverbal message.** Rolling your eyes or exchanging a "knowing" glance with others implies a secret or private communication that is perceived as negative or dismissive.

6. **Verbally attacking and piling on.** Verbally tearing down a person or idea starts with one person and builds as others express similar comments. For example, *"I agree with Todd. You didn't handle this situation well, and as Cheryl said, you left us hanging out to dry."*

7. **Rescuing.** Co-conspirators form a closed ring and rescue, protect, and save each other. For example, *"You can stop attacking Marcus. He did what he needed to do, which is more than I can say for you."*

The Language That Ignites Victim Mentality

Victim language is designed to avoid accountability and commitment by protecting one's story and interpretation of what happened. This shows up in blaming, hedging, and defensive language that allow victims to wiggle out of any situation.

Consider the power of language and how it influences how we think, listen, and behave. We forget that speaking is an action and that language is a powerful tool for changing how people respond to the world around them. The words you choose construct and define your reality, and they form your interpretation.

There is a distinct difference between *victim language*, which focuses on external factors and blame, and *owner language*, which focuses on taking accountability. Exhibit 4-3 provides examples of both.

Victim language frequently starts with a reference to an outside party and uses words such as *you, they, he, she,* and *this group* at the beginning of a sentence. For example, "You never listen to me." Further, the victim attributes a causal relationship, such as "Your actions caused me to react this way."

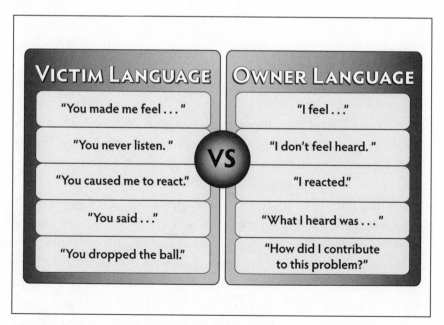

EXHIBIT 4-3: *Examples of Victim Language versus Owner Language*

In owner language, the word *I* is used frequently to take personal accountability: "I am accountable for my impact." Owners take accountability for what they experience, hear, and see, and they do not blame others.

SILOS, DIVISIVENESS, AND THE VICTIM TRIANGLE

The victim triangle describes how silos and divisions are formed within a company: roles are defined, impenetrable boundaries built, and an us-versus-them atmosphere created. Each group—the victim, persecutor, and co-conspirator—defends its position, has the need to be right, and gathers evidence to build a case. Warring factions escalate the conflict by persuading others to support their position and conspire against the enemy. Classic examples of adversarial relationships include sales versus marketing, operations versus corporate, staff versus operations, and global corporate leaders versus individual country leaders.

The moment a group perceives itself as being thwarted by an outside force, the outside force becomes the persecutor. Those who agree with the victimized group become the co-conspirators. The victim triangle is now complete—the three roles have been filled, and all hope of collaborating to resolve differences vanishes. Positions become embedded and entrenched, and fighting against the enemy keeps the silo and boundaries locked in place.

Let's return to the automatic listening loop discussed in Chapter 3 to identify the exact point where victim mentality emerges. You may recall the six steps: (1) something happens, (2) you have a reaction (an emotion or feeling), (3) you form a judgment, (4) you make up a story, (5) you search for evidence, and (6) you predict the future. Can you identify the precise point when victim thinking takes hold? If you answered step 4— making up a story—you are correct. Although you form a judgment in step 3, you assign roles and build your case in step 4 by inventing a story in which *you* decide who is the victim, co-conspirator, and persecutor.

The central point here is *everything hinges on how you tell the story.* Inside the closed loop of automatic listening, you interpret and distort the facts to support what you believe. The *story* you invent determines whether you are operating out of a small context (victim mentality) or a big context (owner mentality). You are controlled by the story you invent; you are lost the moment you believe your interpretation is the truth. When you slant the story to make yourself or your group the victim, you abandon personal accountability and surrender your power to others. Once you place yourself in the victim role—consciously or unconsciously—you will behave in a way that undermines and sabotages. You will play small, be right, and be petty.

How Victim Mentality Drives a Wedge between Groups

A conspiracy in one part of the organization can corrupt the entire system when groups take sides and fight against one another. We encountered this situation while working with an exploration group in a gold mining company. The head of exploration was a strong but frustrated leader who perceived corporate and senior leaders as the persecutors. Members of the exploration department were co-conspirators and gathered evidence to prove they were the victims of an unfair senior management team. They affirmed their victim mentality in comments such as *"They* always cut our group's budget first; no wonder we can't succeed."

Senior leaders became increasingly frustrated with the constant complaining and battle that never seemed to end with the exploration group. The victim triangle between exploration and senior leaders left people embittered, and it contaminated other parts of the organization. An either-or question emerged, and people asked each other, "Whom do you support—exploration or corporate?"

The victim triangle is another example of automatic behavior, but it does not have to end in "divorce." When teams and organizations learn how to build committed partnerships and work together in an extraordinary way, they break out of the victim triangle and find new solutions. This is what occurred during an acquisition in which the CEOs of the two companies demonstrated fearless leadership.

Breaking Up the Victim Triangle and Building Trust during a Merger

We were working with a company in the oil and gas industry that was acquired by a company seven times its size. While going through the acquisition, leaders and employees in the smaller company felt they were not being listened to or valued.

What Happened. Conspiracies formed quickly against the acquiring company, and rumors began to spread: *"They are unfair," "They don't care about people,"* and *"They are going to fire most of us and dismantle our company."* Applying the victim triangle: leaders in the smaller company became the victim; their families, friends, and coworkers became their co-conspirators; the leaders in the acquiring company became the bad guys or persecutors. The tension was high among senior leaders in the two companies, and meetings were unproductive.

Breaking Up the Victim Triangle. We worked with the CEOs of both companies to resolve this situation and ensure a successful merger. Because both CEOs were fearless leaders, we were able to bring both senior leadership groups together for a session and face the issues head on.

When we started the session, the group of 35 leaders was resigned, skeptical, and discouraged. Leaders from the acquiring company were exasperated with the resistance they were experiencing, and they were concerned that the merger was going to be a long and difficult process costing millions of dollars. Leaders from the smaller company felt as if their company was being swallowed by a big fish and they had lost complete control of its future.

The CEO of the acquiring company opened the session with the following: *"The statistics for successful mergers are not on our side, with over 50 percent ending in complete disaster. If we don't resolve the issues between us, this could happen to us. I believe it is the 'people' part that makes the critical difference in the successful integration of our companies. We have exceptional talent in this room, and by the end of this session, I want us to be one company and one team. Working in partnership is the only way we will succeed, and that begins with an honest dialogue about our concerns and fears."*

What the two groups had to face was how they had applied the victim triangle to each other and had made each other the persecutor. Each group was trapped in victim mentality, which came as a surprise to both groups. Once they recognized this, they were able to see how they had created barriers to cooperating and collaborating. They took on the task of building authentic partnerships where previously none had existed.

The Result. In three days, the two groups eliminated victim mentality and built strong committed partnerships. Even though everyone knew there would be many changes in the next 12 months including a number of changes on the senior team, the two groups united as one leadership team. The acquisition was highly successful and the senior group directly attributed this to their breakthrough in working together as an aligned and cohesive team.

Lesson Learned. When leaders are fearless in confronting what people are experiencing but not saying, issues can be quickly resolved and a new future created. In this case, senior leaders moved from thinking as separate companies to a larger context of working together as committed partners. By quickly integrating senior leaders, the parent company was able to eliminate the barriers that commonly prevent success during a merger.

The salient point to bear in mind is that a victim triangle can form in an instant, creating silos and "enemies" where there should be none. Any group or individual can unwittingly become the persecutor, victim, or co-conspirator. That, of course, leads to resignation and the loss of focused and aligned people. This jump is automatic and seriously damages the ability of the organization to perform.

DELUSIONS OF ADEQUACY: 50/50 ACCOUNTABILITY DOESN'T WORK

We have now come full circle back to the topic of accountability, which is the foundation of fearless leadership. What is typically referred to as "accountability" in organizations today is actually 50/50 accountability, on which the victim triangle is based. This carries the familiar mantras "It's not our fault, it's theirs," or "I'll do my part if you do yours." The 50/50 model requires another party to take action before something can happen, and as a result, it slows down or stops progress altogether.

In a culture of 50/50 accountability, responsible and committed people work hard but in opposition to someone or something. People listen and speak against others, an idea, or a group, and you seldom hear people speaking "for" something. All energy is focused on fighting a foe—real or imaginary.

In a 50/50 environment, leaders expend a great deal of time refereeing conflict between people competing for resources. Being the mediator or arbiter in decision making and conflict resolution costs considerable time and money. Nothing is easy, efficient, or fast, decisions are subpar, and execution is inconsistent.

100% ACCOUNTABILITY: NO BLAME, NO SHAME

Owner mentality is based on taking 100% accountability and looking from the enterprise perspective. But before we go any further, let's distinguish between accountability and responsibility.

You are responsible for the areas in which you are in charge, such as fulfilling your job expectations. Accountability is a larger context, and it is the choice to adopt an ownership mentality and think of the organization as a whole, not as its parts. Although you may not be responsible for another group's results, as an owner, you take accountability for the organization's results and what needs to happen. When you build a culture of 100% accountability, people shift from the automatic behavior of victim mentality to being owners in how they act and engage.

A culture of 100% accountability unites people with a team-based mindset: all team members take accountability for business results and their impact on people, even when others accept *zero* accountability. You severely inhibit your ability to influence change when you expect others to take accountability and restrict your choices based on what *they* do. Using the model of 100% accountability, you can make things happen even when others choose not to take action. This requires that you think as an owner and focus your attention on what you *can* do, not on what others *should* do.

> **100% Accountability**
> Being personally accountable for business results and your impact on people, even when others accept zero accountability.

There is no blame or shame in the model of 100% accountability; there is only taking accountability, working in committed partnerships, and learning from your mistakes. This model reverses the automatic process of shrinking the game and playing small, and it introduces a way to recover quickly. Instead of an environment in which people form and harbor resentments, and wallow in regrets about what they or others should have done, positive and aligned action advances the business.

Transformation can happen quickly once you learn how to intervene between what happens and your automatic behavior. This is what transpired when a company faced a community crisis in which senior leaders could easily have become defensive and been seen as the persecutor.

Taking Accountability with the Customer and Community in a Crisis

A crisis occurred when a fire broke out in a residential neighborhood resulting in numerous injuries and a death. Although negligence was not clear, many in the community assumed that faulty equipment owned by our client sparked the fire. As happens often in a crisis, leaders must make a clear and decisive choice: either accept accountability (not blame) and take ownership, or avoid it and become the persecutor by default.

What Happened. We were in a leadership session with the top six leaders of the company when the CEO, Larry, received the call about the fire. The leaders were shaken by the news and their legal counsel advised them to prepare for media interviews and not to admit culpability. But taking the standard approach of "No comment; there is insufficient information to determine what caused the fire" simply fuels the reaction and makes the company and its leaders the persecutors. On the other hand, "taking accountability" allows leaders to express their concern, compassion, and commitment without defending or blaming.

The CEO and senior leaders asked: *"How can we take accountability and care for our community in this difficult situation?"* They demonstrated fearless leadership and shifted their focus from the standard response to being committed partners to the community. In a series of difficult interviews, company leaders never once defended, justified, or rationalized what happened. Instead, they expressed their sympathy and compassion, and they took accountability.

The CEO responded brilliantly to the media and said, *"We deeply regret what has happened, and we offer our sympathy to the families and community. As a company, we are accountable for your safety— for the safety of our customers. The investigation will identify what and who is responsible for the malfunction, but regardless of what is discovered, we care about our community and you."*

The Result. There were no angry phone calls, letters to the editor, or public backlash. A remarkable thing happened: as company leaders took accountability, there was a resurgence of community spirit and partnership. One customer commented, *"It took guts to do what the company leaders did. They took responsibility at a time when all the facts were not in. This is something we can all learn from."*

Lesson Learned. You can always take accountability (not blame) for a situation, even when you do not have all the information. Taking accountability is an act of courage that demonstrates your caring for people and your willingness to "be big" in a difficult situation.

Victim mentality cannot exist inside an environment of 100% accountability; there is nothing to feed it and keep it alive. When leaders act as owners, thinking and behavior change, and the question becomes "How can we accept accountability?" Just as the leaders took accountability— and not blame—in a community crisis, companies can operate in the same way. Accountability is not blame or shame; it is acting as an owner and taking a stand.

YOU ASK FOR WHAT YOU WANT, BUT YOU CREATE WHAT YOU BELIEVE

Leaders tend to be clearer about what they want than what they believe. It's easy to identify goals and aspirations: "I want to be rich," or "I want to be successful." But when we ask leaders what they believe, they are at a loss. Beliefs operate below the surface of conscious awareness where they influence how we behave. Examples of widespread beliefs are "Leaders should have all the answers" and "Leaders should be right." If these beliefs are part of your repertoire, they influence how you speak, listen, and act. Beliefs are self-fulfilling prophecies, and in this way, you get what you believe, not what you want.

Let's look at an example: If you believe that an individual is making it impossible or difficult for you to succeed, your behavior will be consistent with your belief. Even if you say you want a good relationship with this individual, your belief that he or she is "out to get you" will influence your behavior. You will unconsciously adopt a victim attitude and treat the individual as the persecutor. Not only will you distrust what he or she says, you will change how *you* behave because you certainly behave differently with someone you trust than with someone you don't. You may withhold how you feel, turn everything into an argument, or ask questions that cast doubt or suspicion on the individual's credibility.

The person who is your "persecutor" begins to react to your behavior, mirrors your distrust, and withholds information from you. This feeds your belief that the individual cannot be trusted, and now you have even more evidence for your case. Of course, what you cannot see is that your evidence is tainted by your self-fulfilling prophecy. You have changed your behavior, and then you have used the individual's reaction to your behavior as evidence that you are right and that he or she cannot be trusted. Your words "I want an effective relationship" hold no weight. When you do not believe it is possible to have a trusting relationship with a specific individual, you will create what you believe to be true, not what you want.

Getting Stuck in a Rut Is Normal; *Choosing* to Get Out Is Extraordinary

There is a story about a sad little frog that was mired in a deep, muddy wagon track. His frog friends came by every day and tried everything they could to encourage him to get out of the rut. But the poor little frog was a victim of circumstances and believed that he couldn't do anything to get out. Finally, after several days, his friends gave up hope and left him alone.

Then one day his friends walked by the side of the road and saw the little frog sitting by the pond bathing in the sun. He was chipper, happy, and very pleased with himself. His friends asked, "How did you get here?

We thought you couldn't get out of that rut." The little frog replied, "I couldn't, but when I saw a wagon coming toward me, I had to."

The little frog reacted in a hurry *only* when his survival was threatened, but up until that point the little frog was powerless. When you fall into victim mentality you *react* to circumstances and *self-fulfill* what you believe. There is an important distinction that must not be missed: fearless leadership is based on being proactive and decisive; victim mentality is based on blaming and reacting.

Transformation is a moment-by-moment process. You have the capacity to transform yourself every time you make a choice to be or do something different and to rise above your automatic behaviors. The moment you pause and examine *how* you are interpreting a situation and the role you have cast yourself and others in, you expand your personal context and find new ways to get out of old ruts.

If you think that transformation is something that can be mastered and forgotten, let me disabuse you of this notion. Transforming yourself and your organization is an ongoing process that must become a way of life, not another thing to do or to check off your list. Fearless leadership is the ongoing commitment and process to continually transform yourself and others to reach higher and excel.

As we move into Part II, our focus is on taking a stand, building committed partnerships, and learning how to recover quickly when breakdowns occur. We will not spend any time on how to achieve the unattainable state of perfection because the quest for perfection is in itself a trap. But you will learn how to master the ability to powerfully influence and interact with others.

Let's draw a clear line about what fearless leadership is and is not. Fearless leadership is not the absence of fear; it is standing strong and resolute in the face of fear. Certainly there are times when you feel powerless and resigned, and fearless leadership will not eliminate challenges or breakdowns in your work. But *you* will be different in how you meet and address these challenges and breakdowns. It is your personal transformation that gives you the power and freedom to alter anything.

You cannot control or change others, and if you persist in pursuing this path, you will be constantly disappointed and frustrated. The good news is that others have no control over you. You have a choice over how you focus your attention, how you choose to act and react, and whether you choose to play big or play small. You may be powerless to change others, but you are not helpless. You always have a choice.

To be a fearless leader, you must be willing to get out of your rut and overcome automatic behaviors that limit you—your blind spots, the need to be right, and victim mentality. You must take a bold stand; define how you want to play the game and the difference you want to make.

If you choose to play big—and this is definitely your personal choice—then act decisively, and decide where you want to focus your attention and what you want to accomplish. Identify where you have been conspiring against others and change *your* behavior without expecting others to change theirs. Rewrite your story and change your interpretation so you are no longer the victim, and others are no longer the persecutors. In doing this, you will expand your personal context and, therefore, expand your ability to play big. Although it may not appear possible right now, you will be able to build committed partnerships, even with those you currently perceive as your opponents.

LEADERSHIP EXPLORATION

The purpose of this assignment is to identify where you are resigned, shrinking the game, or engaged in victim mentality. As with all assignments, do not rely on your point of view only. Ask others to provide you with candid input, and listen to what they have to say. If you are not willing to authentically listen to input from others, you are not ready to do this assignment.

1. **Answer the following questions to identify *if* you are resigned.**
   - Do you feel that no matter what you do, it is never enough and will not change anything?
   - Has your enthusiasm or energy changed recently? When did it change?
   - Are you abrupt and short fused on small matters that normally would not bother you?
   - Do you isolate yourself from others by doing such things as closing your office door, working at home, or avoiding conversations?

- Are you quiet in meetings, saying only what needs to be said but not fully communicating?
- Is your normal optimistic approach replaced with pessimistic comments?
- Do people who usually seek you out avoid you or work around you?
- Do you feel emotionally drained, as if you are running on empty?
- Do small things annoy you that usually don't bother you?
- Does everything seem to take a lot of energy and effort?

2. Answer the following questions to determine *where* you are resigned.

With Whom Am I Resigned and Shrinking the Game?

- A direct report or a coworker?
- My team?
- The organization as a whole?
- Senior leaders?
- The next level up?

Where Am I Trapped in Victim Mentality?

- In what circumstances have I become the victim? Whom have I made the persecutor: the company, senior leaders, a group, the community, a customer, a supplier, a colleague?
- Who are my co-conspirators? How have I actively enlisted them in my view?

What Payoffs Am I Receiving in Being a Victim of Circumstances?

Behavior serves a purpose, and if you are engaging in victim mentality, you are receiving certain benefits or payoffs. What are they? Examples:

- *"No one can hold me accountable."*
- *"I get to be right."*
- *"I win; others lose."*
- *"I avoid conflict and confrontation."*
- *"I don't have to deal with difficult people or situations."*
- *"No one interferes with me or my team."*

What Price Am I Paying in Being a Victim of Circumstances?
Just as you receive payoffs when you engage in victim mentality, you also
pay a price. What is the cost of your behavior on yourself and others?
Examples:

- *"I neglect my health and well-being."*
- *"I am discouraged and frustrated, which impacts my coworkers
  and family."*
- *"I am underperforming by my standards. I know I can do much
  more."*
- *"I am not motivated or excited about the future."*
- *"I feel emotionally drained. I am running on empty."*
- *"I feel alone and misunderstood."*

Once you recognize that you are engaged in victim mentality, you have
two choices: (1) continue to be right and remain stuck in defending and
justifying your behavior, or (2) take accountability and expand your personal context and results.

LEADERSHIP ACTION

Rewrite Your Story and Create a Different Ending

Identify a circumstance in which you have become trapped in victim mentality. With a coworker (or team), apply the following steps:

Step 1. Tell your story with all the details that describe how you have been
wronged, treated unfairly, or have been unappreciated. Hold nothing back,
and express all your frustration, upset, and disappointment. At the end, ask
your partners how your story impacted them. Were they persuaded and
ready to be your co-conspirators, or did they recoil as they heard you take
the victim role?

Step 2. Retell the same story, but now cast yourself as a fearless leader
instead of a victim. Do this by (1) presenting the facts only (what actually happened) and deleting your victim interpretation; (2) eliminating
all blame (including blaming yourself, others, or circumstances); (3) taking accountability for how your action (or lack of action) contributed to
the situation; and (4) letting go of your need to be right and focusing on

what you need to do to be effective. Ask your partners how your story impacted them. Was your story believable and credible? Did you truly shift from victim to owner mentality, or did your need to be right still show up in your story?

Step 3. Answer these questions:

- Which story ending do you want?
- Which version represents who you are and what you stand for?
- Which version allows you to produce the business results you want?

In the course of history, there comes a time when humanity is called to shift to a new level of consciousness, to reach a higher moral ground. A time when we have to shed our fear and give hope to each other. That time is now.

—WANGARI MAATHAI (1940–)

PART

II

TAKING A STAND AND TRANSFORMING YOUR ORGANIZATION

Building a high performance organization based on 100% accountability is possible only with committed partnerships—an extraordinary partnership in which leaders commit to the success of each other, take a bold stand, and emotionally and intellectually align. Part II of this book provides you with the methodology for breaking the cycle of automatic and unproductive behavior and building a framework of uniform behavioral standards that transform a company's fundamental values from concepts into practical applications.

Chapter 5 starts off by tackling how to create an environment in which leaders take 100% accountability for business results and their impact on others. In this chapter, we explore how taking a bold stand creates the organizational context needed to unite and mobilize people to action.

Chapter 6 introduces the five agreements of committed partners and the extraordinary way in which they work together. In this chapter, you will learn what it means to stand for the success of others, how to recover quickly from breakdowns, and how to work together as a cohesive team.

Chapter 7 examines how the rigor of honoring and fulfilling commitments is the foundation for a culture of accountability. In this chapter, you will learn how a promise-based management approach—where people can unequivocally rely on one another—builds trust and leads to effective execution.

Chapter 8 shows you how to talk straight responsibly and manage sensitive issues rather than allowing them to fester and undermine performance. This chapter provides you with the skill sets needed to resolve relationship issues and build a committed partnership where all parties share an urgent and focused commitment to delivering business results.

Chapter 9 takes us to the heart of high performance—authentic and sustainable alignment. In this chapter, we explore what is required to achieve both emotional and intellectual buy-in. You will learn why group decisions don't stick and what you can do to achieve authentic and sustainable alignment that turns your business strategy into focused delivery.

Chapter 10 focuses on holding one another accountable for the best in performance. Here we discuss how a culture of 100% accountability is self-correcting, where people constructively interevene and hold themselves and others accountable for both business results and their impact on people.

Finally, Chapter 11 culminates with the pervasive message of fearless leadership: you have the power to influence change and shape the future. This chapter focuses on what you can do right now to achieve the results you want. It brings together how committed partnerships and 100% accountability are the indispensable keys to sustainable leadership and organizational transformation.

Chapter
5
Changing Your Direction and Taking a Bold Stand

*The question isn't who is going to let me;
it's who is going to stop me.*

—Ayn Rand (1905–1982)

We have it backward. The conventional view is to apply a logical approach to the complex dynamic of aligning leaders in advancing organizational objectives. This keeps leaders focused on changing structure, processes, and systems without fully considering the capacity of others to implement and sustain them. We seek the comfort of known methods and incremental approaches over the discomfort of discovering something new, and perhaps, infinitely more effective.

To the casual observer, our automatic behaviors are mere examples of unproductive actions, but taken together, they lead us in a disturbing direction *away* from leadership and organizational effectiveness. Our natural impulse is to pull back, withdraw, and step *away* from situations that leave us feeling uneasy, uncomfortable, anxious, or fearful. These avoidance behaviors buttress us from taking accountability, working in partnership, and operating with integrity. The net effect is that we contract our thinking, behavior, and participation, which dilutes our prospects for success.

We must overthrow the notion that conventional thinking and automatic behavior are sufficient to solve problems at the speed at which they are emerging today. While this may sound discouraging, there is a remedy. We must reverse the instinctive reaction of *avoiding* discomfort and fear and instead usher in a new era in which fearless leaders step into the fray and solve problems from a radically new perspective.

This counterintuitive thinking of moving *toward* the very things that make us uncomfortable in order to create something more effective is potent and must be learned. For some it may appear risky. But the greater risk is to remain on the proverbial treadmill of solving recurring problems with solutions that are unequal to the task.

In this chapter, we investigate how to reverse the instinctive behavioral urges of avoiding, escaping, and evading and replace them with extraordinary behaviors that move us *toward* reconnecting people with one another and the larger mission of the organization. In stark contrast to the automatic behavior of avoiding, fearless leaders confront the real issues and embrace new solutions.

This chapter is designed for you to learn the shortest and most effective path for working together in a new way. We explore how organizational capability expands when leaders demonstrate their commitment through uniform behavior.

In an unpredictable environment, your most powerful approach is to counterbalance high levels of uncertainty with a stable standard of behavior. When people know the rules for how everyone is expected to behave, they are able to focus on pressing business needs. Articulating a compelling stand for how you expect people to work together is the first step in defining personal and organizational context. This strategy puts you in control and gives you the power to produce breakthroughs—sudden transformations of what is possible—and achieve unprecedented results.

> Fearless leadership is not the absence of fear. It is the courage to confront fear and solve problems from a radically new direction.

Reengineering your thinking and behavior starts with an undeniable premise: there is nothing wrong, missing, or inadequate with you; you do not need to be fixed. Our quest is to transform what you can achieve. "Fixing" puts a Band-Aid on the symptom where wounds are temporarily patched but never healed.

Perhaps you are resigned, frustrated, or disillusioned, but this is normal. By now it is clear that you have automatic and unproductive behaviors that undermine what you want to achieve. But if you have strength of character and strong core values of accountability and integrity, you have what is needed to be a fearless leader. My goal is to offer you a methodology that transforms your capacity to play a much bigger game.

MOVING *TOWARD* CREATING SOMETHING INSTEAD OF AVOIDING SOMETHING

This drift of moving away from uncomfortable situations reveals our natural protective instinct of avoiding perceived threats. The only road out of this milieu is to step into the discomfort and solve problems from a new direction.

Conspicuously, our instinct is to trust only our intellect and depend on what has worked before to save us. But this more-of-the-same philosophy leads us *away* from what will resolve today's problems. Limiting perceptions harden, and we become even more convinced that we are right about people and situations. We stop looking for the possibility and see only sharp and chiseled boundaries that prevent us from confidently taking action. Fear, uncertainty, and anxiety undermine performance, and our instinctive reaction is to run for cover. But it is here that we must change our direction and move *toward* our discomfort in order to find more effective solutions.

Think of your behavior as fitting into one of two categories: moving toward generating something, or moving away from discomfort and fear. Many consider *avoidance* behavior to be smart, normal, and natural. And from a rudimentary perspective, they are correct; avoiding is a natural behavior that appears to reduce the expenditure of energy and resources. But the truth is that avoiding takes considerably more energy than creating a new reality.

Consider the amount of time you spend worrying or thinking about a sensitive conversation, a difficult person, a potential conflict, a tough decision, misalignment of leaders, or an unresolved situation. It takes a substantial investment of energy to defend, be right, and avoid—much more than is required to step into your discomfort, take a bold stand, and act decisively. When you change your direction, you change what is possible for you and others.

Moving *Toward* Transforming and Emotionally Engaging Others

Leaders are blissfully unaware that by approaching things backward they disconnect people from their desired goal and purpose. This is based on an erroneous view that all bases are covered when leaders focus solely on their accountabilities and objectives. "I try to connect with people," said a CEO, "but they just don't seem to like my humor." "What makes you think people want humor from you?" I asked, "Is that what your wife wants when she wants to connect emotionally with you?" The CEO was momentarily perplexed and then replied, "No, she wants me to listen to her and include her in what's going on for me." "Then, you need to listen to others and include people in what you are experiencing so they can connect with you as a person, not a figurehead CEO."

To transform a team or organization, people need to feel emotionally connected to one another, the organization, and its leaders. They need a larger context: a way to belong and be part of a winning team. Logic does not deliver this, and more often than not, it pushes people over the edge into resignation and disengagement.

At the heart of the dilemma is our confusion between changing an organization versus transforming an organization. Change initiatives play an important role in creating greater efficiency and effectiveness, but seldom do they alter behavior and how people relate to one another and the organization's mission. When people are not emotionally engaged, their behavior does not change in lasting ways.

The context for change must be radically overhauled if leaders want to expand and accelerate what their organization can achieve. Resignation, silos, victim and entitlement mentality, and complacency keep the playing field small and engagement low. To attack the problem at its core, you must provide people with a method of self-mastery based on the behaviors of 100% accountability and committed partnerships. The only way to capture this high level of alignment and emotional connection is to transform, not change, how leaders work together.

Transformation is not a soft science; it is a methodical, disciplined approach to optimizing leadership and organizational effectiveness in a remarkably short period of time. The concept of speed is perhaps the most misunderstood aspect of transformation. When you provide people with an opportunity to profoundly expand their personal context and capability, they instantly reengage and redirect their newfound enthusiasm and confidence into organizational goals. This explains why organizational and personal context are interdependent factors in helping an organization reach optimal effectiveness.

Exhibit 5-1 provides an overview of the *different focuses* needed to change an organization versus transform it.

Leaders who push the organization to deliver more and try vainly to squeeze extra effort out of people who are emotionally disconnected and unaligned are disappointed with the results. This push to get more gives you less, especially when you are fixated on the wrong things.

The root of the problem lies in thinking that results are separate from relationships. There is no equivocation that business results are, and must be, the measure of success in any organization. However, relationships—how people work together—are the *foundation* for business results. Most leaders give lip service to relationships, and at best, they provide detached or disjointed efforts that do not connect people to business objectives. The leaders are ignoring the fact that *how people work together* must be placed at the heart of the business mission, not on the periphery.

How often do you think of relationships or teamwork as "nice to have," "something that can wait until the crisis blows over" or "something that is working fine and can be tweaked later"? Most leaders, if they are honest, put business results and people in a hierarchical order in which results must be achieved in order to have the luxury of developing people—and these leaders are going backward again.

Instead, leaders need to operate from the principle that *people* are both their business concern and their vehicle for delivering results. If the people of the organization are not front and center of a leader's thinking and strategy, then it is time to consider a new direction. When leaders focus on building committed partnerships, they produce a seismic shift in behavior and organizational results.

Changing the Organization	vs	Transforming the Organization
Pursue business results first; relationships last: *"We'll work on culture and building a constructive work environment after everything else is done, if there's still time and money."*		**Build strong working relationships to guarantee business results:** How leaders work together—their relationships with each other and the organization—is the foundation for business results and success. When you build aligned teams and leaders, business challenges and opportunities are resolved with speed and efficiency.
Launch more initiatives: *"After we complete these initiatives, we can start new ones to fix other problems."*		**Expand context and capability:** People are change fatigued and resistant to more initiatives. However, they are energized and replenished when they have a compelling context and a methodology that expands their personal capability and effectiveness.
Accept relationships of convenience: *"You don't have to be friends with people to do your job. Just do what needs to be done, and work around people who get in your way."*		**Build committed partnerships:** Committed partnerships connect people and give them energy and ability to influence change. People stand for the success of one another, eliminate silos, and embrace enterprise thinking. They act with urgency and tackle the organization's greatest challenges.
Stay aloof to maintain objectivity: *"As a leader, I need to keep a distance from people to maintain my objectivity and be strong for them."*		**Emotionally connect with people:** People want to emotionally connect with leaders, and they have respect for leaders who are courageous in taking accountability for their impact and mistakes. Leaders who openly confront and discuss their blind spots are perceived as authentic, transparent, and accessible.
Convince people with logic or fear tactics: *"I need to make a case with people so they are convinced that I'm right. If they don't line up behind my point of view, I make sure they are aware of the consequences."*		**Inspire people by engaging them emotionally and intellectually:** Fear paralyzes most people and prevents them from acting. Likewise, attempting to convince others with logic does not inspire people to do more and reach higher. You must reconnect people to one another, the organization, and the grand mission. When people are emotionally and intellectually engaged, they *choose* to give their discretionary effort.

EXHIBIT 5-1: *Changing the Organization versus Transforming the Organization*

Using Counterintuitive Thinking to Produce Big Results

Transformation requires counterintuitive thinking that goes against our natural instinct of protecting and avoiding. Recognizing your automatic instinct to pull back and avoid gives you the ability to press the pause button and override this reaction by asking

- What am I avoiding or deflecting?
- What am I resisting and trying to prevent?
- How am I shrinking the game and limiting what is possible?

Our penchant to avoid is unconscious and manifests in our behavior. You can change direction by including others in a new and more effective partnership and thereby avoiding the downstream threat. The following two examples are of fearless leaders who turned difficult and messy situations into opportunities to build a new foundation of committed partnerships.

Moving in a New Direction with Community Leaders. Zari was the head of the community relations group in a sizable operation. Her team encountered persistent difficulties with leaders in the community and ran into obstacles that prevented resolution of conflict between the company and the community. Zari's group believed that the community leaders were the problem and if the community leaders changed their ways, everything would be fine. The "conspiring against" behavior of Zari's group—their judgments about community leaders—was a primary contributor to the breakdowns and constant tension between the groups.

Zari also engaged in the conspiracy against the community leaders. We asked her, *"Are you aware that you are acting as a victim and making the community group the persecutor?"* Zari retorted: *"I'm not a victim at all. They're just very difficult to work with and we can't do our job."* *"But that's the point. You're not doing your job. Your job is to build a partnership, not fight with community leaders,"* we pointed out. *"Well, that's what we're trying to do,"* Zari said defensively. *"Here's the problem, Zari. You want a partnership with community leaders, but you blame them for the problems. You can't build a partnership when you've made others the persecutor, your group the victim, and you conspire with one another. Is this what you call accountable behavior?"* we asked. Zari, a highly responsible leader, said, *"When you put it that way, I can see how my behavior has not been accountable or an example of the leadership I expect from others."*

Zari's breakthrough led her to ask her group a question that confronted the real issue: "Where do we need to take accountability for our partnership with community leaders by changing our behavior?"

The Committed Partnership Created. Zari and her leadership team changed their behavior and took accountability for their impact which produced an immediate and positive change in how community leaders responded. This started the process of building a new partnership with one another. It must be noted that Zari's success was in large part due to her courage to take accountability for her behavior and how she had allowed her team to become the "victim."

Moving in a New Direction with a Major Distributor. Clarke, a senior vice president, and his group were resigned about working with a "controlling and demanding" distributor. *"It's a waste of time to try and change the ways of the distributor. They are stubborn and inflexible and tell us 'that's the way we do things around here.' We avoid them every chance we get and just work around them,"* said one of Clarke's team members. Problems smoldered and grew between the two firms with each company judging the other as inflexible.

In a fit of despair, a member of Clarke's group halfheartedly said, *"Maybe we could talk with the distributor group about 'how' we work together and find a new solution."* The group spurned the idea and called it "a moment of insanity" and said, *"They'll never listen to what we have to say."* But as is so often the case in transformation, the most unimaginable becomes attainable when you change direction and look from a different perspective.

After incredulity and doubt receded, Clarke's group reconsidered. *"What have we got to lose?"* asked a team member. Indeed, what is there to lose when the lines are drawn and partners have become opponents? Our fear in these cases is of going from bad to disastrous and upsetting the delicate balance in the relationship. This is where fearless leadership is needed most: to turn into the storm and *toward* the discomfort in order to break through the barrier and create a new reality.

Before Clarke's group was ready to talk to the distributor group, they had to examine their own blind spots. We asked Clarke and his team, *"How has your behavior—how you talk to one another about the distributor and how you work around the distributor—contributed to this breakdown?"* The moment a member began defending the team's actions, we stopped the conversation and redirected it back to the team's accountability. After a while, they began to see how their fixed and rigid viewpoints about the distributor had perpetuated the breakdowns. Prior to the in-depth exploration of blind spots, Clarke's group perceived the distributor as the "persecutor" and responded as the victim, thereby feeding the cycle of constant breakdowns and tension.

The Committed Partnership Created. The change in the behavior of Clarke and his group paved the way for a new way of working with the distributor. Clarke's group changed their thinking and actions without expecting the distributor to reciprocate. This genuine display of 100%-zero accountability captured the attention of the distributor group, which did, in fact, respond in kind. This underscores a key to transformation: when one individual or group authentically takes accountability, it alters the conversation between all parties and opens up new possibilities.

In the above stories, fearless leaders overrode their automatic instinct to play small and protect their own interests. In each case, the leaders purposefully chose to move *toward* what others believed was improbable and impossible. This highlights the antidote for automatic behavior: lean into your discomfort, fears, and concerns, and purposefully engage with others in an extraordinary way.

The Shortest Path to Success: Taking Decisive Action Despite Discomfort

Counterintuitive thinking is difficult to comprehend because it does not seem logical. For example, you may postpone having a difficult conversation because you feel uncomfortable and unsafe. Your logic tells you to wait for a better time, or the right moment, when the other party will be more receptive and you will feel more confident. So you wait, but the right moment never appears, and you do not feel comfortable having the conversation anywhere but inside your head.

The quandary is that you cannot feel comfortable or safe until you have a responsible and forthright conversation with the appropriate person. It is the act of having a frank conversation that creates safety in your relationship with others.

Let's take another example of counterintuitive thinking: how we relate to taking accountability and apologizing. Conventional thinking leads us to believe that an apology is an admission of guilt or a sign of weakness. The words "I'm sorry" or "I apologize" catch in our throat and come out as a constricted sound that embarrasses us or others, and we quickly move on to another topic. But here again, apologizing and taking accountability are not admissions of blame, weakness, or frailty. They are, in fact, the opposite. When you apologize for your impact, you demonstrate courage and offer the gift of recovery. You reach out to others to repair possible damage and restore the relationship.

Another small but telling act is how you listen to others. You may think, as many do, that listening means paying greater attention to *exactly* what is being said, the content of the story. By focusing on the literal message, you get to be right and say, "That's not what you said—I heard your precise words, and you can't weasel out of them now." By not listening to the real message—the emotional content and commitment—you miss what is really being said. In Chapter 6, we explore listening for positive intention which is a method for listening beyond the words to the commitment and contribution being expressed. As with all extraordinary behaviors of fearless leaders, you must lean into your discomfort—for example, by listening for emotional meaning—in order to expand your capability and effectiveness.

There is also a natural aversion to commit, a fear that we will be locked into something or trapped in some way. That explains why we have multiple types of "casual promises" and only one type of commitment, which we explore in detail in Chapter 7. Our avoidance of committing is multifaceted: we don't want to get trapped, look bad, fail, be embarrassed, or lose the support and respect of others.

Finally, let's examine the counterintuitive thinking needed to take a bold stand and decisive action. Your courage to take a bold stand is what galvanizes others and ends the "will we or won't we" debate. Your declaration is what moves people into pure focused action. The moment you take a stand, you personally gain freedom and power because it moves you out of questioning yourself. Until you fully commit, you live in the question "should I or shouldn't I" and you are unable to act. Later in this chapter we talk about how taking a stand—a bold and public commitment—is the first step in transforming people and organizations.

THE PRICE OF ADMISSION: FIVE REQUIREMENTS TO BECOME A FEARLESS LEADER

At this point, it should be clear that there are no half measures in fearless leadership. This is not a spectator sport where you can sit on the sidelines and watch the game. Being a fearless leader has a price of admission that requires staying in the game and playing at all times, even when you would like nothing more than to crawl back into the stands, grab a hot dog, prop your feet up, and yell at the referee.

You're either in or in the way.

—MUSICIAN OZZY OSBOURNE

Fearless leadership is a big game; it has a higher purpose and operates with a different set of rules. The price of admission is based on five choices only you can make:

1. Take *100% accountability* and act as an owner.
2. Take a *bold stand* and act decisively.
3. *Be courageous* and openly discuss your blind spots.
4. Build *committed partnerships* to achieve business results.
5. Be *unreasonable* and make the tough calls.

Choice 1: You Must Have the Courage to Take 100% Accountability and Act as an Owner

Fearless leaders have an extraordinary level of ownership and accountability. In defining themselves as part of the whole enterprise, and not as a separate entity, they see themselves as more than their role, function, or title. Their behavior is consistent with this larger personal context, which allows them to take 100% accountability. How would you answer the following questions?

- Do you work with others to help achieve the enterprise objectives and mission? Or do you limit your contributions to your department, group, or business unit?
- Do you take accountability for your organization's partnership with customers, stakeholders, and suppliers? Or do you limit your focus only to the partnerships that involve you?
- Do you align with decisions and initiatives as if you authored them yourself, even when you would have preferred a different course of action? Or do you comply in public and complain privately to others?
- Do you speak powerfully about the excellence and commitment of your organization? Or do you feel a lack of pride and ownership in your organization?

If you're asking the question, "What's in it for me to act as an owner?" let me answer that. It's easy to see how a CEO or executive could act as an owner because most are financial owners vested in stock options and equity in the company. With a major portion of their financial portfolio tied to the success of the company, ownership is easy. But what about leaders and employees who do not have this financial incentive?

The compelling reason to adopt the mindset of an owner is because it directly impacts your performance and how others perceive you. And if that's not enough, let me add another reason: being an owner expands your capacity and your potential to succeed.

Without leaders acting as owners, the game of business shrinks and people focus on their individual areas of responsibility. Victim and entitlement mentality set in and become a permanent part of the landscape.

Leaders who take 100% accountability and behave as owners are emotionally mature; they think critically about the impact their words and actions have on the abilities of individuals and groups to progress toward achieving their goals. They demonstrate what it means to play big and operate from an enterprise perspective. And, they instill the same behavior in their team.

Choice 2: You Must Have the Courage to Take a Bold Stand and Act Decisively

Nothing happens in an organization until leaders take a public and unshakable stand that emotionally engages people and focuses them on the critical mission. Taking a stand is the act of publicly declaring your commitment and steadfast resolve to bring a new reality into existence.

Your stand as a leader must connect the aspirations of people to the aspirations of the organization. In this way, your stand must expand both organizational and personal context. Most leaders are skilled at creating the business context, but much less so at creating a personal and emotional context that captures the hearts and minds of people.

Imagine the consequences of not taking a bold stand: the organization vacillates, individuals and teams lose faith, and business results falter. Taking a bold stand is a subject that warrants additional attention and we cover it later in this chapter.

The following example illustrates how acting as an owner and taking a stand changes the behavior of others.

Being an Owner Is Not Just a Concept; It's a Group Practice That Boosts Profits

Safety is always an issue at mining sites. In one mining camp the director of safety, Randy, complained incessantly about being the only person who cared enough about safety hazards to constantly police the site. Randy was a victim of a familiar mindset and behavior.

What Happened.   At a meeting of the senior mine site team, Randy attacked the group for not being proactive about safety. Sparks flew and one leader said pointedly to Randy, *"When you decide you want my job, I'll consider doing yours."*

Intervening to Expand Group Ownership.   Randy was not the only person who had a victim mindset; the group was also displaying the same victim mindset and blaming one another. Titles and job responsibilities were being used as the red herring to avoid taking 100% accountability for safety.

High performance attacks the victim mindset. It takes courage; and in this case, Carson, the team leader, took a strong stand and intervened in the conversation: *"Safety is the job of every person in this room. Each person in this room is the owner of safety—so you can add that to your title."* At first the group complied but they had not bought in, so we asked: *"What is stopping you from taking 100% accountability for safety as a team?"* One team member said, *"How can we do our job and Randy's job too?"* *"As a group you've said that you want to be a high performance team and this is not how a high performance team behaves,"* I responded. *"So what are we supposed to do,"* asked a team member. Carson jumped in and said, *"Think about what would happen if Randy fails in his job? What would you do then?"* *"Well, if Randy fails,"* said another team member, *"then we all fail. We need one another to succeed. That's what it means to stand for the success of one another."* As a result of this dialogue, the team recognized that they had not been behaving as owners of safety.

Lesson Learned. Being an owner means taking 100% accountability for the "whole," and not *hiding* behind the "parts." Carson's team transformed from operating as individuals within their own roles and responsibilities to standing for one another and operating as a team. Carson remained steadfast in his stand that safety is everyone's job, and not surprisingly, the safety record of the mine steadily improved and was a demonstration of the commitment of the team. Organizations that do what it takes to build a high performance culture are the companies that successfully achieve and maintain a competitive edge.

Choice 3: You Must Have the Courage to Openly Discuss Your Blind Spots

It is exhausting to be with leaders who deny they have blind spots, are unwilling to be coached, or who cover up their own shortcomings and mistakes. Without a doubt, it is uncomfortable to discuss mistakes and breakdowns, but when you talk openly about your blind spots and take accountability for your impact, you instantly transform a tense and closed environment into a constructive and safe environment. When leaders are authentic, transparent, and human, and not afraid to say, "I made a mistake and I apologize for my impact," people are inspired to give more and do more.

Everyone knows leaders make mistakes, but when there is no freedom to discuss them, people cannot recover and move forward. If you want an organization that is flexible and agile, you must be open, honest, and authentic in talking about your blind spots and owning your impact on others. Your courage to move in the direction of your discomfort and talk openly helps others learn how to turn breakdowns and mistakes into opportunities to learn and grow.

Choice 4: You Must Have the Courage to Build Committed Partnerships to Achieve Business Results

The predominant area in which leaders operate backward is by separating relationships and results. Let's be clear: the relationships between people—their committed partnerships—are what produce business results and success. Every time people and results are put in two separate buckets, a false dichotomy is created. Your leadership stand must merge relationships and results, and it must place an emphasis on people working together as committed partners.

Two questions determine where you stand:

1. How would you handle an individual who delivers great business results but damages people?
2. How would you handle an individual who delivers unacceptable business results but has great relationships with people?

Many leaders are tempted to excuse poor behavior in order to save someone who delivers great business results. When this happens, a message is sent to the organization that business results trump how people work together, but in reality this is not the case. Although you may achieve short-term gains as your star performer leaves dead bodies in his wake, you lose long-term business results and the goodwill of people. You also lose credibility when you do not provide and adhere to consistent behavioral standards.

If you have a leader who delivers great business results but has a negative impact on others, there is an option other than tolerating poor behavior or firing the individual. You can provide the individual with the resources to honestly examine his or her blind spots, make a new choice about how to engage with others, and master new skill sets for repairing relationships and building committed partnerships. For the vast majority, when people feel supported and safe to explore their impact on others, they take accountability and permanently change their behavior.

Choice 5: You Must Have the Courage to Be *Unreasonable* and Make the Tough Calls

Are you a reasonable leader? This is an obvious trick question because if you tell me you are reasonable, my response will be, "That's unfortunate. Let's see what we can do about your condition."

Most leaders consider *reasonableness* to be a positive trait, but even the words used to describe being reasonable—sensible, rational, and realistic—return us to tolerating "good enough." Leaders are expected to be reasonable. They set *reasonable* goals, *reasonable* expectations, and make *reasonable* demands on others. Their objectives and commitments are based upon not exceeding the comfort zone of the past. Reasonable leaders accept excuses, rationalizations, and justifications as a way to explain why things are the way they are. Moreover, reasonable leaders rely on logic to find their answers and distrust the emotional side of intelligence. But in the long run, being reasonable keeps leaders stuck in behaviors of enduring and avoiding, instead of confronting and transforming.

Unreasonable leaders demand much more of themselves and others, and refuse to use circumstances as an excuse for the lack of results. They make the tough calls, hold themselves and others accountable for explicit behavioral standards, and set a clear direction. In times of turmoil, fearless leaders rally people by taking a bold stand and bringing a fierce determination to get through anything and everything together.

DECLARING A BOLD STAND AND RECONNECTING PEOPLE TO THE ORGANIZATION

A participant in one of our leadership sessions asked, "How do I believe again?" Her question is telling and significant. Even when people are resigned and disheartened, they continue to search for a way to believe in the organization. No one wants to feel powerless and wait for others to act, or hope that the tooth fairy will deliver a pleasant surprise. People want to know: "What can I do today that will make a difference?" They want to do more, give more, and be more. And they want to be proud of the organization and help make it wildly successful.

People want to believe, and the stand you take tells them what they can believe in. It defines the organizational and personal context and either expands or shrinks the game. Merely communicating tactical objectives leaves people disengaged and moves them away from the outcome you want to achieve.

Taking a stand is a bold declaration—a public commitment—about what you believe in, what you can be counted on for, and how you will focus your energy and the energy of your group. When you take a stand, you set a clear path. For example, you can take a stand about who you will be as a leader in the organization. An example of a powerful, personal stand is, "I am 100% accountable for business results and my impact on others." Your stand is a promise first to you, then to others. In a personal stand such as this, you are declaring how *you* will play the game.

Your stand is your stake-in-the-ground, and it is not about what you *hope* will happen but what you will *make* happen during your watch. It is your rallying cry to unite and mobilize people to action. You must believe in it; it must resonate with everything you personally stand for and be consistent with your personal values. If it does not create a "fire in the belly" for you, it will not for others.

Whether you are a leader with a formal title or an individual contributor, you can take a bold stand. The example in this section is of an executive who takes a courageous stand and leads his organization to greatness. However, the same methodology applies to taking a personal stand with your group or as a member of the organization.

In order to perform at their highest capacity, people need a big context with clear boundaries, a galvanizing purpose, and a stable set of behavioral agreements. Together, this provides people with a secure base so they can focus their energy on tackling your organization's most pressing challenges.

Your stand provides the context and purpose; it is the nerve center for *what* you want the organization to accomplish and *how* you want people to work together. If the connections and synapses are not unmistakable, people will comply or intellectually align, but they will not fully commit with heart and mind. The behavioral agreements of committed partners and the road map for achieving emotional and intellectual alignment are introduced in Chapter 6 and developed in each subsequent chapter.

> Nothing happens until you publicly declare your stand.
> People do not take up arms until the General calls for action.

Many leaders think they are declaring a stand when what they are really doing is stating a position. Providing a list of objectives does not fulfill the need for a human and emotional purpose—a higher purpose. A compelling stand must be a worthy goal that inspires people to lift their vision to a higher standard, something that goes beyond normal limitations.

Don, a senior executive, asked me to watch his presentation to a group of leaders and provide him with feedback. He was articulate, clear, and provided a detailed presentation on his business strategy. By the end, his leaders got the message, but the room was flat; there was no energy, enthusiasm, or passion for the game. And as we all know, even the best players on a team must have passion for the game or they do not perform at their optimum capacity. Like most leaders, Don presented an intellectual message designed perfectly for the rational, logical mind. I asked him, "What were you thinking about when you were speaking?" He said, "I was thinking about how much information I needed to cover." "Well, there's your problem," I responded. "You think speaking is about you, not about the audience. You need to personally connect with the people you are speaking to. All the information in the world does not boost your credulity unless people are engaged."

It wasn't that Don lacked emotional commitment; what he lacked was the ability to *express* his emotional commitment and connect with the group. As with so many leaders, Don defaulted to relying on logic to carry the weight of his message.

Stop Convincing and Start Enlisting

Why do leaders feel they have to argue for business results and convince people of urgency? Is it a blunted ability to deal with the dual sides of emotional and cognitive intelligence, or is it the discomfort of expressing emotions and self-disclosing? The answer lies in both camps.

It is amazing to me how many leaders think that a logical appeal, bolstered by a dependency on PowerPoint slides, will move and inspire people. For the record: it does not; it never has; and in the foreseeable future, it never will. No matter how much data or evidence you have, you cannot convince people about how they should *feel*. There is a maxim that is indisputable: people may not remember what you say, but they will never forget how you made them *feel*.

If you are satisfied with compliance and intellectual alignment, then go ahead and present a few more slides. But if it's emotionally engaged people you want—those who give their discretionary effort and passion—then you must give them your emotional commitment and stand.

Not surprisingly, this is another area that we have backward. We fall into the quagmire of convincing people by throwing facts and information at them, instead of helping people personally connect to the business mission. When you communicate, remember that people are asking these questions about you.

- Can I *relate* to the leader and connect with his or her experience?
- Can I *believe* the leader?
- Is the leader approachable, real, and genuine?
- Does the leader *inspire* me to do something different?

Using logic to "convince" people does not work. This is an area in which leaders must learn new skill sets that are distinct from traditional "speaking" skills. Remember, speaking is an action that either accelerates or diminishes the results you want to achieve.

How to Take a Bold and Compelling Stand

Enlisting the support of others and connecting people to the organization requires being *confidently open and available*. To a fearless leader, being open and available means talking openly about your experiences, blind spots, and missteps so others can connect to *you* and emotionally engage.

When you take a stand, you commit yourself emotionally and intellectually, and you ask others to learn with you so together you can achieve the business objectives. People want a challenge, and they need new tools and skills for expanding their capacity. People enthusiastically engage when they discover that they have the power to make a difference. When you provide people with the tools to learn how to work effectively together and quickly eliminate barriers, they will surprise you with their results.

To gain a fuller understanding of what it means to take a bold stand, let's break down the elements for uniting and aligning people to take productive action. The primary elements are these.

- **Be open and talk about your blind spots.** One of the reasons we provide leaders with a list of common blind spots, and encourage them to use it is that it provides them with a way to easily communicate. It starts them on the path of self-disclosing their struggles, sharing what they have learned, and taking accountability for their impact on others. When all members of a group share a common understanding of blind spots, they have a way to powerfully communicate and make course corrections to get back on track quickly.
- **Call for committed partnerships first and engage people emotionally and intellectually.** This may sound backward, but you must talk about "how" people are expected to work together before you delve into the details of "what" they are to do. There is a reason for this. Understanding the strategy of a game is useful only after you have a team that is aligned, knows how to play as a team, and shares a stable set of rules. When you engage people as committed partners, you establish a uniform set of agreements, expand their personal context, and emotionally connect them to the larger organizational context. (In Chapter 6, we cover the five agreements of committed partners.)
- **Focus the committed partnerships on your mission-critical objectives.** The point of forming committed partnerships is to focus them on your business needs. It is a wake-up call to the organization that moves people into action. What makes this different is how you are asking people to relate to one another and the organization. You are calling on their emotional commitment to accomplish a major business objective or tackle a challenge.

- **Learn how to be a committed partner and ask others to do the same.** There is a reason we call this special type of partnership a "committed" partnership. As with any significant commitment, there are agreements and a formal acceptance, which provide the infrastructure for holding each other accountable. You will need to help people learn what it means to work in committed partnerships, so you must also learn. But what comes first is the commitment to learning and working together as an invincible team.
- **Leave them with an inspired vision of the future.** Although you will need to explain what you don't want, as well as what you do want, make sure you leave people with a positive message. End with what you want them to do, and give them a sense of how the future will be different. Describe what will happen when you achieve the objective: what business results will be different, how attitudes and the environment will change, and how the behavior of people will transform. You must send a strong and consistent message that communicates: how we work together as committed partners is the foundation for producing exceptional business results.

Let's turn to an example of a courageous leader, Scott, who went far beyond his comfort zone to emotionally connect with people. As an experienced leader of a large manufacturing site, he anticipated major problems during a ramp-up. A sister site had just experienced significant burnout and loss of employees during their recent ramp-up, and Scott wanted to avoid those problems.

After trying many different approaches, he tried the one that he had avoided—moving *toward* his own discomfort and learning how to emotionally engage with others. His technical background did not equip him with a template for being confidently open and accessible, so he had to learn how to express himself in a new way.

Below is an excerpt of what Scott said to his extended leadership group. If you had been in the room, you would have felt his emotion, caring, and passion. I can tell you that his leaders were so moved by his message that they cascaded it throughout the entire organization.

In the example below I have used brackets to highlight the elements Scott used in taking a bold stand.

"We behave as if people and business results are mutually exclusive. We are afraid that we will not have enough time to do both things. What we are not paying attention to is the time it takes to deal with problems, breakdowns, and burnout. We need to learn new skills and behaviors to save time and avoid loss of productivity. I see two challenges: the first is how I need to be a more effective leader, and the second is how we need to be more effective together."

[Be Open and Accessible, and Talk about Your Blind Spots.]
"Let's start with my leadership: I stay up at night thinking about what I'm not seeing. My wife tells me that I am unbearable—curt and distant. Then she threw in that I don't listen. Something clicked for me. I realized I don't listen and don't include you either.

"My blind spot is going it alone, and that's what I've been doing. I've been trying to solve this problem by myself. I have isolated myself from my family and from you, at a time when we need one another."

[Call for Committed Partnerships First, and Engage People Emotionally and Intellectually.]
"How to be more effective is now clear to me: we must work together as committed partners and cease all behavior that keeps us separated, working in silos, and going it alone."

[Focus the Committed Partnerships on Your Mission-Critical Objectives.]
"Our business challenge, as you know, is not on the technical or business side—we know how to produce great results, and we have a proven track record. Our challenge is on the people side of the equation where we also have a proven track record—but not one that we want: we burn people out during a start-up and lose the very resource that is most important to us.

"I want us to answer two questions: (1) how are we going to create an environment where people feel good about how we get the job done and (2) how are we going to engage people so they want to do this again?"

[Learn How to Be a Committed Partner and Ask Others to Do the Same.]

"I don't have all the answers. What I do have is a commitment to learn how to be a more effective partner with you. I will screw up, but I promise you I will own my mistakes and share them with you. I am asking you to do the same: take on learning how to be committed partners with each other and everyone in our organization. Let's tear down the walls and be an unbeatable team."

[Leave Them with an Inspired Vision of the Future.]

"We will be the prototype manufacturing facility and others will come to us to learn how we accomplished so much in so little time. We will create an environment where people are fully engaged, energized, and on board before, during, and after the ramp-up. Our people will say, 'We kicked our competitors' butts, and we're going to do it again.'"

The entire mood of the site changed. People who had previously been skeptical and resigned were now fully engaged. They were doing whatever they could to achieve Scott's vision because it was now their vision too. People enthusiastically put in extra effort because they *believed* something new was possible. Scott motivated them by demonstrating his unwavering commitment to work together in a new way and care for people.

Scott achieved exactly what he set out to accomplish. Their manufacturing site became the model for other operations in the organization. Scott built a culture of committed partners where people learned together and succeeded beyond all expectations.

What makes taking a stand so powerful is living it every day and demonstrating new behaviors that inspire everyone. A stand is not a one-time message; it is *the* message. You must express it in your actions and your words so it becomes the norm for how you expect others to behave. Think of your stand as taking people on a journey where the path is uncharted and you are leading the way. At each step, you must demonstrate unshakable resolve and confidence. You must describe *your* personal journey and experiences so others can learn from you and not make the same mistakes. You must also encourage others to talk about what they are learning—their breakthroughs and breakdowns—so the entire organization can learn and grow together. This powerful way of learning cements the committed partnership. People make the course corrections necessary to achieve the greatest success possible.

There is comfort in knowing that once you take your stand and emotionally engage others, they will also step up and take a stand. In short order, you will have countless ambassadors who are disseminating your message because it is what *they* believe in and want to create. This explosion of commitment and engagement gives your organization the power to effect rapid change. The bigger your stand and commitment, the more you must expect your mettle to be tested. But because you are working with committed partners, you will not be alone, and your partners will see you through any daunting situation.

When you take a stand for building a culture of accountability, do not treat culture as an initiative. Instead, make culture—how people behave—the larger context and framework for achieving business results. For example, you might say: "How we work together determines what we can achieve." By speaking about how culture is the context for achieving business objectives, you effectively raise the standard of behavior and connect business results to how people work together. In this way, culture becomes a way of life and part of the fabric of the organization.

However, taking a bold stand is only the start of the transformation process. You must also have a way for individuals and teams to learn a uniform and consistent standard of behavior that applies across the organization. There is a limit to what you will achieve by talking about concepts versus learning new skills and integrating them into daily behavior. In the following chapters, we talk about the new behavior that is needed to transform leaders and the organization.

INSPIRE PEOPLE TO *BE* MORE, AND THEY WILL *DO* MORE

We often hear leaders say, "We can't place one more demand on people to change—they are already overwhelmed." It is accurate to say that more demands—initiatives—are not the answer. We have it backward. We put pressure on ourselves and others to do more, achieve one more thing, take on one more project, or add one more responsibility to our list. But the container is already full and spilling over the edges into a change-fatigued workforce that is emotionally drained.

Your attention needs to shift from *doing* more to *being* more. The question is not, "What do you need to do?" The question is, "*Who* do you need to *be* in order to expand your personal context?"

Your behavior is the barometer that measures your personal context— it tells you and others if you are playing small or playing big. Your behavior defines your trajectory, for better or for worse. How you behave and relate to people and circumstances is something you can influence every moment of every day. It is not one more thing to do; it is something *to be* and *express* in your actions.

The task that lies before you is to change direction: stop moving *away* from what you want to avoid and move *toward* what you need to confront in order to create the future you want. Stop holding back, and stop complaining about what's not working, and take a bold stand. Do not be deterred by not having all the answers. All bold stands begin with an uncharted path and a willingness to be fearless and make course corrections along the way.

Take all the energy you use to avoid, resist, and escape, and reroute it into building a new way of working with people. When you get stuck, identify what you are avoiding and change your direction. By making this one small adjustment in direction, you can transform anything.

This is the time to put your insights to rest and take action. Act without hesitating—take a bold stand and build committed partnerships—and trust yourself to recover when you make a mistake. Throw yourself into learning how to be a fearless leader and you will experience the sheer power that can come only from self-mastery.

LEADERSHIP EXPLORATION

Your stand defines the context or game. If you want to play big, you must have a greater purpose and larger mission that inspires you and others. Ask yourself the following questions, and ask a coworker to provide you with his or her perceptions about your behavior:

1. Are You Willing to Take a Bold Stand?

- Are you playing a game that is big enough, or are you being reasonable and holding yourself back?
- What stand do you already have that you are not expressing publicly?

- What prevents you from taking this stand? What are you avoiding (fears, concerns, repercussions, consequences)?
- What could you achieve if you took this bold stand and *succeeded*?

2. What Is Your Stand about the Connection between How People Work Together and Business Results?

Do you believe that how people work together directly impacts business results? Do your words and actions send a consistent message? Do you clearly articulate the connection between relationships and business results, for example:

- *How we work together* determines the results we produce.
- *Relationships* are the foundation for business results.
- Working together as *committed partners* is how we will achieve a new level of performance.
- *How we work together* is our competitive edge.
- Our *committed partnership* is our key to accomplishment.

LEADERSHIP ACTION

Declare a Bold Stand and Speak the Future into Existence

With your committed partner or group, share a bold stand with one another. Remember that speaking is an action: your words shape reality and influence the results you produce. Taking a bold stand is the act of expressing your commitment out loud to mobilize yourself and others into action. Speak courageously with conviction, confidence, and passion.

- **Include the five elements in stating your stand:** (1) be open and talk about your blind spots, (2) call for committed partnerships first, and engage people emotionally and intellectually, (3) focus the committed partnership on your mission-critical objectives, (4) learn *how* to be a committed partner and ask others to do the same, and (5) leave the group with an inspired vision of the future.
- **After you express your stand, ask the group for feedback.** Find out how you impacted the group and ask what would make your stand more powerful. Also share how it felt for you

to publicly declare and articulate your stand. Did it inspire you to new action?

- **Now turn your stand into action by answering the following questions:** (1) With whom do I need to declare my stand? (2) Who else do I need to include? (3) By when will I publicly declare my stand? (4) What actions do I need to take to turn my stand into results?

> *The ultimate measure of a man is not where he stands*
> *in moments of comfort and convenience,*
> *but where he stands at times of challenge and controversy.*
>
> —MARTIN LUTHER KING, JR. (1929–1968)

Chapter
6
Standing for the Success of Each Other

The most dangerous strategy is to jump a chasm in two leaps.

—Benjamin Disraeli (1804–1881)

To raise the level of performance, you must foster an environment in which aligned leaders and engaged people are bursting with enthusiasm to help the organization excel. For this, you need *committed partnerships:* people who act as owners and stand for the success of each other and the organization.

The causal chain is clear: it is the relationship that people have with one another and the organization that drives business results and makes system and process changes viable. The success of your organization or team depends on the willingness of people to change their behavior and expand their capacity to work together in a focused and disciplined partnership.

It is troubling that most business-as-usual associations are relationships of convenience or unstable alliances in which people work together only when absolutely required. These traditional relationships, for the most part, are politically motivated or pursued for reasons of personal gain. What is disturbing is that they are pervasive throughout organizations and representative of the low quality of relationships. The debilitating downside is that most businesses operate with an inherently defective platform for aligning and mobilizing the very faction that determines what the organization can achieve: people.

Without committed partnerships throughout your organization, you cannot achieve the interconnection and synergy needed between people, strategy, and operations. But when you provide people with a disciplined methodology for working together, they will successfully navigate any challenges and achieve the objectives of the company.

> **Committed Partnerships**
> Standing for the success of each other both privately and publicly.

Because relationships are in a constant state of flux, often vacillating between breakdown and recovery, leaders must have the ability to talk about concerns and fully resolve them so they are not carried into the future. Decision making and alignment must be effective and swift so flawless execution is ensured.

This chapter explores how to transform traditional business relationships into committed partnerships. Two factors are required: (1) a leadership stand to build a constructive and empowering environment, and (2) a way for people to learn how to be committed partners and stand for the success of each other.

BUSINESS SUCCESS HINGES ON COMMITTED PARTNERSHIPS

Business success hinges on people working together in committed partnerships. Unfortunately, automatic behaviors eclipse productive behaviors, and people tolerate relationships of convenience. Because of the unstructured and temporary alliances between people and groups, the organization or business unit experiences breakdowns the instant there is misalignment.

The lack of a disciplined way of working together became evident in a global information organization we encountered. As a result of constant breakdowns in client proposals, leaders did not trust business units in other countries to deliver consistent high-quality presentations to the client. Each business unit defended its approach and directed its anger and frustration at each other instead of resolving the problem.

Leaders were resigned for two reasons: (1) having to deal with a recurring breakdown, and (2) not having an effective method for correcting the situation. Breakdowns and challenges are to be expected. But a predicament occurs when the resolution of a problem requires a change in behavior that no process or system can correct.

In another organization, leaders could not align on a new process for connecting customer interactions and product delivery from beginning to end. Each group had their own approach and did not want to change their system which became particularly apparent with the financial group. When the financial group dug their heels in and argued for the status quo with only small modifications, everyone became demoralized and frustrated. Not once was the question asked, "How will our process impact our customers?" All eyes were focused on what was best for internal groups and the customer—the end user—was left completely out of the equation.

Finally the CEO threw up his hands and said, "We're keeping the current system for now, and in a couple of years we'll review what changes are needed." He avoided taking a stand and compromised for fear of upsetting people.

From these two examples we can see how unresolved breakdowns lead to inferior decision making. Why do we have structured and disciplined processes for every aspect of business from project management to quality control, yet we have nothing for how people work together to achieve efficiencies for the business? In the most important area in which we need structure and guidelines, we have none. People cannot be held accountable for a standard of behavior that can be conveniently manipulated, is applied inconsistently, or does not exist. Missing this important point keeps us operating backward and paying the price for substandard organizational effectiveness.

> When the going gets tough, fearless leaders have compassion for people but they hold the line on high behavioral standards.

We wonder why instability exists and people become resigned. Let's face the problem squarely: it is not because of breakdowns or challenges. People are ready for those events. It is because of the enormous amount of energy required to deal with those who are not taking accountability, are not aligned, or are unresponsive. But who is accountable? Is it the individual whose behavior we judge as ineffective or unproductive, or is it the organization that fails to provide a consistent, uniform method with which people can align and resolve problems?

Let's return to the question: Why is it we have specific guidelines, measurable milestones, and explicit accountabilities in all areas of business, but we think we can build a high performance culture without this same rigor? Committed partnerships are not naturally occurring phenomena; people must learn how to build stable and effective partnerships.

In building a high performance culture, committed partners learn new behaviors and raise the standard of behavior throughout the organization. Leaders and employees insist on holding one another accountable for high standards. You will no longer need to referee conflict between people and groups because they will have a clear and unambiguous process for working efficiently and effectively together.

You can look the other way, but until a high behavioral standard for working together is firmly embedded into the organization's DNA, people will compensate and deliver the best they can in a dismal and dysfunctional environment.

FROM "I CAN DO THIS ALONE" TO "WE ARE IN THIS TOGETHER"

Fearless leadership starts with seeing what you cannot see and taking accountability for your impact. Committed partners create an environment in which it is safe to say "I have a blind spot," "I made a mistake," or "I need help." This environment of trust, openness, interdependence, and active mutual support eliminates the façade of pretending to have it all together. Committed partners have their attention on *recovery*, not perfection, and they learn how to move swiftly in identifying and resolving breakdowns. Here is the key: their commitment is to being effective, not being right.

Committed partners develop a relationship in which they are *for* each other, both privately and publicly, and operate with the conviction that when one person fails, every one fails. They do not allow conspiracies against one another or the organization to form; they stomp out doubt, gossip, and skepticism, and they stand for company initiatives. Team members understand that their personal success is inextricably tied to the team's success. They know one another's blind spots intimately so they can quickly spot automatic behavior and transform it into extraordinary behavior that forwards the action.

> ### The Stand of Committed Partners
> We commit to the success of one another and we take 100% accountability for business results and our impact on people.

Committed partners know that day by day they must overcome the dominant automatic behavior of going it alone, which is corroborated by the leadership myth "I should be self-sufficient and able to handle anything." Myths have power. Although they have no basis in fact, their power comes from a body of traditional beliefs that accumulate over time. Like the air you breathe, myths are transparent and appear to be "the way things are." These myths become part of your belief system and determine how you speak and act. You don't consciously choose to believe myths; instead, you inherit them. They are foisted on you from the unspoken culture of leadership.

It's easy to discount a myth as some historical superstition that has no modern-day relevance, but in our work with leaders we discover the full extent of their grip. As we discussed earlier, although you ask for what you want, you create what you believe: your underlying assumptions and beliefs form the core of how you lead and interact with others.

This explains why committed partners are well schooled in automatic behaviors—theirs and others. They want their hands on the mechanism that allows them to anticipate problems, steer clear of breakdowns, and recover quickly when they occur. They share a set of agreements and skills for attacking the real issues.

Here is the shift that is needed in thinking: committed partners measure their success and effectiveness by what others say, not by their own self-assessment. This means that in a committed partnership, *your* point of view is irrelevant; the only valid measure of your impact on people is what *others* say. When there is a disconnect between how *you think* you have impacted others and what *others tell you*, throw your opinion out.

Committed partners accept 100% accountability in all matters. This means keeping your attention on what *you* can change, not on what *oth-*

ers should do. Let's clearly define what 100%-zero accountability means by comparing it to the traditional way in which people behave: 50/50 accountability. Typically, people are willing to take accountability and meet others halfway as long as the other party exhibits some sense of accountability or remorse. This is what happened when a problem occurred between an operations group and a human resource group. Each group was willing to take accountability providing the other group accepted their fair share. A stalemate occurred as both groups grew defensive waiting for the other to act. In a 50/50 model of accountability, individuals and groups adopt a victim mindset and, as a result, are powerless to effect change. All action depends on what others choose to do, and taking accountability is viewed as accepting blame.

In the model of 100%-zero accountability, it does not matter what others choose. Accountability is viewed as owning the problem or situation. It is irrelevant who is to blame or what caused the problem. With the owner mindset firmly in place, people quickly resolve problems by confronting breakdowns and blind spots and operating with an enterprise perspective.

In the example between the operations and human resources group, the human resources group ultimately set aside their assumptions and judgments and took 100% accountability. They went to the operations group and said "Our actions impacted your project deadline and each of you personally, and we apologize. We would like your coaching and input so we can make corrections." The statement of accountability from the human resources group is a demonstration of 100%-zero accountability because (1) there is no condition or expectation that other individuals or groups respond in kind, (2) there is a clear and unambiguous statement of accountability for impact (intended or not), and (3) there is an authentic request for feedback and coaching on correcting the immediate and long-term situation.

Taking 100%-zero accountability is an example of giving up the need to be right about your point of view. When you do this, your behavior is not dependent on what others do. The "zero" in this formula makes you the master of your fate. You can choose what you will do, what you will stand for, and what action you will take without waiting for others to act.

The power of 100% accountability and committed partnerships comes not from having *a handful* of these special relationships but from having *an entire organization* of committed partners. However, telling people you want them to think differently will not change what they do. Instead, help others learn how to engage with a new set of rules for working as committed partners. Committed partnerships must become a permanent part of your organization so people say "This is the way we do things here—we stand for the success of each other."

COMMITTED PARTNERS: AN EXTRAORDINARY LEVEL OF TRUST AND OWNERSHIP

In case you believe that a committed partnership is a luxury item rather than a necessity, let me set the record straight. You cannot build a high performance organization or team without committed partnerships: it is simply not possible. A high level of ownership from leaders and employees is required to reach world-class status and outperform competitors, and all of this requires committed partnerships. People must learn how to work as interdependent teams. Committed partners look out for each other and the organization, and they go far beyond their formal roles and responsibilities.

To get a fuller understanding of committed partnership, let's explore it in practice. Committed partners do not tolerate blind spots such as blaming others. They are quick to hold each other accountable for rising above circumstances and not getting trapped in victim mentality. It is this exceptional level of ownership that allows partners to look out for the welfare of the entire organization, rather than resorting to the automatic behavior of turf wars and unhealthy competition.

Committed partners apply a disciplined methodology that safeguards against the damage of blind spots and gives them the tools to act with speed. The operative factor is that individuals and teams *learn* how to work together. This learned behavior transforms traditional teams into high performance teams.

As we discussed in Chapter 5, your job is to fuse people and business objectives together so they are interdependent factors for achieving long-term success. Without exception, you must elevate *how* people work together to the level of critical importance.

You do not need to have all the answers to initiate committed partnerships. In fact, you must be willing to lead *without* having all the answers. However, you must have a clear goal: making committed partnerships and 100% accountability your new organizational norm.

Purposefully Expanding the Circle of Trust

Here is another area in which we think backward. Our automatic behavior with trust is "You must earn my trust." But for many, earning trust takes a long time, sometimes years or even a lifetime. If we must wait to develop trust in working relationships, we have a problem. We must reverse our thinking of expecting trust to be earned, for which we place the burden of proof on the other party, and learn how to grant trust based on shared commitments and agreements.

One of the distinguishing features of committed partners is the way in which they grant trust to one another. All issues are put on the table; nothing is taboo. If the issue impacts performance, execution, or the quality of relationships, it is immediately discussed and resolved.

I must warn you: granting trust is not natural or comfortable; it is outside our scope of "reasonableness." Why would you trust anyone when you do not have sufficient information or data? Common wisdom says do not trust until you have evidence, and a lot of it, that a person is trustworthy. But here is where we must blot out the "logic" of demanding that trust be earned and supplant it with an urgency to grant trust in a partnership based on shared rules of engagement.

Pure and simple: committed partners do not have the need to earn trust. They act with urgency and grant trust based on precise and shared agreements for how they will work together. Committed partners understand the significance of trust as displayed in the sidebar "Granting Trust in Committed Partnerships."

How many trusted colleagues—people you can count on unconditionally—do you have on your team or in the organization? If you are like most people, you have only a handful of trusted partners. If you imagine trust as a large circle with concentric circles inside of it, whom would you place in your inner circle—the bull's-eye portion? And whom do you distrust—those in your outer circle?

Most people have only a small fraction of the people they interact with on a daily basis in their inner circle of trust. When people and teams do not trust one another, they compensate for low trust levels by second-guessing leaders, making redundant efforts, micromanaging, and locking on to tactical issues rather than maintaining a strategic focus. The cumulative

Granting Trust in Committed Partnerships

- **Trust is commitment based.** Committed partners grant trust based on specific agreements and a shared commitment to the success of each other and the organization.
- **Trust is self-confirming.** When a committed partner grants trust to another, that person, knowing he or she is trusted, is more trustworthy. This demonstrates the 100%-zero accountability formula: a change in the behavior of one person can alter the trust in the overall relationship.
- **Trust is transparent.** Committed partners are persistently attentive to the quality of their relationships. They manage trust, and the moment it appears to waver, they discuss concerns without delay and restore the partnership.
- **Trust is a requisite.** Committed partners recognize that trust is a requisite for effective teamwork and innovation. The quality of their partnerships is the foundation for producing business results.

effect: the lower the trust, the higher the automatic and unproductive behaviors.

The circle of trust (Exhibit 6-1) gives people a way to talk about a topic that is ardently avoided: the truth about whether they trust one another. Until a committed partnership is formed and explicit standards are set, the circles of trust are based on unspoken, individual criteria. The risk is that you seldom know when you are in another's inner circle or when you have been ousted to some gulag in Siberia for a passing comment, unfortunate behavior, or unintended impact.

It is typically and tragically true that you will rarely know what happened when you are removed from a person's inner circle of trust because you failed to live up to unspoken criteria. The same applies when you are in the outer circle of trust and are moved into the innermost circle. At all

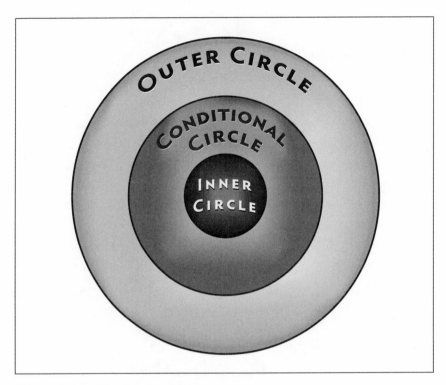

EXHIBIT 6-1: *The Circle of Trust*

times, you are moving in and out of others' circles of trust, as they are with you. The problem is that the circle of trust is an implied construct that is not discussed or examined. When people suddenly find themselves not trusted, they have no idea what happened or how to regain the trust that has been lost.

Let's start by understanding the automatic nature of the circles of trust: the inner circle, the conditional circle, and the outer circle.

Inner circle of trust. We place people in our inner circle whom we trust unconditionally to do the right thing. This emotionally based trust does not mean that we view these people as perfect, just that we trust their intention even when they make mistakes and are imperfect. The truth is that you are far more forgiving of people in your inner circle, whether wise or not, because you have an unfaltering belief that you share the same commitments, beliefs, and values.

Conditional circle of trust. The conditional circle gives us the latitude to test people and see if they can make it inside our privileged group. Or we use the conditional circle to toss out those who were once in our inner circle but no longer meet our personal criteria. The conditions people impose for this part of the circle vary. Some label others as conditional based on such past experiences as the individual not keeping his or her commitments. Others put people in the conditional circle to see if they can live up to their personal standard of behavior.

Outer circle of trust. Typically we place people in the outer circle who have not demonstrated sufficient evidence that they are worthy of progressing toward our inner circle of confidants. They may be in our outer circle simply due to a lack of information and experience. But we also place people in this circle when we lose confidence in them and feel we can no longer count on them. In these cases, we move from viewing individuals or groups as neutral to seeing them as detrimental to obtaining our goals. We doubt their commitment and do not trust their intention to do the right thing regardless of circumstances.

We seldom stop to consider where people are in our circle of trust. We simply respond automatically and in a different way with those we trust than with those we don't. When was the last time you said to someone "You are outside my circle of trust"? You probably do not consider or talk about who is in or outside your circle of trust. But your behavior sends the message anyway, and others interpret whether they are trusted or not by your actions. Likewise, others are constantly sending you a message about where you are in their circle of trust. Unless we form committed partnerships and have a way to build and restore trust, we are left with the devastating automatic fluctuations that occur when people are shuffled in and out.

You already know the value of trust on teams and in organizations. When unconditional trust is not present, automatic behaviors are.

And as so often happens, distrust leads to resignation, and the only thing that rectifies this situation is building committed partnerships. Marco, the president of an integrated solutions company, knew that his "good" team was not a high performance team. Here's how he addressed the issue of trust and initiated the process of building committed partnerships.

How a Leader Recognized the Lack of Trust and Established Committed Partnerships

Marco relied on the individual expertise of his direct reports and interacted with them as a group of individuals and not as a team. He felt he had a good group and simply wanted to move them a couple notches up the scale. But a problem, simmering below the surface, would not allow this to happen.

The locus of the issue was Marco's exclusive and protective relationship with Kevin, a brilliant marketing strategist. He gave Kevin carte blanche to operate as a separate entity and make unilateral decisions that undermined the team's effectiveness. A frustrated member of the team said, *"Kevin is not linked to all points in our operating strategy, and we pay the price."*

What Happened. Several senior leaders expressed their concern about Kevin and asked Marco to discuss it at the next group meeting. The meeting opened with several comments from senior leaders who said they felt blindsided by not being included in a recent change in marketing strategy that directly impacted their business units.

Marco was defensive and responded, *"Things happen fast around here, and you're included as soon as time permits."* The room got quiet and not a word was said. Now it was our turn to facilitate the dead-end conversation. I asked Marco: *"Is this what you want—leaders who comply with you even when they don't agree?"* *"No, of course not, I just want them to agree with me,"* answered Marco half jokingly. I responded, *"But you can't achieve agreement unless you're willing to listen to how your behavior has impacted the group. Right now the group does not trust you to listen and resolve a situation that is affecting everyone."*

This time Marco listened. And he turned to the group and said, *"I reacted too quickly. What do you guys want to tell me?"* This time the group talked and fully disclosed their concerns.

The Result. The group meeting surfaced many issues that had impacted trust and working relationships. Marco took accountability for his impact and the splintered group had an honest conversation without finger-pointing and blaming one another. Even Kevin demonstrated his willingness to be part of the team. The group of individuals began the process of becoming a bona fide team and building committed partnerships with one another.

Lesson Learned. Even groups of talented individuals have trust' issues that must be resolved in order to build high performance teams. Because trust is not a one-time event, team members must learn how to talk about trust, be attentive to the relationship, and restore trust quickly when it is compromised.

Without committed partnerships, teams cannot form and people become isolated. With no ability to confront blind spots or to gain and restore trust, they move from being a lame duck to a dead duck. When you take a stand that your team or organization will work together as committed partners, instead of a group of individual experts, you begin the process of transformation in earnest.

THE AGREEMENTS OF COMMITTED PARTNERS

Committed partners operate at the highest level of integrity and accountability. They agree to a high standard of behavior for how they will interact, align, and deal with breakdowns. They stand for the success of each other, privately and publicly. They are fearless and relentless in putting an end to conspiring against others.

They grant each other trust and agree to immediately talk to the appropriate person if they feel they can no longer stand for them. The declaration of committed partners is "I am granting you trust. If at any point I feel I cannot trust you, I will talk with you immediately and not to other people. I will not gossip about you or undermine, conspire against, or blame you. If there is a breakdown between us, you have my commitment that I will address it immediately with you to restore our partnership."

There are five agreements that committed partners align on and use daily to hold each other accountable. This chapter discusses the first agreement—standing for the success of each other both publicly and privately. Chapter 7 discusses honoring and fulfilling commitments; Chapter 8 focuses on talking straight responsibly; Chapter 9 explores aligning emotionally and intellectually; and Chapter 10 examines holding each other accountable.

The Five Agreements of Committed Partners

1. We stand for the success of each other both publicly and privately.
2. We honor and fulfill commitments.
3. We talk straight responsibly.
4. We align emotionally and intellectually.
5. We hold each other accountable.

Committed partners agree to stand for the success of each other in all conversations—one-on-one, meetings, and electronic. They master specific skills for strengthening the working relationship: conspiring *for* each other, listening for positive intention, and cleaning up and recovering quickly when breakdowns occur.

Conspiring For Each Other at Every Opportunity

Your first accountability as a committed partner is to transform the automatic behavior of conspiring *against* others to the extraordinary behavior of conspiring *for* others. Committed partners stop conspiracies against each other by actively intervening, taking a stand for the person or group, and facilitating *clean ups* in derailed relationships.

As a committed partner, you must be willing to honestly identify where you have not supported others and have conspired against them. Remember that *mere* intention does not matter; people respond to your impact, not your intention.

I will tell you right now that you unintentionally engage in conspiracies against others. It happens in an instant. Most leaders are unaware of the imperceptible statements their behaviors make that broadcast the message they do not support a colleague or a corporate initiative.

The rub is that you cannot form committed partnerships until you clean the slate and take accountability for how you have conspired against each other. Even then, you must continually be on the lookout for how your behavior may communicate a lack of support or alignment. Always remember: you are accountable for the *perception* you create and the *impact* you have. Your job as a committed partner is twofold:

1. Intervene and stop yourself when you are conspiring against others whether through silent or active participation.
2. Intervene and stop others when they are conspiring against a person or group.

Nothing is gained by judging behavior as good or bad; instead, think of behavior as effective or ineffective. In this way you can be more forgiving of your mistakes as well as those of others.

But before we go further, we must recognize that this is yet another area in which we have it backward: we judge others by their behavior but expect them to judge us by our intention. As a fearless leader, you must operate with a new standard: you must give others the benefit of the doubt by listening for *their* positive intention and be accountable for your impact without defending and justifying *your* intention. This may seem completely unfair but it is totally necessary to meet the conditions of 100%-zero accountability. It is a difficult concept to grasp because it requires that you give up the belief that others should automatically understand your intention. You must stop explaining what you really meant to do or say and take accountability for how others experienced your behavior. What may appear "unfair" is that you are being asked to do it all: take full accountability for your impact *and* listen with positive intention to others. This is what the "zero" means in 100%-zero accountability: you must completely own the problem or breakdown without blaming others or expecting them to take accountability. When you take 100%-zero accountability you hold yourself to a higher standard. You focus on your behavior, not the behavior of others. It is your high behavioral standard that inspires and catalyzes others to follow your example and make *their choice* to be 100% accountable.

Isabel, a member of a leadership team in a pharmaceutical company, learned how to intervene and end conspiracies against others. She took a stand for the leadership team and their commitment to people and the organization.

Changing Direction by Conspiring For Others

Isabel's peers did not trust her, at all. They felt that she undermined the team at every opportunity and formed alliances with others against the team. From Isabel's perspective she felt as if her team was ineffective and she distanced herself from their decisions. *"I always hear a lot of grumbling about our leadership team. Although I am a member of the team, I think of myself as 'one of the people,' and I defend the underdog,"* explained Isabel in her private leadership session. After explaining the victim triangle to Isabel, she cautiously said: *"Maybe I am a co-conspirator because when others complain, I climb on board and make myself the good guy and my peers the bad guys."* *"Let's be clear about what you are saying,"* I responded. *"This is not a 'maybe' situation. You are definitely a co-conspirator and a victim, and you have lost the trust and support of your team. Are you aware of the damage you have created?"*

Isabel was stunned by my statement; however, the feedback from her peers that she had rationalized intellectually started to sink in at an emotional level. She was troubled as she began to understand the extent to which her peers did not trust her. Although it took a rigorous intervention, Isabel had a significant breakthrough and took accountability for undermining the efforts of her team.

We coached Isabel in how to clean up the conspiracies she had participated in against her team as the first step in building a committed partnership.

The Result. Isabel met with each member of her team, apologized, and took accountability for her impact. Because she had created considerable damage and ill will, one apology was not enough. She had to demonstrate authentic remorse and a noticeable change in her behavior before others were willing to trust her again. Isabel was determined to stand for the success of her team and she did not give up. One by one, team members began to stand for her success.

To build committed partnerships, start by ending conspiracies against others and redirect underground conversations to the appropriate person or venue so the issue can be resolved. Fearless leadership is a methodology for quickly changing direction and taking accountability to get things back on track. But even so, do not be deluded into thinking that a high performance team and committed partnerships are the panaceas for curing all ills. The cure is to build an organization in which people are resilient and agile. High performance teams are not models of perfect behavior; they are imperfect teams that know *how to recover quickly*.

Listening For Positive Intention

In standing for the success of others, committed partners listen for positive intention. They start with the belief that people want to do their best. They trust others and recognize that there are times when people are unable to clearly articulate what they need or want to contribute. Committed partners listen generously and focus on the positive intention to discover the spoken or unspoken commitment.

Let's contrast this with the *automatic* way of listening which is to be right and have a know-it-all attitude. It takes work to genuinely listen to others while the mind is judging what they are saying. Notice the chatter in your head (judging, criticizing, assessing), and realize that you need to override it in order to hear what people are attempting to communicate.

The first step is to catch when you listen against others. For example, you may find yourself frustrated in a conversation or meeting and your mind is screaming loudly "This is absolute crap." The moment you have this reaction, you stop listening, and your attention is on what you want to say. If you can recognize when you are listening against a person or idea, you can self-intervene and turn your behavior around.

The power in fearless leadership is intervening in your automatic behavior and making a more effective choice. I watched Zach interact with a peer, Raoul, in a conversation about selling a major portion of the business. Zach was becoming increasingly agitated. When he responded to Raoul, he took accountability for the fact that he had been listening *against* and said, "I need to apologize because I haven't been listening. I had a reaction to what you were saying and I began judging you rather than listening. I'm telling you this because I want to let go of my reaction and genuinely hear what you have to say."

Now I know this is not a normal conversation, but fearless leadership is not normal behavior. Committed partners master communicating in a way that allows them to do what Zach did. They take accountability and "own" their behavior. They eliminate ambiguity by being forthright and emotionally honest. Even when they are reacting, they say that they are reacting, and they remain unwavering in their commitment to listen for positive intention. This transparency lets people know where they stand, increases trust, and opens the door to having "unusual" conversations where real issues are discussed and resolved.

When you notice you are listening against, take accountability and own your reaction. Then refocus your attention on listening for positive intention. Move beyond the literal message and listen for what is behind the individual's impassioned plea, complaint, or less than clear message. This is easy to understand but difficult to apply. In the moment when we are listening against a person or idea, we are triggered by our need to be right. This strong automatic behavior keeps us from hearing another person. The first step is to intervene with yourself and ask, "Am I more committed to being right than being effective?" Then honestly answer this question.

100%-Zero Accountability in Action
When you do not feel heard, it is your accountability.
When others do not feel heard, this is also your accountability.

If someone says "You haven't listened to me," fight the urge to say "I heard every word you said; in fact, I can repeat it word for word." Although you get to be right, the other person will not feel heard. Stop defending your behavior and start listening. You are accountable not only for what you say but also for how others hear what you say. Until the other person experiences being fully heard and understood, you have not listened.

Leaders are most powerful when they share what they are learning with others. Learning from missteps is as important as "doing something right." William, the COO of a large enterprise, talked about his automatic behavior of not listening or, more accurately, listening against. In speaking to a group of leaders he said, "A trap I fall into is preaching, telling others what they should do, and being judgmental. When I do this with my daughters, they either shut down and stop talking, or argue with me. When I remember to listen for positive intention, they open up and tell me about the challenges they're facing. I'm amazed at the difference, and I'd like to say it's because my daughters are behaving differently. But the truth is it's because I'm listening differently. My commitment is to listen for positive intention with each of you. But I am judgmental and I will fall into old behaviors. I need your help and coaching when I do. Oh, and I promise not to bite your head off!"

The atmosphere of the meeting changed to laughter and warmth the moment William talked openly about his tendency to judge and not listen. The leaders became talkative, responsive, and engaged. In essence, William gave permission to the group to hold him accountable and no one had to tiptoe around him. William courageously opened the door for others to identify their own blind spots and limitations. This is fearless leadership. William used what he learned as a way to help others learn and grow. He led his entire organization to a new level of financial performance by building a culture of accountability. His bold stand, decisive action, and commitment to partnership were real and believable because he walked the talk.

Let's bring together what we know about standing for the success of others. Committed partners conspire *for* each other in all matters, public and private, and listen for positive intention. In the following section we examine how to build committed partnerships and add another practice: cleaning up and recovering quickly when there is a breakdown or problem.

HOW TO BUILD COMMITTED PARTNERSHIPS

When you give your word that you are a committed partner, you make a series of promises. Of course, making the promise is easier than *fulfilling* the promise. You must have the highest level of integrity to keep your commitments and communicate immediately when you feel you can no longer support a person, group, or initiative. When breakdowns occur, the explicit intention is to rapidly restore the relationship so partners can quickly remedy the business situation.

An example of a committed partnership is marriage. There is a clear set of rules and boundaries that both partners agree to maintain. Yet in working relationships, we seldom define the type of partnership we want and instead work with an implied and inconsistent set of rules. It's a small wonder that there are so many problems, assumptions, and breakdowns that interfere with effectiveness. This is why committed partners make formal commitments and live by their agreements. They establish a clear set of guidelines for maintaining the committed partnership and ensuring alignment.

Establish the Context: Commit to the Success of Each Other Privately and Publicly

Everything starts with your commitment and creates the context for the partnership. You cannot overstate your commitment to the partnership any more than you can say "I love you" too much to your significant other. A sincere commitment is meaningful and reinforces the context that committed partners share.

There are two levels of commitment—the commitment you have to the success of each other and the commitment to mutual organizational goals. You cannot have a committed partnership without both commitments firmly in place. The following questions are useful in establishing a committed partnership.

Questions for Building a Committed Partnership

Committing to the Success of Each Other

1. Are we willing to stand for the success of each other both privately and publicly?
2. Are we willing to end conspiracies against each other?
3. Do we promise to communicate immediately and restore the relationship if we feel we can no longer support each other?
4. Are we willing to grant trust?
5. Are we willing to listen for positive intention?
6. Do we agree to actively coach each other on blind spots and graciously accept coaching?

Committing to the Success of the Organization

1. Are we willing to set aside our personal agendas and commit to the enterprise mission and initiatives?
2. Are we willing to eliminate silos and build committed partnerships throughout the organization?

Clean Up the Past: Operate with a Clean Slate

When there are trust issues, committed partners address and resolve them rather than allowing them to fester. They do not use the past as an excuse for the lack of an effective working relationship. Committed partners clean the slate so that the working relationship is not contaminated by old assumptions, beliefs, and judgments. The agreement to stand for the success of each other includes communicating immediately the moment you notice something is off in the relationship or when you need to take accountability for your impact.

Keep in mind that our automatic behavior is to avoid talking about difficult or sensitive issues; we withhold our feelings and hope everything will blow over. This is where the skill of *clean up* is useful: it provides a way to efficiently clean the slate and make amends so problems do not escalate or persist.

The skill of cleaning up is simple and direct. Take accountability for your impact, apologize, and make a promise about your future actions. Then behave consistently with what you have promised. When should you clean up? Any time you "wonder" if you have had a limiting or damaging impact on another person or group. Act immediately the moment you sense that something is off. Do not wait; override the automatic lure to avoid or postpone action. As soon as you hear that nagging voice in your head about something you said, or wish you had said, talk to the appropriate person. It's as simple as that. Make the decision to communicate, and take decisive action.

The act of cleaning up demonstrates that you value the relationship. When you clean up and apologize, you remove the opportunity for people to hold onto negative experiences or build assumptions and stories. It strengthens your credibility as a leader when you increase safety for others to speak up and take accountability.

> **Clean Up**
> Immediately taking accountability for your impact on others and restoring the relationship.

Taking accountability for a mistake or undesired impact gives others the freedom to deal with their mistakes in a productive and healthy way. You want people who are willing to take calculated risks and correct their behavior immediately when something does not work. Most importantly, you want people who are focused on achieving business objectives rather than preoccupied with managing or hiding unresolved issues.

Below is an excerpt from a speech given by Dominic, a CEO of a business consulting company, to his leadership group. Six months prior, he had taken a stand for building a high performance culture and committed to learn everything he had asked of others. His speech demonstrated his commitment to action and inspired others to learn and grow.

"Here's what I have learned about mistakes in my life:

1. It's just as easy to make a big mistake as it is to make a small one.

2. *In order to profit from your mistakes, you have to get out and make some.*

3. *And my favorite—why make the same mistake over and over again when there are so many new ones that you could be making?*

"*On a more serious note, I want to apologize for a mistake I made. I did not include you from the beginning with my vision for a new culture and did not plan effectively to make sure I put you at the front of the process. Things happened fast, and I did not realize my error until we were well down the road.*

"*Joan and Al pointed out my mistake, and they were correct. I need you as my committed partners. I cannot build our high performance culture alone. This mission requires all of us working and thinking together. You can count on the fact that I won't make this same mistake again. However, I will make new ones.*"

Dominic is a powerful leader. People felt that if he could own his mistakes and recover, then so could they. He demonstrated that the way to rebuild trust is to immediately address the issue, clean up, and make a commitment to new action.

A word of warning: clean ups never work when used as a technique. They must be authentic and from the heart. As you begin doing clean ups, do not expect that your *mea culpa* will engender a similar response. This never works, and it will be seen for what it is—a manipulation. Treat your clean up as *your* action for taking accountability, without expecting that others will clean up with you.

Relationships require maintenance and attention. Put all issues, assumptions, and judgments on the table. If you wonder about something, say it. If you have questions about how another person perceives you, ask.

Don't leave relationships to chance. Even if you do not have something specific to clean up, check with others to see if anything is missing. Ask "Do we need to clean up anything with each other?" or "Are there any unresolved issues that we need to address?" Take accountability and initiate a relationship *check in*; do not wait for others to come to you.

Use the "Cleaning Up the Slate" questions in the sidebar when you want to repair a relationship and ensure that all past issues are resolved. Use this as a guide in a conversation with committed partners and listen for positive intention as they give you feedback.

Cleaning Up the Slate

Building Trust and Standing for the Success of Each Other
- Have I let you down or disappointed you? How have I impacted you?
- Have I damaged our trust? What can I do to restore your trust?
- What do I need to clean up? Where do I need to take accountability for my impact?

Listening Against and Making Assumptions and Judgments
- Do you feel that I listen against you?
- Do you feel that I judge you and make assumptions?
- What do I need to clean up? How can I take accountability?

Withholding Emotional Commitment
- Do you feel that I talk straight?
- Do you feel that I withhold my commitment and support?
- Do you feel as if I am talking straight with you right now? What do I need to correct?
- What do I need to clean up?

Conspiring Against
- Do you feel that I have conspired against you or undermined you in any way? What do I need to clean up?
- Have we conspired against each other? How has this impacted others?
- What do we need to clean up with each other? Whom do we need to include in our clean up to end our conspiring against each other?

Holding Each Other to Account
- Are we willing to hold each other accountable for our committed partnership agreements?
- Is there anything else we need to clean up?

Shape the Future: Align on Action

As in any partnership, you will have breakdowns. Committed partnerships are like any other relationship in that respect. The difference is that committed partners anticipate the breakdowns, and they align on how to recover.

Most breakdowns occur due to unmet expectations. It is essential to make sure your expectations are clear and explicitly communicated. Always recheck your alignment to ensure that you are on track and heading in the same direction.

Leaders skip the most fundamental principles and forget to ask the important questions, such as "Who is going to handle this?" "By when will it be complete?" and "Who needs to be included?" Perhaps we consider these questions to be too elementary or basic, but the lack of rigor in asking and answering these questions is what leads to breakdowns, incomplete action, unmet expectations, and disappointment. The discipline in a committed partnership is to be explicit in all matters to eliminate the automatic act of filling in the blanks, making up stories, and distorting facts.

The Long-Term Advantage of Committed Partnerships

The agreements and actions of committed partners offer a long-term advantage: you create the stability needed to achieve business results by building stability in how people work together. Let's face it: all of this is easy to understand but difficult to apply. But when a fearless leader emerges and raises the standard of his or her organization to 100% accountability and committed partnerships, business results soar. Leaders change direction and think and behave in a new way. Escape hatches and excuses are eliminated, and everyone is accountable for expanding the game.

When you keep relationships solid and stable, you balance the unpredictability of a changing environment. A solid behavioral platform gives people a way to optimize performance. When you allow relationships to disintegrate, you can count on bedlam inside your organization. The stable agreements of committed partners and the way in which they constantly attend to the quality of their relationships give your organization the power to survive any storm and prosper.

LEADERSHIP EXPLORATION

Where Do You Need to Clean Up and Take Accountability?

Misunderstandings and unresolved conflicts make it impossible to build committed partnerships unless you clean up first. You must start by asking, "Where do I need to take 100% accountability for my impact?" Remember that 100% accountability is not accepting blame; it is the act of taking charge and adopting an owner's mindset. Answer the following questions and identify the actions needed:

1. **Where have I engaged in conspiracies against others?**
   Where have I actively or silently supported a viewpoint that is negative, destructive, or damaging to an individual or group? What individuals and groups do I need to clean up with?
2. **Where have I been trapped in the victim mindset?**
   Where have I been feeling hopeless, resigned, or frustrated? Who have I blamed as the persecutor—an individual, a group, senior leaders, the company? With whom do I need to take accountability and clean up?
3. **Who do I need to clean up with?** Where have I tolerated a working relationship that is less than great? Where have I not taken accountability for resolving issues that are in the way of building a positive and constructive relationship?

Where Do You Already Have Committed Partnerships, and Where Do You Need to Build Them?

As a fearless leader, your role is to build committed partnerships throughout the organization. You must consistently demonstrate your commitment to high behavioral standards and stop tolerating relationships that are derailed or insufficient for playing big. As always, engage in this leadership exploration with a partner who is willing to push you and challenge your thinking. Ask the following questions and identify actions needed:

1. **Who are your committed partners?** Whom do you trust unconditionally on your team, the level below, and the next level up? Do you stand for each other's success both privately and publicly?

2. **Where do you need to build committed partnerships?** Think broadly and consider your peers, direct reports, team, customers, community leaders, key suppliers, and other stakeholders. What committed partnerships will you build, and by when?

3. **Who are you avoiding building a committed partnership with?** We all have people with whom we believe it is not possible to form a committed partnership. And we have evidence to prove this. Set aside your assumptions and identify key people with whom a committed partnership would make a significant difference to you and the business.

LEADERSHIP ACTION

1. **Initiate Clean Ups with Individuals and Groups.** Before you attempt to build a committed partnership, you must clean up unresolved issues and conflicts. The most difficult task you will encounter when doing a clean up is not the act of cleaning up, it is whether you have the courage to give up your need to be right. If you are stuck in a rigid point of view and believe that you are right and others are wrong, a clean up will not work. You cannot authentically clean up a situation unless you take 100%-zero accountability. Anything less will be viewed as contrived and inauthentic. Examine and suspend your judgments and assumptions so you can genuinely listen to the perspective of others.

    Identify three individuals and/or groups that you are willing to clean up with and take action. When doing a clean up, always start with your commitment to the person and your relationship. Apologize without defending your behavior or explaining what you intended. Then take 100% accountability without expecting others to do the same. Every time you authentically clean up a relationship, you pave the way for building or restoring a committed partnership.

2. **Initiate a conversation.** Explain your purpose (what you hope to achieve), establish the context (why you are having this conversation), state your commitment to the success of the other

person, and take accountability for your impact. Remember that the emphasis is on opening the conversation and listening for positive intention. By listening carefully to the other person, you will discover where you need to clean the slate so you can build a committed partnership.

3. **Initiate a discussion about the circle of trust with an individual or your team.** A genuine conversation about trust requires a safe environment. You must have the courage to listen without reacting or judging. Your outcome is to expand the circle of trust for the partnership or team. This will not work if you are not authentic and not willing to suspend your judgment. People withhold and are not emotionally honest when the environment is unsafe. If this is the case, do not put people on the spot; do this activity privately with an individual instead of a team.

Using the three circles of trust in Exhibit 6-1, follow the steps below:

- **State where you believe you are in the group's circle of trust.** First, talk about the group as a whole and where you believe you are in *their* circle of trust. Next, if the environment is conducive, talk about where you believe you are in each individual's circle of trust.

- **Ask the other person or team to share where they believe they are in *your* circle of trust.** Listen, and acknowledge their willingness to begin the process of building a committed partnership. Use this opportunity to learn how you impact others.

- **If you are ready, and others are willing, find out where you need to take accountability for your impact and clean the slate.** Trust, or the lack of trust, must be honestly addressed for a team to move to a new level of performance.

Do not follow where the path may lead.
Go instead where there is no path and leave a trail.

—RALPH WALDO EMERSON (1803–1882)

Chapter
7
Honoring and Fulfilling Commitments

To predict the behavior of ordinary people in advance,
you only have to assume that they will always try to
escape a disagreeable situation
with the smallest expenditure of intelligence.

—FRIEDRICH NIETZSCHE (1844–1900)

We must start with the undeniable problem: we have destroyed the meaning of the word *commitment*. It used to be a significant pledge, a vow, a duty. The word *commitment* meant something; it was our word of honor. Today, we are consumed with trying to sort through *real* commitments versus casual, throwaway promises.

We make far too many casual promises. And we speak with little or no regard for carrying out the words we communicate. You put your integrity in the balance every time you commit. Others judge the fabric of your character by whether you keep your commitments and follow through on them in a timely manner. Casual promises and broken commitments are the quickest way to undermine your credibility.

In this chapter, we explore how committed partners honor their agreements, and when necessary, responsibly revoke them in a way that supports business results and working relationships. We explore the factors that build a commitment-based culture where people behave consistently with their words. This includes examining the link between honoring commitments and credibility, breaking the automatic behavior of accepting excuses for results, separating authentic commitments from casual promises, and learning how to elicit commitments from others by making clear and direct requests.

HOW COMMITTED PARTNERS RELATE TO COMMITMENTS

Committed partners have a distinctive and potent relationship to commitments. They do not resort to automatic behavior of treating commitments casually. Instead, they reaffirm the power of their word by treating commitments with great care. They swiftly crush anything that threatens to erode the integrity of their word, and they do not tolerate from others or themselves broken commitments, empty promises, or slippery conditions for fulfilling commitments. In a committed partnership, people hold themselves and others accountable for doing what they say they are going to do, or when appropriate, responsibly revoking a commitment.

These leaders have a high level of credibility and foster an environment that exudes trust and confidence. They balance uncertainty in the world with their conviction, assurance, and a sense of calm in the midst of a storm. People follow these steadfast and impassioned leaders because they can trust that their word is their bond. Fearless leaders send a consistent message: *together* we will overcome any challenge and any daunting circumstance, and when tested, we will not falter.

Our automatic reaction is to shrink the game, take shortcuts, and settle for less. How you rise above this reaction is dependent on how you relate to commitments—yours and others—and sets the course for business success or failure. Our worst and most ineffective behaviors are activated when we feel our survival is threatened, yet this is the very time when we must stand for something that is greater than our individual needs. We must soundly defeat pettiness, small-mindedness, and divisive thinking to resurrect strong core values of integrity, accountability, and commitment where our word will once again be synonymous with consistent action.

You cannot be 100% accountable if you do not honor your commitments and behave in a way that is consistent with your words. Your relationship to commitments—both big and small—defines your character and decides your fate. It determines the sustainability of your committed partnerships. Leaders eventually fail when they leave a trail of broken promises and diminish their word to the point where they are no longer trusted.

How do you relate to commitments? Read the following statements and determine if any reflect your attitude about commitments:

- **"I don't trust others to deliver what they promise."** "People around here are lousy at keeping their commitments so I don't expect people to do what they say."
- **"I keep others' expectations of me low."** "Commitments are overrated. That's why I don't make them. My motto: no commitment, no expectation."
- **"I only commit so I won't let people down."** "I like to please people and don't want to disappoint them. I say 'yes' when I think that's what they want to hear, and I regret it later."
- **"I do what I say I am going to do."** "I don't mince words. When I say I'm going to do something, I do it. If I'm not willing to commit, I say so. People know where I stand at all times."

The question in fearless leadership is not simply whether you make commitments or even keep them. The question is "Will you keep your commitments even when circumstances are tough and you are uncomfortable?" This is the true test of your mettle.

Credibility, Trust, and Confidence

When it comes to assessing leadership effectiveness, there are only two legitimate measures: the business results you produce and how others respond to your leadership. Your effectiveness as a leader is based on the extent to which others perceive you as credible and trustworthy, which, in turn, is what inspires confidence and generates results.

Agreements, commitments, promises, pledges, and pacts—call them anything you want. When you say the words "*I will*," you are promising something to someone. The words *commitment*, *promise*, and *agreement* are pledges to do something. Respecting your word and honoring your commitments are expressions of your integrity and values. When your word means something, you can create anything. People whose word is respected are perceived as trustworthy, reliable, and credible. It takes strength of character to consistently demonstrate that your word is your bond.

Credibility is a multidimensional construct that consists of your expertise and your trustworthiness. If you are credible, people believe the truthfulness and correctness of what you say. Credibility is based on trust: can others count on you to do what you say you are going to do? You may be the best in your field with regard to knowledge and proficiency, but if you avoid making commitments or treat commitments casually, people will not trust you. When you do not keep your word in all matters, you destroy confidence. Your credibility at all levels in the organization is determined by how you relate to commitments. All people have is your word. What else is there?

A Team Is Frustrated by a No-Commitment Leader

"Sorry, folks, but I need to take off," Dana said to her direct reports. *"But, Dana, we don't have closure on this decision. What action are we taking?"* asked a frustrated direct report. *"I'll get back to you in a couple days,"* Dana said as she breezed out the door.

Dana is a senior vice president in a global chemical company. Her plate is always full—so full that her team works overtime to make up for her lack of follow-through and broken commitments. When Dana is not in the room, here's what her team says about her:

- *"Dana is not respectful of others—she cancels meetings or overextends them by an hour or more. We stay late or come in early just to complete our work."*
- *"The only thing that decisiveness and Dana have in common is that they both start with 'D.' Dana leaves everyone hanging; she postpones decisions and never makes a timely one."*
- *"Dana has a commitment problem—she doesn't commit. She makes vague promises such as 'I'll get back to you soon.' We all know that 'soon' means: 'Whenever I feel like it, so don't bother me.'"*

A leader's credibility requires living by his or her word. If you are of the misguided opinion that it is acceptable to break small commitments as long as you keep the big ones, you are heading for a huge fall—a fall in credibility. You might classify "I'll call you tomorrow" as a small commitment that is not worthy of worry or angst should you neglect to follow through. But your thinking is flawed. It does not matter how *you* think your broken commitments will impact others. The only relevant data is the experience *others* have when you break your commitments.

Use any classification system you want, but when you separate important commitments from the not-so-important ones, you are creating a false dichotomy. When you say "Yes, I will do this," you have committed. Your words carry weight, and you lose credibility each time you break or irresponsibly revoke a promise. The people around you tally commitments the same way one maintains a debit or credit ledger. When you break a commitment, others put a check mark in the debit column. When you keep a commitment, they put a check mark in the credit column. From the perspective of others, you are either a leader who keeps his or her word or one who does not. There is no gray area. The question you must answer is "Do you have the courage to live by your word, and to recover quickly and responsibly when you do not?"

A Good Excuse Is Not a Result

When people do not fulfill their commitments, most have a good excuse. They will tell you about the effort they put into the project or the circumstance that impeded them. They will justify the lack of results with explanations and excuses. But an excuse is not a result that almost made it. An excuse is an excuse. It is the cover story or pretext intended to explain why the result or commitment was not fulfilled. It is intended to vindicate and pardon the person who did not do what he or she promised. And we fall into the trap of accepting effort as a reasonable excuse for the lack of results.

Have you noticed how conditioned we have become to accepting excuses and explanations? We frequently ask others "Why is this late?" as if the answer to "why" justifies the lack of a result. The word *why* routinely leads to an explanation, reason, or excuse based on the individual's interpretation of events. Why do we waste our time asking for interpretations and listening to excuses, rather than illuminating the facts so we can correct the situation and hold each other accountable?

We have become so conditioned to excuses masquerading as legitimate justification that we can no longer separate them from the facts. Not to belabor the point but we have it backward again. Who cares if there is a good excuse? A good excuse is not a result and never will be. Let's move on to solving the problem, stop wasting time bickering and defending what we did, and learn what we need to do to correct the situation and prevent it from occurring again.

We accept what appears to be sensible, justifiable, legitimate, or rational. Our *reasonableness* is what gets us into trouble. We have lowered the bar on what is acceptable behavior in the same way that we have become seduced into paying for effort instead of paying for performance. We have become complacent and reasonable to the point that we are not mindful of the consequences. We accept "good enough," take shortcuts, and settle for less from others and ourselves.

> **Axiom of Fearless Leaders**
> Circumstances are not an excuse for the lack of results.

When leaders tacitly approve of an environment in which good excuses are tolerated, the organization gets into trouble: (1) leaders make excuses when they do not deliver on their commitments, and (2) they accept excuses when others fail to fulfill their commitments.

Until we resolve to honor and fulfill commitments, we cannot hold ourselves and others accountable. The "good excuse" approach is indulged, and everyone is given a reprieve. "Too bad the business result did not get produced, but circumstances were such that it just wasn't possible" becomes the voice of reason inside the organization. People learn to apply low standards to commitments, and even those who take commitments seriously inadvertently drop their standards when no one else is playing by the same rules.

The "good excuse" approach becomes the norm in the organization and the substitute for performance and business results. The organizational blind spot of tolerating "good enough" becomes firmly rooted in place, and leaders are easily roped in by excuses. People imitate how leaders behave and poor behavior becomes the cultural norm.

A CEO Stops Accepting Excuses for the Lack of Business Results

Derek was the managing director of a business unit in South Africa. He had been in the job for four years, and his unit was continuing to falter. He had a litany of reasons for why the business was not doing well, such as *"I inherited people who were not competent," "My family is having trouble adjusting to a new country,"* and *"I don't have enough time to put out all the fires created by my predecessor."* The list went on and no one held Derek accountable. Although there was much grumbling about his underperforming business, "reasonable" excuses were tolerated.

What Happened. Nothing changed until the company's new CEO intervened. He stopped accepting excuses and set a new and higher standard of behavior. He told Derek, *"Your results are unacceptable."* Derek jumped in and started to explain the reasons for recent failures: *"We had a lot of trouble with our customers . . ."* The CEO interrupted and stated, *"Let me repeat, your results are unacceptable. The purpose of this conversation is to align on what is needed, what actions you will take, and when they will be implemented."* Derek fervently agreed, *"I'm completely aligned with you. All we need to do is get rid of a few more people and bring in competent folks who can deliver."* The CEO, not dissuaded with this tactic, stood by his guns: *"I want to hear how you are personally accountable for the lack of results and what you are going to do about it. I'm willing to work with you, but you need to take accountability first."*

When Derek realized this new CEO was not going to allow him any leeway and that his excuses where falling on deaf ears, Derek made the choice to change his behavior. In less than a year, Derek's unit began turning around. No excuses, just results.

Lesson Learned. Fearless leaders cut through the nonsense and do not tolerate disingenuous behavior, nor do they accept "reasonable" excuses as a substitute for business results. When leaders hold others accountable for their commitments and performance, not for activities and effort, they hold people to a higher standard and most will change their behavior.

When leaders change the rules of the game and raise the bar on how people are expected to behave, a few may leave the organization, but the overwhelming majority will stay and become passionately engaged. People want to do their best, and tolerating poor behavior in some lowers the standard for everyone.

Words are actions, and we use the words *accountability, integrity,* and *commitment* as if we are sprinkling sugar on cereal, adding a splash of flavor with no real substance. The words that represent our highest ideals and values no longer have potency. Without recognizing it, we accept a low standard of behavior that undermines business results.

Every time you accept an excuse, you send a message: a good excuse plus a reasonable explanation equals the result. This is no way to run a business. Until our behavioral standards for accountability and commitments are significantly raised, becoming a world-class organization is a pipe dream. It is a castle in the air that will remain unachievable until committed partnerships are formed and leaders build a culture where commitments stand for action and results.

We need fearless leaders who are not unfair or arbitrary, but who take accountability and refuse to accept low behavioral standards. We need leaders who have the courage to restore the true meaning to the words *accountability, integrity,* and *commitment.*

Your Word Is Your Bond

In a culture of accountability, your word is your bond. Individuals and teams are caretakers of their promises, and they do not give or take commitments lightly. They treat commitments with respect and do not let circumstances or challenges stop them.

Your relationship to the words that come out of your mouth determines the extent of your power. If talk is cheap, and words are empty and hollow, then committing is not a powerful action. On the other hand, when commitments are kept or responsibly revoked, they are the linchpins for producing business results and the keys to greatness.

A person who keeps his or her agreements, commitments, and promises without excuses is living 100% accountability. Yet how many times have you been late to a meeting and dismissed it due to traffic or forgetfulness or blamed it on another meeting that went longer than expected? How much integrity do you have in keeping your word to yourself and others? As a leader, you are always sending a message to others. When you habitually break your commitments, you are saying "You are not important. Circumstances dictate my behavior." There are legitimate urgent circumstances that justify breaking or altering a commitment. However, when circumstances determine your behavior daily, others will not trust your leadership.

A CEO Demands That People Live by Their Commitments

A technology company faced a worldwide meltdown in how its client service teams supported the customers. Cross-functional teams did not trust each other to keep their commitments on consistently bringing high-quality new products to market on time. Leaders in all parts of the world were resigned that nothing would change. It was commonplace for people not to keep their commitments.

What Happened. The CEO intervened and took a bold stand about how he expected leaders to behave and relate to customer commitments. "We—and I am including myself—have done a lousy job of keeping our commitments. We spend more time arguing about who is accountable for what than delivering what our customers want. This behavior needs to end. Your word matters. My word matters. All we have is our word. Beginning now, I expect each of us to honor and keep our commitments. You must make a choice: Care for your commitments to our customers and one another or find a company that doesn't care. Because in this company, we care about commitments and what we say is what we do."

The Result. This CEO is a fearless and inspirational leader. His message galvanized people to alter how they interacted with the customer and one another. Global teams developed a motto: *"We Live by Our Commitments."* Whenever there was a breakdown, someone always asked, *"Are we living by our commitments?"* With this change in attitude and behavior, global teams cut time to market significantly while boosting product quality on all platforms.

To be a fearless leader, you must respect the power of commitments. The first rule is to keep commitments that you make to yourself because *you said you would.* The second rule is to keep commitments you make to others because *you said you would.*

Speaking Is an Action

Language shapes reality and words shape our thinking and actions. Every time you use phrases such as "I'll try" or "I'll do my best," you diminish the probability of a successful outcome. The definition of the word *try* is "to attempt." When you say "I'll try" instead of "I will," your thinking and behavior adjust to match your words. *Try* is not a commitment or action: it is a statement of no accountability with a back door to escape any consequences. When an individual does not deliver on an "I'll try" promise, he or she is saying "I said I would try. I did not say I would do it."

Have you noticed how many words are designed to hedge and avoid taking accountability? Here are just a few:

- try
- maybe
- perhaps
- sometime
- possibly
- probably
- most likely
- almost certainly
- in all probability
- doubtless

Each hedging word or phrase provides a clean exit and ensures that the individual can avoid accountability simply by saying "I never committed." Now examine how few words and phrases we have to express commitment:

- "I will."
- "I promise."
- "You can count on me."

There is a stark contrast between the plethora of words for hedging and the scarcity of those for committing. Language reveals a great deal about culture and beliefs. This explains why transforming companies into high performance organizations requires a new language: leaders must master specific distinctions—such as the difference between a casual promise and an authentic commitment—in order to raise behavioral standards and clearly articulate what is expected. The language of high performance transforms speaking into an action rather than a description of an event. Everyone shares the same language and methodology for acting swiftly to overcome challenges.

THREE PROMISES AND ONLY ONE AUTHENTIC COMMITMENT

I am unwilling to use the word *commitment* to apply to statements that are not commitments at all. I have identified three types of promises, and only one authentic commitment. My intention is to restore the word *commitment* to its rightful place as a fundamental driver for output and productivity.

Before going any further, let's discuss the cost to an organization of a culture of no accountability and no commitment. In this type of business culture, not everyone in the company avoids taking accountability or committing, but there is sufficient critical mass to tip the scales. People continually shift the blame to others. You can count on an enormous amount of wasted time and inefficient action, or as one client put it, "*heat in the system.*" Rework is high, and people are frustrated. Cultures that are sloppy about managing commitments will never be world-class organizations.

In the sidebar there are three promises and one authentic commitment. As you read the descriptions, consider how they apply to you, your team, and your organization. High performance organizations reach elite status when leaders make authentic commitments and keep them. Anything less is not acceptable.

The Difference between Promises and Authentic Commitment

- **Casual promises.** These are statements made with no intention to act. For example, Ralph, a salesperson in a software company, made lots of nice-sounding promises such as *"Just tell me what you need, and I'll get it to you."* When people told him what they needed, he smiled—but did nothing.
- **Slippery promises.** These are statements made with a built-in escape hatch. For example, Nadia had no trouble at all committing. She just made sure she could back out of her commitments quickly. When she failed to deliver, she simply responded, *"I'm sorry. I must have misunderstood what you wanted."*
- **Pie-in-the-sky promises.** These are statements made with no completion date or deadline. For example, Warren had no trouble committing, but he conveniently left out the due date so he had room to maneuver. His motto: *"No deadline, no problem. I'll get to it if something more important doesn't come along."*
- **Authentic commitments.** These are clear and explicit statements with the intention to deliver regardless of circumstance. For example, Barbara did not commit lightly. When she said, *"Yes,"* she meant it. When asked to cut next year's budget by 20 percent, she said, *"I will."* No conditions, no escape hatch, no unnecessary words.

Casual Promises

A casual promise is thrown off in the moment with no thought other than to please or avoid. Considered to be social niceties, casual promises are anything but nice, and they do not result in action. A casual promise is easily identifiable: it is vague, there is no intention to act, and both parties accept the pretense of this promise. Hedging language used in casual promises includes

- "I'll give it my best shot."
- "I'll try."
- "It's conceivable that I could have this done today."

- "I hope I can complete this tomorrow."
- "I will do this, but I wish I had more help."
- "It might be completed by the end of this week."

Hedging language, such as *perhaps, maybe, hope, wish, try, might be, could be,* and *conceivably* are used in casual commitments. Again, *try* is the biggest culprit in casual promises. If *try* is a word you frequently use, then pay attention to how you feel about making commitments. When you make a commitment, do you feel boxed in, stuck, or trapped? Many people experience commitments as limiting and taking away their choices. Interestingly enough, the exact opposite is true. The condition of "trying" is limiting and stagnant, whereas taking a stand and committing open up boundless possibilities.

The Leader Who *Tried*

Malcolm hedged practically everything he said. He changed his mind frequently and liked the flexibility of not tying himself down. When he was promoted to the position of assistant director in a mid-size government agency, he opened a meeting of leaders with the following statement:

"We have a lot of challenges ahead of us. In the next 20 minutes, I'll try to describe what we must address. And, if I miss anything, I'll do my best to get you the information you need. I hope to set up a follow-up meeting soon to check in on our progress. And feel free to stop by any time I'm in the office."

Hedging and Casual Promises. When you listen for hedging words or conditional language, the real message practically screams at you, *"I am not committing to anything, not now, not ever."* Malcolm used multiple hedging phrases—*try, do my best, hope, soon*—and he even used a conditional statement, *"any time I am in the office."* Malcolm was an expert at hedging. When we asked him to eliminate hedging language in his speaking, he replied in complete sincerity, *"I'll try."*

If you discover that you make a lot of casual promises, then decide now to make only those commitments you plan to keep. Eliminate casual promises for which you have good intention but no commitment to action.

Slippery Promises

Just as the name implies, slippery promises are cunning, tricky, and often treacherous. These promises are carefully constructed with a back door. People make promises but always have a way to retreat. Examples of back-door escapes—the exit strategy—include these:

- "I did not receive the information I needed."
- "I thought you said Thursday, not Tuesday."
- "I was under the impression you wanted a preliminary report, not a final report."
- "I wish you had clarified this before. I had a different understanding."

Slippery promises are designed to place accountability for failure on other people and to make them wrong in the process. The response "I wish you had clarified this with me before" makes the other person responsible. In contrast, an accountable statement is "I did not hear you correctly."

Be aware, there are those who use slippery promises to manipulate. It is difficult to hold someone accountable when he or she tells you "I remember our conversation differently." To avoid this situation, do not accept slippery commitments. Document the specific agreements when the commitment is made and make sure all parties are fully aligned. Documenting an agreement in detail eliminates the easy "exit" strategy of those who make slippery promises.

How about you? Do you slip and slide out of promises and agreements? If one of your blind spots is treating commitments casually, you will not see how this occurs in your behavior. Most likely you view yourself as someone who responsibly keeps commitments. To raise your level of awareness, ask people you trust to point out when you make casual or slippery promises.

The CTO Blames Others for His Failure to Keep His Commitment

A CTO in a manufacturing company committed to providing a comprehensive report for the executive team regarding a major overhaul of the company's logistics system. When the analysis was due, the

CTO did not have the report. He took the offensive and said, *"My people didn't get the report to me on time, but I can give you an overview."*

What Happened. This is an interesting backdoor strategy. The CTO blames others for his failure to keep a commitment. He does not take accountability for the failure of his team to deliver on time or the impact it had on the executive team. He simply makes the problem everyone else's except his.

Pie-in-the-Sky Promises

A pie-in-the-sky promise has no deadline; it is a deliverable that is not grounded in a specific time frame. Therefore, no one can be held accountable. Without a specific "by when" promise, there is no commitment. For example, the phrase *"I will call you soon"* is a pie-in-the-sky promise. "Soon" is not a date, but we treat it as an acceptable nuance in our language. The statement "Let's have lunch sometime" means, "Let's pretend this is a meaningful agreement that we both know will never happen."

An effective way to determine if someone is making a pie-in-the-sky promise is to ask for a specific time and date. For instance, if a coworker says, "Let's have lunch sometime," answer right away with "Great, how about next Tuesday at 11 a.m. at the High Street Café?" The moment you attempt to tie down this type of promise, you will uncover the real intention of the speaker. He or she will respond by either withdrawing the offer or hedging and saying "Let me get back to you after I check my calendar." Examples of pie-in-the-sky promises are

- "I'll call you soon."
- "I'll get this to you as soon as possible."
- "It is almost completely done."
- "You'll have this before long."
- "No problem—I'll get this to you immediately."
- "I'll have this done right away."
- "You'll get this in short order."

The English language is full of vague references to time. With such an abundance of words and phrases, we can keep just about every promise unanchored with no deadline in sight. Consider the following:

- any minute now
- before long
- in a little while
- in a second
- in due time
- posthaste
- shortly
- immediately
- instantly
- presently
- promptly
- quickly
- directly

Many of these phrases sound quite accountable, but in business, they are inexact and problematic. No one is clear about when the promise will be delivered, ergo no one can be held accountable. Without a "by when" date, you do not have a deliverable.

A Leader Avoids Action with a Promise, Not a Deadline

Incomplete or pie-in-the-sky promises are easily mistaken as commitments. In making the promise, the individual throws out tidbits that *sound* like commitments but are actually empty promises that lead to falsely inflated hopes. For example, a manager talked to her CIO about meeting an outside consulting group to get help with the integration strategy. The CIO hedged and said, *"The organization may not be ready to change, but if you want, I can meet with these consultants at some point."* But no meeting date was promised, and the manager did not tie down a deadline.

The Result. A pie-in-the-sky promise does not produce action—at least not action that anyone can count on. Without an explicit deadline, no one can be held accountable; everyone simply wastes time. Several weeks later, the manager went back to the CIO and asked if he was ready for the meeting with the consultant. The CIO said,

"No, but we'll get to it soon." Six months later, the CIO was still promising, and the manager was still waiting.

Authentic Commitments

In a culture of 100% accountability, there are only authentic commitments. Committed partners either commit or do not. "Yes" is a clear and unconditional statement with no strings attached. In this type of culture, committing is not a weak promise; it is a high performance action. When people commit in a high performance culture, others take the commitments seriously and respond with full support.

> **Honoring Your Commitments**
> Doing what you say you will do and communicating responsibly when you don't.

Committed partners learn to quickly recognize casual, slippery, and pie-in-the-sky promises. In their place, they insist on authentic commitments without conditions or an escape hatch. They ensure that commitments have clear actions and deadlines, and a responsible way to revoke them when appropriate.

Let's start by defining what a commitment is in a high performance culture. A commitment is an action designed to turn ideas into reality. It is a clear stand to deliver a specific result within an agreed-upon time frame, regardless of unforeseen circumstances or challenges.

> **Manage commitments and you manage results.**

One of the reasons people do not commit is that they are worried about failing. This is another example of backward thinking: in order to bring a new reality into existence, *you must first commit.* A commitment is a stand and an action in high performance. It is not elusive and vague. Commit first, then work out the complete plan on how to fulfill your commitment. A commitment—big or small—sets new thinking and behavior in action. For example, if you commit to your team that you will be on time to meetings, and you authentically communicate this, you have taken an action.

You have publicly declared your intent and stand, and your committed partners will support you and hold you accountable.

Committing requires the courage to say "Yes, I will" and then take action to achieve it. Declaring your commitment *energizes* and *empowers* you and others to act instead of sitting on the sidelines wishing and hoping something will materialize. Making and managing promises is a discipline that is essential for producing business results.

In contrast, giving your word in a culture of 50/50 accountability means only that you will try to do your best. In this culture, people allow circumstances to dictate results, and they use excuses to cover up poor performance. For example, "If only we had received this information sooner, we could have . . ." Commitments in a 50/50 culture are easily avoided by blaming others or the situation. There is always an escape hatch to avoid being held accountable.

In a culture of 100% accountability, commitment drives results, and circumstances do not get in the way. An authentic commitment means "We will deliver in spite of challenging and tough circumstances." So-called good reasons and excuses are not used to avoid fulfilling a commitment.

COMMIT OR DO NOT COMMIT

The culprit is that we do not communicate a clear yes or no. If you cannot say yes unconditionally, then your answer is no. Saying *"Yes, but"* or *"I'll try"* are not commitments. *"No, I cannot"* and *"Yes, I will"* are both clear and acceptable statements about what others can count on you for. It is as simple as saying yes when you mean yes and saying no when you mean no. Except that we do not do this. We say yes to get out of a conversation, be polite, buy time, or avoid conflict. In business today, a yes is often reduced to being a strategy for placating and avoiding.

If you want to commit but have reservations, then say "My answer is no, I cannot commit at this time. I'm willing to commit once I clear up my concerns." If you cannot authentically commit, say so, and discuss what is causing you to hesitate and avoid committing.

People need to trust what you say. They listen to your promises, watch your actions, and *then* decide if they can trust you. When your commitments are inconsistent with your behavior, people throw out what you say and believe only what you do.

The Language of Commitment

Commitment language is strong and direct and says "I accept accountability for producing this result." If you are not ready to commit, say no instead of using a watered-down or conditional yes. There is integrity in saying no; it tells people exactly where you stand and paves the way for a discussion on what is needed to move forward. Exhibit 7-1 shows the difference between committing and not committing.

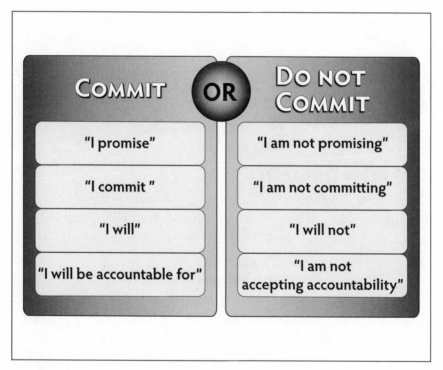

EXHIBIT 7-1: *Commit or Do Not Commit*

Unfortunately, in business today, many leaders use words that are imprecise, sloppy, and noncommittal. As a result, misunderstandings and reactions muddy the water, and people spend an inordinate amount of time trying to sort through mixed messages and breakdowns in communication. For example, when you hear the word *try* come out of your mouth, stop and self-correct. Tell the truth, which is either "*Yes, I will commit*" or "*No, I will not commit.*"

In high performance organizations, words have precise meanings and purposes. They are an efficient shorthand communication. They are tools for working together in a new way to seize opportunities, innovate, and act with urgency.

Commitment language is action oriented and sends an unequivocal "I will" message. The language of commitment tells others you are giving your word and can be counted on to keep it. Examples of commitment language include

- "I commit."
- "I will . . ."
- "I give you my word."
- "You can count on me to . . ."
- "I'll make it happen."
- "I'll take care of it."
- "I'll be accountable for . . ."

Think before You Say "Yes"

Only you are accountable for deciding when to commit and when not to. Before committing, identify how this will impact commitments you have already made, and determine if you have any conflicting demands on your time and energy.

Be clear about your purpose and priorities. Commitments take energy, and every time you commit, you are focusing your energy on a particular area. Ask: "What is most important to our team and our organization?" Align your commitments and actions with the business objectives you want to achieve. Keep the big picture in front of you at all times to ensure that your commitment is consistent with your purpose.

Guidelines for Authentic Commitments

The requirements for authentic commitments listed in the sidebar are used by committed partners as a checklist to ensure that all criteria are met. Any commitment that does not meet these standards is not accepted. Companies that formally adopt and implement these requirements often post them in meeting rooms and offices to make sure that everyone is using consistent guidelines.

Guidelines for Authentic Commitments

1. **Align with the enterprise mission.** *Does our commitment forward enterprise objectives?*
2. **Tell the truth.** *Is this a commitment we are willing to keep, regardless of unforeseen circumstances?*
3. **Be responsible about your capacity to deliver.** *Can we deliver on this new commitment given other commitments we have made?* Before committing, make sure the group is willing to manage conflicting demands on time and energy.
4. **Identify possible negative impacts.** *What unintended consequences could this commitment have on business results and people?* How will we minimize or eliminate any possible negative impact?
5. **State a specific time agreement.** *By when will this commitment be fulfilled?* A commitment is not real without a deadline or due date.
6. **Agree to include others and commit publicly.** *How will we include others in our commitment?* A commitment begins to produce results the moment leaders take a stand and communicate it publicly.
7. **Agree on how to revoke the commitment should it become necessary.** *How will we handle a change in our commitment or a change in the due date?* Sometimes there are legitimate reasons for withdrawing or revoking a commitment. When this occurs, immediately communicate to everyone prior to the due date and take accountability.

Revoke a Commitment Responsibly

There are times when it is responsible to revoke a commitment. However, having an attitude that it's OK not to communicate or treating missed deadlines as "no big deal" is unacceptable. When you made the commitment, you set up an expectation; therefore, when you break a commitment, you must manage the expectation as well as your impact on others.

When revoking a commitment, communicate *prior* to the promised deadline, not after you failed to deliver. Be honest about why you are not keeping your promise, apologize for your impact, take accountability for how your behavior has affected others, and recommit to a new action, deadline, or alignment. The only exception to this guideline is when something urgent prevents you from communicating prior to the deadline. When this occurs, communicate and take accountability as soon as possible.

Revoking a commitment is not a one-sided communication. A simple "I'm sorry" is insufficient. A cursory acknowledgment is not an example of *responsibly* revoking a commitment. You must be accountable for your impact on others. You can do this only by finding out how your broken commitment created a domino effect on *their* results and *their* commitments.

In summary, responsibly revoke a commitment by using the following guidelines:

1. Communicate prior to the deadline.
2. Communicate to the appropriate person.
3. Be accountable for your impact and clean up where appropriate.
4. Realign on what is needed, and establish a new commitment.

MAKING AND MANAGING REQUESTS THAT FORWARD THE ACTION

A request is a clear and concise question that moves the action forward regardless of whether it is accepted or declined. The very act of making a request "calls the question" and forces clarity and defines what action and commitment others are willing to make. It takes courage to make a request. You must be willing to clearly ask for what you want, even when you believe your request will not be accepted. A clear and direct request puts an end to circular discussions and demands a specific, committed action.

Making a request is only half of the action. You must also manage the response to your request by asking for one of four acceptable replies:

1. **Yes**. I accept the request.
2. **No**. I am declining the request.

3. **Counteroffer**. I have a counteroffer.
4. **Redirection**. I am redirecting your request to the appropriate person.

When committed partners make and manage requests, they turn complaints or disappointments into positive action. Requests add rigor to everyday conversations, provide clarity, and move people into action. Nothing can move forward until action is called for and a specific request is put on the table.

Making and managing requests requires that you are willing to accept a "no" response to your request. It is not a real request if people do not have the freedom to say no.

To make an effective request, clearly state what you want. Be precise and exact. Eliminate all hedging and ambiguous language such as "I'd like to have" or "Is it possible?" A clear and direct request is clean communication—for example, "I request that you meet with my group within the next two weeks." Be straightforward and put your request on the table so people know exactly what you want.

The discipline of making commitments and requests breathes new life and vigor into people and how they work together to manage results. Commitments provide structure, direction, and boundaries, all of which are essential for producing results and unleashing the power of people. What makes commitments powerful is that they move us out of inertia and into action. When this disciplined behavioral template is overlaid on an organization, initiatives work, change happens quickly, and processes go into high gear.

LEADERSHIP EXPLORATION

Responsibly Making, Keeping, and Revoking Commitments

Authentic commitments are distinct from casual, slippery, and pie-in-the-sky promises. They represent a high standard of behavior that requires you to be rigorous and disciplined in making and keeping commitments. You must be willing to honor and fulfill your commitments and responsibly revoke them if it becomes necessary. Examine your behavior in this area by answering the following questions, and ask others to assess your behavior:

1. Do I avoid making commitments? Do I only make commitments when I have a convenient exit strategy for not delivering?
2. Am I a person of my word in all matters—large and small? Do I only make commitments that I plan to keep, and do I keep the commitments that I make?
3. Do I hold others and myself accountable for honoring commitments, or do I allow commitments to slide?
4. Do I use "good" excuses or explanations to justify not fulfilling commitments?
5. Do I deliver my commitments on time or do I miss deadlines?
6. Do I responsibly revoke commitments when necessary by communicating prior to the deadline and taking accountability for my impact?

LEADERSHIP ACTION

1. **With your team, or with a committed partner, examine if you honor and keep commitments by answering the following questions:**
   - Do we trust each other's word in all matters—large and small?
   - Do we keep our agreements to team members?
   - Do we keep our agreements to nonteam members?
   - Do others perceive us as keeping our word?
   - Do we explain or justify our lack of delivering on a commitment, or do we take accountability?
   - Do we responsibly revoke commitments or do we just allow them to slide and disappear?
   - Do we hold each other accountable for commitments?
   - Is our current behavior effective? Are we demonstrating the behavior we expect from others? If not, how do we need to change our behavior?
2. **Identify specific requests you want to make of others.**
   To elicit a commitment from someone, you must be willing to ask for what you want. However, we are seldom direct in asking for what we want. Instead, we complain, imply, or

expect others to read between the lines. Identify what requests you have of both team members and nonteam members that you have not explicitly made.

3. **Make a clear and direct request, and manage the response you get.** Decide whom the appropriate person is that you need to talk to; then be direct and make your request. Make sure you get a clear yes, no, counteroffer, or redirect. Ensure that your request ends with committed action and a specific deadline to which all parties agree.

4. **Here is a challenge: Think of a request that you would like to make but have not made because you are concerned about the response you will receive.** Examine what stops you from making this request and talking straight responsibly to the appropriate person. What story are you making up about the response you *think* you might get? Are you willing to be uncomfortable and make your request? How can you deliver this request in a responsible manner?

We limit our effectiveness when we withhold communication and do not trust our instinct. We keep many great ideas, brilliant thoughts, and brave requests under a tightly sealed lid either because we fear they will be rejected *or* we fear they will be accepted. Which applies to you?

No sooner said than done—so acts a man of worth.

—QUINTUS ENNIUS (239–169 BC)

Chapter
8
Talking Straight
Responsibly

*I am more afraid of an army of 100 sheep led by a lion
than an army of 100 lions led by a sheep.*

—CHARLES MAURICE DE TALLEYRAND-PÉRIGORD (1754–1838)

How many issues are hidden from sight and remain unresolved, waiting to explode with devastating consequences for your organization? How many times have you found out too late that there is a problem? And how many times do you find yourself intervening to get things back on track? For companies that do not have a methodology in place for handling breakdowns and talking straight responsibly, that sequence of events is a daily occurrence.

We *think* we talk straight, but in practice, we fall far short of the mark. We dance around the real issue and dole out information as though we are dealing with the infirm, who in their weakened state are incapable of handling straightforward communication. We think we are "protecting" people from hurt, so we do not talk about things that add to their distress.

But our real concern is for ourselves, not others. We avoid the discomfort of confronting sensitive issues and broaching what appears to be unsafe territory. We keep our real thoughts and feelings to ourselves, or hand them out to a privileged few and tell them to keep it private. But there is a significant gap between what leaders *think* is effective communication and what people want to hear.

People have a burgeoning capacity to hear the truth, but leaders have been taught to restrict and massage what they say. When leaders are not forthright and direct, people do not trust them; committed partnerships break down and teamwork crumbles. In a guarded and closed environment, there is a burning necessity to protect one's own interests at the expense of others, and people revert to unproductive, automatic behaviors.

This chapter provides you with the tools to manage indirect or emotionally charged conversations with responsible straight talk. By the end of the chapter, you will gain confidence in quickly handling difficult concerns and issues, instead of postponing or avoiding them altogether. You will learn how to communicate in a way that is direct, responsible, and supportive.

THE PRICE OF AVOIDING DIFFICULT CONVERSATIONS

Talking straight responsibly is simple in principle but difficult to apply. Some leaders soften their message. Others dump their reactions on coworkers saying whatever is on their mind, thinking they are talking straight. Both are incorrect: Talking straight responsibly—with emphasis on the word *responsibly*—is not a license to say whatever you feel. It requires that you be authentic, emotionally honest, and accountable for what you say and how it impacts others.

Most leaders, by their own admission, avoid difficult or sensitive conversations. I have two questions for you:

1. Do you want people to talk straight to you and provide you with candid and complete feedback?
2. Are you willing to talk straight with others and provide them with candid and complete feedback?

The common response is to answer yes to the first question but no to the second. We want "straight talk" from others, but we are reluctant to talk straight to others. In interviews with leaders from diverse industries, we asked, "Do you want people to talk straight to you?" Not surprisingly, the vast majority answered with an unequivocal, "Yes." The consistent comment was "I don't want a sugarcoated or watered-down message. I want others to be forthright and honest with me." Clearly, these leaders are not afraid to *hear* straight talk.

However, when we asked, "Do you consistently talk straight to others?" their answers were littered with explanations and reasons for not talking straight. The typical rationale was "I don't want to damage the relationship," "I don't like to hurt people," or "Talking straight in our company is a career-limiting move." When we pressed the point and asked leaders if they consistently talked straight to others, few answered with a definitive yes.

The obvious conclusion: it is much easier for leaders to hear straight talk than to give it. The probability is high that this also applies to you. How would you answer the following questions?

- Do you find it difficult to be emotionally honest and direct?
- Do you postpone or avoid difficult conversations?
- Do you withhold your thoughts and feelings waiting for the right moment to speak?
- Are you careful and guarded in what you disclose?
- Do you talk openly with only a select handful of people?

While you may be uncomfortable having difficult conversations, your discomfort will be far higher if this costs you the support of others. If you have the blind spot of avoiding difficult conversations, you can expect that it will have a negative impact on your credibility and foster an environment of distrust.

Karla, a senior vice president in the energy industry, was tight-lipped and closemouthed. She took the phrase "flying solo" to an extreme and did not provide her direct reports with information about key decisions nor did she provide candid feedback about their performance. Her personal strategy was not to exclude; it simply was not to include. The most troublesome aspect of Karla's behavior was her unwillingness to be straightforward and candid. As one of her direct reports said, "You never know where you stand with Karla. She'll say one thing to your face and then do something that leaves you feeling that she was not honest. I never trust that I'm getting the full story from her."

When we asked Karla if she talked straight to others, she said, "I tell people what they need to know, when I feel they need to know it. With performance reviews, I try to keep the feedback positive so people feel I'm supportive." In our interactions with Karla, it was clear that she was more committed to controlling information and looking good than she was to being authentic and talking straight. But the irony is that Karla did not succeed in looking good. Her direct reports did not trust her, she lost credibility, and word spread to others outside of her group to "watch your back" with Karla.

The obvious conclusion: People want straight talk from you and are disappointed when they discover they cannot trust you to be emotionally and intellectually honest with them. When you soften a message, withhold important details, or fail to provide full disclosure, you significantly diminish your ability to build powerful teams and relationships with others. People trust leaders who are transparent, inclusive, and straightforward. Your credibility depends upon the degree to which others perceive you as direct and accessible.

Talking straight responsibly is an absolute requirement in building a productive work environment. When leaders dance around the real issues and put a positive spin on what they communicate, people feel that they are being spoon-fed pabulum. Unless organizations attack leadership behaviors directly, they get more of the same. There is nothing worse than an organization led by leaders who are blind to their blind spots.

High Uncertainty, Low Productivity

It is important to understand the construct of uncertainty and how it applies to optimizing performance. Most people have an overriding need to reduce uncertainty and guesswork and do not tolerate high levels of ambiguity. It is incumbent on you as the leader to keep uncertainty low so people can stay focused on business needs. People work effectively when they are given complete information and are able to make sense out of what is happening.

The point is that people have a predominant need to increase predictability. This is why closed and guarded leaders generate negative consequences and raise anxiety levels when they withhold information from others. When there is organizational uncertainty, people direct their energy to information-seeking about what is not being said in order to reduce their anxiety. When leaders do not talk straight responsibly, and in a timely manner, uncertainty levels climb and productivity takes a hit. But when leaders provide clear direction, are frank about the challenges, and express their emotional commitment, people do their jobs and do not worry about the environment.

High levels of certainty increase the ability of people to focus on the right things at the right time. But our automatic behavior—avoiding discomfort—results in leaders circumventing anticipated debates or tough conversations, rather than confronting issues head on. This is most obvious in duck-and-weave cultures, where polite and politically correct interactions prevail, making it impossible to address the real issue.

Secrets That Everyone Knows, but No One Is Talking About

We love secrets and being part of a clandestine group that holds all the keys and releases them only when utterly necessary. We covet our secrets and hold on to them tightly, believing that others are not ready to hear them, should not hear them, or cannot hear them.

Let's shed light on the truth about secrets: there are none. A secret is something that everyone knows but no one is talking about. What you do not tell people, they will make up in their minds. What you think is a secret will be discussed in the hallways and embellished in the worst way.

Although people may not know the specific facts about a situation, they sense when something is afoot. There is a palpable reaction in a work environment when leaders are not saying something or are withholding information. People pick up what is called "leaking behavior," where leaders inadvertently leak behavioral cues and information that reveals there is a "secret."

As you know, your every move is scrutinized as a leader. Do not underestimate what others observe about you and how much they already know. Regardless of how skilled you believe you are at concealing verbal or nonverbal cues that advertise your concerns, frustrations, or stress, others pick them up. The only antidote to people filling in the blanks is for you to fill them in first. Talk openly and honestly and eliminate secrets.

This does not mean you should share confidential information; of course, you should not. But you must learn how to reduce uncertainty by sharing the appropriate information. Even in highly sensitive matters, you can reduce uncertainty by addressing the issue head on, as a CEO did when rampant rumors spread about his "early" retirement and threatened to disrupt the cultural transformation effort he was leading. Instead of ignoring the rumors, or trying to quash them by issuing a memo, the CEO spoke directly to folks and said, "I hear that I'm leaving the company. This is a surprise to me since I have no plans to retire or leave. Perhaps you think I'm getting on in years and should think about retiring, but I must confess that I'm much too engaged in what we're creating to stop now. Since I cannot keep my age from climbing upward, there will come a time when I will retire. When this time comes, I'll communicate directly to you. In the meantime, for better or for worse, you have me. So let's focus on our mission, and do what we set out to do."

Postponing important communication is rarely a good idea. I am continually amazed when leaders avoid talking about critical issues thinking that this is an effective way to interact with others. When I ask them why they are waiting instead of taking decisive action, they offer several reasonable replies: "I need more information," or "I don't want to alarm others," or "I need to buy time so we can avoid a bigger problem." They also tell me they fear unrehearsed words such as "What if I say the wrong thing or it comes across the wrong way? What if my words have a negative impact and I can't take them back?" These concerns are valid and they underscore the need to learn how to talk straight responsibly.

If It's on the Internet, It's Not a Secret

An embarrassing situation occurred for Armand, a senior leader in a global health-care organization. A disgruntled ex-employee took Armand to task and viciously attacked him, using an anonymous blog for communication. The senior group met the day prior to a leadership conference of their top 200 leaders and deliberated about whether they should say anything about the Internet fiasco. One leader argued, *"This will blow over and most people will never know what happened. There's no need to mention anything at the conference."*

What Happened.   Armand and the CEO disagreed and said: *"If we say we're committed partners, then we must talk straight. We must acknowledge this issue so there are no secrets or surprises."* On the first day of the conference, Armand addressed the group and said: *"Overnight I have become an Internet celebrity. I want to take accountability and include you in what happened."*

The Result. Not surprisingly, more than half the leadership group had already learned about the blog. It certainly was not a secret, and by ignoring it, the attention on pressing business issues could have been diluted. By talking straight responsibly, Armand and senior leaders eliminated speculation so everyone could focus on the business needs at hand.

Lesson Learned. The best way to dispose of rumors and gossip is to talk about them openly and broadly. When you talk straight responsibly and trust in the ability of others to handle direct communication, they will respond appropriately.

As a leader, you must maintain the integrity and balance between what you can and cannot say. Although you must handle sensitive and confidential matters with great care, there is an easy solution that many leaders miss. When it is not appropriate to include others in the details of a situation, include them in your commitment, accountability, and stand for people.

Jack, the president of a business unit in a service company, spoke to a group of several hundred employees during a time of cost containment when people feared they would lose their jobs. Although Jack did not have any specific details about whether downsizing would actually occur, he took a stand and said, "I know that many of you are worried about your jobs and whether we will downsize. No decision has been made about this and I have no new information. But you have my commitment that we will do everything possible to contain our expenses and streamline our business so we can avoid losing the talented and loyal people who work here." At a time when people could easily have become demoralized, they cheered Jack and partnered with him to find new solutions to contain costs and keep the company, and their jobs, intact.

POWERFUL, HONEST CONVERSATIONS: TALKING STRAIGHT RESPONSIBLY

The CEO knew something was off between members of his senior team, but he couldn't quite put his finger on it. We worked with him on how to lead a straight talk conversation with his group in which he took the following stand:

"I'm unwilling to settle for less than what I know we can achieve. And I'm unwilling to settle for less than the high performance team we can be. I want us to have an open and honest conversation about how we work together. I have questions that I'll ask each of you, but before I do that I want to hear how I've impacted you. I'd like your honest feedback so I can be a more effective leader. Let's start with how you would answer the following questions about my leadership:

1. *What impact do I have on you, individually and as a team? Do you feel that I listen to you and that I'm committed to your success?*
2. *Are there unresolved issues that I need to address with you so we have a strong partnership?*
3. *What do you need from me that I am not providing?"*

The conversation had a slow start, but it picked up speed as people began to feel safe in speaking up. After answering the questions about the CEO, each team member asked the same questions about their impact on one another. This discussion started the group down the path of learning how to talk straight responsibly.

Let's define talking straight responsibly in precise terms. It is being emotionally honest and communicating responsibly as soon as you recognize there is an unresolved issue. There are two criteria for measuring your success:

1. Your communication advances the business objective.
2. Your communication strengthens the relationship with the individual or team.

Talking straight responsibly is a learned skill that demands a high level of accountability and trust. Not only are you accountable for the content of your message, you are also accountable for its emotional impact. If you are saying to yourself "How people react to what I say is beyond my control," then let me remind you that you are accountable for making sure your message is understood in the way in which you intend it. Of course, you cannot control how people react, but you can make an extra effort to ensure that you are doing everything possible so that your message paves the way for a more effective partnership.

Talking Straight Responsibly
Being emotionally honest and communicating responsibly as soon as you recognize there is an unresolved issue.

Be Willing to Be Uncomfortable

Your discomfort is not an acceptable excuse for avoiding what needs to be said. Our mission is not to eliminate your discomfort but to increase your comfort with being uncomfortable. This is another marker of fearless leadership—the ability to persevere even when a situation is unpleasant or disquieting. At all times you must remember that fearless leadership is not the absence of fear or discomfort; it is doing what needs to be done in spite of these feelings.

Most leaders imply or soften a message, drop hints, or demonstrate their displeasure in countless small ways. Their hope is that others will read between the lines and get the real message so they will not have to deal with it. If you are indirect or roundabout in your communication, you are giving others the power to interpret your message and infer meaning. You will be extremely dissatisfied with how people fill in the blanks. While *you* may be more comfortable using indirect or implied communication, others will reduce their uncertainty and anxiety by making up their own meaning, and innumerable breakdowns will follow.

When you leave communication to chance, you are saying "I am not accountable for the accuracy, precision, and impact of my message." People need to know where you stand and how you feel. Err on the side of *overcommunicating* and be known as a leader who courageously, and swiftly, addresses any issue or concern.

The question that must be answered is: *"Are you willing to talk straight responsibly even when you are uncomfortable?"*

Be Emotionally Honest

Leaders who talk straight responsibly leave nothing to interpretation. They know that saying something or writing it in an e-mail does not mean that others heard or understood their message. You must act as the responsible agent for how others respond to your communication. Everything you communicate must be consistent with your agreements as committed partners and with your stand for the success of one another.

Being emotionally honest is powerful. People cannot argue with how you feel, but they can always argue with your point of view or position. When you are emotionally honest, everyone listens. In observing leaders speaking to large and small groups, it is easy to see when the audience believes the leader is speaking from the heart and talking straight. The moment the leader talks directly about the "real" issue and self-discloses his or her experience, the room changes, and the audience transforms from being passively engaged to sitting on the edge of their seats.

For instance, Sharon, the head of human resources, said to a large group of leaders, "I have two conflicting concerns about speaking to you today: I'm both nervous and confident. I'm nervous that I will not live up to your expectations. And I'm confident that I don't have to because I know I'll get your candid feedback either way." Sharon's communication was authentic. Instead of trying to pretend that she was not nervous, she told others exactly what she was experiencing. People listen when you include them in what you are feeling, not just in what you are thinking.

To master talking straight responsibly, you must be willing to self-disclose and speak from your heart. Using logic or intellect to mask what is really going on builds walls between you and others. For most people it is much easier to hedge and say, "I need more information before I can give you my answer," than to say, "I need to feel confident that you're committed to this course of action, and I'm unsure about where you stand."

What we normally call straight talk is an intellectual message containing logic and facts that has little to do with how people are emotionally engaged and motivated. When you feel concerned, disappointed, or upset, you need to state what you are feeling in a responsible manner, not pretend that everything is fine. Your behavior and words send a message. People are amazingly resilient, supportive, and results driven when they emotionally connect with you and feel included as your committed partner.

Be Precise and Speak Responsibly

An area in which leaders often run into difficulty is when they react to a crisis or urgent need by using generalizations, such as *all, everyone, always*, or *never*. Seldom do leaders literally mean *all* as in every case or *never* as in no case. But you may find yourself using these words to empha- size a point, only to discover that your words are taken literally.

When the CEO spoke to the leaders of a business unit, she said, "We're cutting costs immediately and eliminating the use of all consultants." Immediately following her talk, she took off for a two-week vacation and panic set in. More than 30 percent of the workforce was hired on a con- tract basis, which fit the definition of consultant, and people were fright- ened about losing their jobs. Fortunately, the business unit leader learned of the reaction and quickly clarified the CEO's comments by saying, "I've learned that the CEO's use of the word 'consultant' has created some con- cern. What our CEO wants is a reduction in overall costs such as elimi- nating the use of external consultants. She was not referring to internal contractors such as yourselves. Your job is not in jeopardy."

When the CEO returned from her trip, the business leader explained how he had clarified the CEO's communication to his group. The CEO said, "Good call—that's exactly what I meant to communicate."

Say what you mean, and mean what you say. Unintentional words, poorly chosen phrases, or generalizations can cause a small or large panic. Eliminate generalizations when communicating messages that have the potential to create apprehension or misinterpretation. Be specific and precise, and when you do not have all the details, tell people exactly that. You must be as def- inite about what you do *not* know as you are about what you *do* know.

Make Private Conversations Public

Making private conversations public is another way of saying that all issues must be put on the table with the appropriate person in order to resolve them. You must be willing to set aside your personal preference and abandon your need to be right. As we discussed in Chapter 6, committed partners learn how to interact in a new way—as a united group, not as splintered factions.

The power in making private conversations public is that it allows the team to learn from breakdowns and generate systemic and behavioral changes to prevent them from occurring again. Conspiracies against oth- ers, which form in an instant, are stamped out as individuals and teams learn how to constructively confront sensitive issues.

How a Leader Insists On Straight Talk from Her Group

We worked with Mei Li and her team on a major breakthrough project. During a meeting, Sean, a team member, pulled Mei Li aside and said, "*I'd like to talk to you privately. I have a concern about how you're leading the meeting.*" Mei Li said, "*Great—I want to hear your concern, but I would like you to share it with the entire group.*" Sean was confused and said, "*I don't want to put you on the spot.*" "*Hold on,*" said Mei Li, "*we're committed partners and we handle breakdowns together. I'm not concerned about being put on the spot. I'm committed to being effective, and I need everyone to hear your coaching so we can learn together.*"

What Happened. Sean had recently joined the team and was new to the concept of committed partnerships. But he relied on Mei Li's direction and gave her feedback in front of the group, saying, "*We're missing important issues that need to be discussed. A couple of folks have mentioned this already, but you don't seem to be listening.*" Mei Li— a fearless leader—thanked Sean for his feedback and asked for additional input from the group which turned out to be quite similar. Together the group reorganized the agenda to focus on the key issues.

Lesson Learned. Making private conversations public gives you the ability to surface and resolve issues as a group that are getting in the way of forward momentum.

Committed partners learn how to provide responsible feedback in the moment when something occurs. Further, they learn how to listen to feedback from others and treat it as valuable coaching, rather than defaulting to automatic behaviors of being defensive, embarrassed, or closed to input. You *save* an enormous amount of time when you and others learn shortcut methods for making private conversations public, in a safe and responsible way.

Be Sensitive to Cultural Differences

There are important cultural differences that must be taken into consideration when engaging in talking straight responsibly or making private conversations public. In some cultures, people talk straight—*irresponsi-*

bly—and engage in brash and presumptuous behavior. In other cultures, it is inappropriate to have certain conversations publicly, and they need to be handled offline. You can build committed partnerships in any culture as long as you respect cultural differences and build partnerships that support the values, beliefs, and practices of the culture.

When you do not respect or understand cultural differences, breakdowns occur, as was the case with a merger between two giants in the manufacturing industry. There were hiccups because of the cultural and language differences between companies from Brazil and the United States. The acquiring company from Brazil was hierarchical with a command-and-control approach, while the U.S. company was viewed as argumentative and arrogant.

The two CEOs and their respective senior teams met together shortly after the acquisition. Joao, the CEO from the Brazilian-owned company, was charismatic and brilliant and had a movie-star quality. He was confident and never took no for an answer. During the meeting, Joao discussed something he wanted done in the next several months. Harrison, the CEO from the U.S. company, saw a problem and spoke up: "That's just not realistic. We can't complete this in the next three months."

Joao graciously listened to Harrison's input. However, after the meeting, he took Harrison aside and said, "It is not the custom in our company to speak of differences in meetings. The next time you have a differing opinion, talk to me off-line, not in a public meeting."

One size does not fit all. Cultural differences must be taken into consideration when building a high performance organization or team. Do your homework and learn what is valued and important to others, and build committed partnerships in a culturally sensitive manner.

HOW TO TALK STRAIGHT RESPONSIBLY

A global company was going through major change and Henrik, the manager of a business operation, was in the midst of tough restructuring decisions. One of his direct reports, Samantha, questioned his commitment to a significant company initiative during a meeting of senior leaders. Henrik was not in the mood for one more problem, and he barked back saying, "You know me better than that. I'm on board. I suggest you stay focused on your area, which needs your attention a lot more than I do."

We had just begun working with the company, and the exchange between Henrik and Samantha, we later learned, was typical of the caustic interactions in the leadership group. Samantha was livid with Henrik's biting retort and stewed over it for days. She finally picked up the phone and called one of our consultants, Ed, and asked for coaching. Ed told Samantha to stop avoiding the conversation with Henrik and talk straight with him.

"Great. I'd like to give him a piece of my mind and let him know what a jerk he is and how he was way out of line. How does that sound?" asked Samantha.

"Like a lot of rubbish," said Ed. "That's the easy way out, not the responsible one. You need to talk to Henrik immediately, but don't go in blowing off steam. Start the conversation by acknowledging how difficult things must be for him. Let Henrik know you recognize how hard it must be for him to maintain a positive attitude every day and help others remain focused."

"But that has nothing to do with what I'm upset about. I thought we were supposed to talk straight instead of sugarcoating everything," retorted Samantha.

"No one is asking you to sugarcoat anything. I'm talking about how you can take accountability and establish a positive context for the conversation so you get the result you want. Dumping your anger and letting Henrik know how ticked off you are is not responsible straight talk," explained Ed.

"OK, let me see if I understand this," challenged Samantha. "You're telling me to focus on his concerns and forget about mine?"

"No, I'm not telling you to forget about your concerns," Ed rejoined. "We haven't gotten that far yet. I'm talking about how to open the conversation. You cannot have a productive conversation until you take accountability first, before you communicate what you want from others. But if you want to try it your way, go ahead, and call me with the results."

"All right, I get the point," Samantha relented, "but this is an unusual approach. I'm the one who's ticked off, Henrik's the one who acted like a jerk, and I'm supposed to take accountability?"

"Yup, and that's the first time I've heard you describe what 100%-zero accountability means. No one said this was easy; it's extraordinary behavior. I know you would like nothing more than to rip Henrik's head off. But I'm not interested in what you like; I'm interested in your being effective.

That means putting yourself in the other person's shoes, taking accountability for how you reacted in the meeting, and sharing how that impacted you, in that order," Ed said.

Samantha learned the first step in talking straight responsibly: take accountability and start with your commitment to the relationship. She had the conversation with Henrik and instead of attacking him, as she wanted to do, she started by saying: "I did not communicate effectively the other day in our meeting when I questioned your commitment, and I did not take into account how much pressure you are under. I'm sure I left you feeling that I did not support you." Henrik jumped in and said, "I'm glad you came by. I didn't feel good about what I said to you and I wanted to apologize."

Henrik and Samantha talked openly and she expressed how she was impacted and said, "Thank you for your apology. I was upset by what you said. And even though I knew you were reacting to my inappropriate comment, I felt that there was something else behind your words. I thought you were telling me that I was not performing up to standards. Is this what you wanted to communicate?" Henrik was surprised by Samantha's interpretation of his comment, but understood how his words raised her doubts. He told her that there were no performance issues but there were other concerns that he had withheld and not discussed with her. They talked through several issues and scheduled another meeting to resolve others.

When you take accountability first, and bring compassion for what the other person is experiencing, you can successfully navigate any difficult conversation.

Take Accountability and Start with Your Commitment

Talking straight responsibly is not a license to dump your concerns or complaints on another person. The "responsible" part requires that you be direct and look at the situation in question from a perspective that is greater than your own. When you step into the shoes of another person and express your concern for his or her welfare, it opens the door to an open and honest conversation.

Nothing is advanced by heated emotions and sharp retorts. Before you react and say something you will later regret, ask for coaching from a committed partner, and talk through where you are stuck, as Samantha did with Ed. Your coach will help you separate your interpretation from the facts. Your job is to trust that your coach can see the situation more clearly than you can, especially when you are reacting. Before you have a straight talk conversation, make sure you are taking accountability for your reaction, and not blaming the other party.

To master talking straight responsibly, you must (1) recognize there is an unresolved issue and (2) take action and communicate immediately when something is off track. Have the courage to communicate despite your discomfort and put all issues on the table. But do not fall into the trap of using the cooling-off period as an excuse for postponing or not having a difficult conversation. Handle your reaction and communicate as close to the event as possible. Unresolved issues escalate when they are not discussed.

When delivering your message, talk in first person ("I feel something in our partnership is off") and eliminate blame statements ("You apparently disagree with my strategy"). By taking accountability for how you speak, you will keep the conversation from becoming a debate, or worse, an all-out war.

When you choose to be a "bigger" person, you can let go of who should apologize first or who is the bigger jerk, and then be accountable for how you contributed to the breakdown or problem. You always have a choice to either play small and be petty or play big and rise above your automatic behavior.

By starting with your commitment, you provide a context for the conversation. You are answering questions such as these:

- What is the purpose of the conversation?
- What do I want to accomplish?
- How do I want to leave the other person feeling?
- What actions do I want as a result of this conversation?

Ask for Permission to Talk Straight and Resolve the Breakdown

After you establish the context and take accountability, but before you jump into the breakdown, ask permission to have a straight talk conversation. Ask: "Would you be willing to discuss what happened in our last meeting?"

If you have a concern, it is likely that the other person has a similar concern. And your concerns may have spilled over into the team. Either way, you must address the issue quickly so residual damage does not occur.

Do not expect every straight talk conversation to instantly produce the result you want. People need time to think about what you said. You may find that you need to clean up and apologize for your impact more than once. Sometimes others may not take accountability, but that should not dissuade you from having the conversation. They must trust that what you are saying is authentic and genuine. Remember that the outcome you are seeking is to strengthen the partnership.

You can encourage others to express their concerns by asking these questions:

- How did I impact you and others?
- What concerns do you have that I need to understand?
- Where do I need to take accountability and correct my behavior?
- What do you want to say to me that you feel I haven't been listening to?
- Where do I need to clean up with you and/or others?

Align on Future Action

The good news about breakdowns is that it gives you an opportunity to have a difficult conversation and strengthen your partnership. All relationships have rough spots and breakdowns; what separates traditional teams from high performing teams is how quickly they recover and resolve issues. An important point to remember is this: members of high performing teams include one another in how they resolve a breakdown so everyone knows the issue has been addressed.

When there is a breakdown between two or more team members that is handled offline, it is important that the team as a whole be included as soon as possible. Making private conversations public is a practice of committed partners because it clears up any issues that get in the way of efficient team alignment. Committed partners keep everyone informed when breakdowns occur and when they have been resolved. People do not need to know the specifics about a breakdown, but they do need to know that it has been addressed.

At the end of a straight talk conversation, make sure you have closure:

- Define the actions you and others need to take.
- Make clear and specific requests and align on what you are agreeing to.
- Identify who is accountable and by when.
- Identify who needs to be included in your resolution of the breakdown.

BUILDING A TEAM THAT TALKS STRAIGHT RESPONSIBLY

By resolving issues quickly, you clear up assumptions, establish new commitments, and restore clarity and partnership. People are enlivened and replenished by conversations that efficiently cut through barriers and conflict. A vast storehouse of energy is released when you communicate directly and responsibly and when you encourage others to do the same.

Practicing responsible straight talk, even when done imperfectly, changes the dynamics of how teams interact. Assess your team's ability to talk straight with one another using the statements in the sidebar "Do We Talk Straight Responsibly as a Team?" You may want to use a rating scale, with 1 as low and 5 as high, to provide a range of responses. Record your answers so you can reassess at a later date.

Do We Talk Straight Responsibly as a Team?

1. We talk openly and honestly about our blind spots.
2. We are emotionally honest with one another.
3. We are culturally sensitive.
4. We speak responsibly and respectfully without blaming or attacking others.
5. When we have a breakdown, we address the issue and recover quickly.
6. We communicate fully and accurately.
7. We talk to one another, not about one another.
8. We include the entire team, in a timely manner, when issues have been resolved off-line between team members.

If you are the team leader, you must be willing to share your assessment first to create a supportive and open environment. Before you begin, share your personal commitment to building committed partnerships and talking straight responsibly, and how these practices will help the team deliver business results.

Fearless leaders talk straight responsibly and do not wait for the *right* moment; instead, they *create* the right moment. They make sure the way in which they communicate advances both the relationship and business results.

LEADERSHIP EXPLORATION

What Critical Conversations Are You Avoiding?

This question will not provoke an endless list, so do not be concerned. However, most leaders have several critical conversations they are avoiding and need to have. To get you started, identify what conversation you are avoiding with (1) your boss, (2) a direct report, and (3) a peer. Ask yourself these questions:

- What is preventing me from having this conversation?
- What reaction am I anticipating?
- What outcome do I want?
- Am I willing to take 100% accountability to achieve the outcome?
- What specific requests do I want to make?

Being a fearless leader is a bold step in trusting yourself to talk straight responsibly, even when you are uncomfortable. Are you willing to have the tough conversations? Are you willing to stop making up stories about how you *think* the other person will respond, and simply have the conversation that needs to happen? Are you willing to act now?

LEADERSHIP ACTION

Act Now; Be Fearless and Talk Straight Responsibly

1. **Identify at least one critical conversation you need to have and schedule a time to talk with the appropriate person.**
   Do not wait for the right time, the right moment, or the right

circumstance. The longer you postpone a conversation, the more difficult it becomes, and minor concerns escalate into full-blown suspicions and doubts. Seize whatever moment you have and dive into the conversation.

2. **Take accountability and be responsible for how you communicate and, above all, listen.** Leave nothing incomplete or unsaid in your conversation. Speak from the heart, be emotionally honest, and invite the other person to do the same. In any tough conversation, start with your commitment to the relationship and resolve the sensitive situation together. It is much easier to resolve a problem when you are standing side by side, facing the issue together rather than placing it between you. Stay in the conversation until all issues are resolved and complete and the relationship is restored.

3. **Immediately include appropriate others in how you and the other party have resolved the misunderstanding or breakdown.** We naively think that a breakdown with one individual does not impact others. This is not true. If you have an unresolved issue with one person, it is likely that others are not only aware of it, but have also been impacted by it. Identify who you need to include in the resolution of the breakdown or issue, and talk with them. Take accountability for the breakdown, and most importantly, let others know that you have restored the relationship. Demonstrate what it means to be a committed partner.

Take time to deliberate,
but when the time for action has arrived,
stop thinking and go in.

—Napoleon Bonaparte (1769–1821)

Chapter
9
Aligning Emotionally and Intellectually

When we are no longer able to change a situation—
we are challenged to change ourselves.

—VIKTOR FRANKL (1905–1997)

There is a lot of talk today about the need for alignment. It is, in fact, one of the few areas leaders universally agree is essential for effective execution. But what is commonly called alignment is nothing more than compliance. The element that is overlooked and misunderstood is the profound level of emotional and intellectual commitment required to achieve authentic alignment. For full alignment to be realized, committed partners must suspend their personal agenda and adopt an enterprise perspective.

Authentic leadership alignment is a learned behavior that most companies rarely experience. They may taste the exhilaration of alignment when faced with a significant threat, but when the crisis has passed, the laws of physics take over and entropy returns. Where there is maximum entropy—heat in a system—there is a minimum amount of energy available for doing work. Fleeting synergy and cohesiveness collapse, and the enterprise perspective that was momentarily attained is lost. Teams and individuals revert once again to automatic behaviors such as victim mentality and conspiring against others. All of this serves to confirm the need for fearless leaders who demonstrate courage, stand firm, and accept nothing less than emotional and intellectual alignment.

> Alignment is not a concept; it is a learned behavior.

Many leaders fail to see that the *behavior* of alignment is the Holy Grail for optimizing leadership and organizational capacity. The quest to achieve alignment is hopeless without the extraordinary way in which committed partners work together. They actively overcome blind spots and rigorously intervene to achieve breakthroughs of major proportion.

Achieving emotional and intellectual alignment allows leaders to turn business strategy into focused delivery. This chapter focuses on how to achieve real and sustainable alignment. You will learn what holds leaders and teams back, and how to master two critical applications: the five levels of alignment and the three decision types. We designed these tools to provide leaders with an effective process for dismantling individual preferences so they could achieve team solidarity and lasting alignment. Then we cover rules of engagement—meeting protocol used by high performance teams.

WHAT IT MEANS TO AUTHENTICALLY ALIGN

What makes fearless leaders so extraordinary is their courage to bring cognitive and emotional intelligence to every aspect of leadership. In decision making, fearless leaders give their full support—heart and mind—and insist on full commitment from others. This exceptional level of ownership is rare and powerful.

As a fearless leader, you cannot commit to keeping everyone happy and making sure that people always agree. That is not your job. Your job is to make sure people have an opportunity to express their concerns, viewpoints, and ideas, and then fully align with what is best for the enterprise. If you rely on group agreement, you will be disappointed. Agreement is fleeting. Its temporary nature leaves you with unsustainable action and the half-measure of compromise. But with authentic alignment you gain sustainable commitment and coordinated action even when people do not agree.

Authentic alignment is an indispensable leadership behavior that requires teams to learn how to interact in a new way where they set aside their personal preferences, political agendas, and pet projects. These teams innovate and discover solutions without compromising the quality of decisions to appease dissenting group members.

In the alignment process, committed partners fully dialogue for the purpose of supporting the decision both emotionally and intellectually, as if they authored it themselves. They agree to (1) dialogue responsibly without holding anything back, (2) support the decision emotionally and intellectually, both privately and publicly, and (3) communicate immediately to the appropriate person if they discover they are no longer aligned. Leaders are committed to sustaining alignment and they are quick to take action the moment they realize they are off track.

> **Authentic Alignment**
> Setting aside your personal preference to support the decision from an enterprise perspective—emotionally and intellectually—as if you authored it yourself.

Authentic alignment is an extraordinary behavior that harnesses the power of people—their energy, passion, and vitality—and focuses it where it belongs: on business objectives. When alignment is used as a technique where people agree but do not emotionally and intellectually commit, it is ineffective. This false sense of alignment lacks the glue for sustainability.

WHAT HOLDS US BACK FROM ACHIEVING FULL ALIGNMENT

"We have a stickability issue around here," complained Nigel, a frustrated CEO. "I meet with my team, we reach a decision, and I think we have agreed to a plan of action. But two months later when I ask for an update I find out that four out of five business unit leaders have not initiated the changes. And, by the way, I have to ask for the update."

This common complaint from leaders, "*Nothing sticks*," refers to decisions about which everyone agrees but that result in no action or inconsistent action. In Nigel's case, senior team members complied and went along with the decision, but they were not aligned. Nigel had confused compliance with alignment. There was, in fact, absolutely no emotional commitment or buy-in from his group and, hence, no follow-through.

Stickability—making sure decisions stick and produce consistent action—is the shared accountability of both the team leader and team members. When you accept compliance from others, you are saying that it is not necessary for people to commit fully. When people comply, they are detached and disconnected from the decision and its implementation, until it impacts their area. Unshackled by any emotional commitment, compliance does not generate urgency. Although *you* may feel urgency, leaders who comply are apathetic and move at a snail's pace.

As a leader, you and your team must be able to identify the difference between complying and aligning. Examine whether you comply with decisions or tolerate compliance from others. Do you settle for "good enough"? Do you look the other way when leaders go along with decisions just to keep the agenda on track? When compliance is the behavioral norm, leaders and teams get mediocre results.

You can make decisions stick by helping your team learn how to align. First, do not blame others for their lack of alignment and follow-through. Blame has no place in fearless leadership; it is an indulgence that does not forward the action. Second, take personal accountability for where you are accepting compliance from others. Third, help your team learn how to achieve authentic alignment.

Complying and Withholding Emotional Commitment

Complying and withholding emotional commitment is the blind spot that prevents groups from achieving authentic alignment. The word *compliance* is defined as a concession, acquiescence, deference, and submission, none of which advance the business objective. Complying is going along with the "pull" of the group without emotionally committing.

With compliance, people conform to a decision for a number of reasons:

- Protecting individual interests
- Making a "politically smart" choice
- Feeling group pressure to conform
- Avoiding conflict
- Feeling resigned or powerless
- Needing to belong and fit in

Our need to belong and be accepted is so gripping that it either forces conformity and agreement, or it expels those who do not fit in. In primitive times, people who were expelled by the tribe were sent into the wilderness where they had to fend for themselves. In modern times, many companies neutralize or isolate people who do not fit in.

For example, Trevor, a senior vice president on the senior team, was recognized by his peers as being exceptionally bright and innovative. Off-line Trevor was a strong proponent of new and more effective approaches for solving organizational problems. But during senior team meetings with the CEO, he stepped cautiously and would not present ideas or endorse others unless he was absolutely certain the CEO would find them acceptable. As a result, many innovations went by the wayside while Trevor complied with the CEO's preference. But complying comes with a cost. The senior team and organization did not get the benefit of Trevor's full talent and expertise. The CEO did not get straight talk from Trevor and was unable to incorporate Trevor's ideas into his decisions. And Trevor's peers did not trust him to speak up and be forthright in meetings.

As a fearless leader you must continually examine how you relate to decisions to determine if you are complying or aligning. Complying is an automatic behavior where we give in to the circumstances and allow others or the situation to dictate our behavior. We go along with a decision but our heart is not really in it, and we feel trapped and resigned. To paraphrase Viktor Frankl: there is a space between stimulus and response where you have a choice. When you raise your level of awareness and recognize when you are withholding your full support of a decision, you have a choice. You can choose to stop the automatic behavior of complying and emotionally commit, or responsibly communicate that you are not aligned. Throughout this chapter, ask yourself this question:

> *"Where am I complying instead of making the choice to authentically align?"*

Complying may appear to be efficient, but it is not. It is used to avoid what most believe is a rocky road to achieve real alignment. One leader explained it this way: "I don't have time to fight every battle. When the decision is not important to me, I go along with the group. I don't go out on the skinny branches alone unless the decision impacts my group directly. Even then, I decide if it's worth my time and energy to fight before I engage."

Have you ever urged colleagues to comply with a decision just so you could end a fruitless debate or an interminably long meeting? The unspoken message in business-as-usual meetings is this: "Just shut up and go along with the program so we can get the heck out of here."

Do you comply and withhold your emotional commitment? Do not be quick to reply; this is a common behavior. Look carefully at the many ways in which you agree with a decision intellectually but do not support it emotionally. For example, let's say your boss wants to alter the pricing strategy for a product and service line, and you disagree. You are faced with a choice to either comply (what appears to be an efficient strategy) or disagree and engage in debate (what appears to be a risky strategy, especially if it annoys your boss or creates a rift in your relationship). What can you do when you are faced with this choice? You can behave as an owner, fully express your concerns, listen to others, and set aside your personal preferences.

> People don't comply because it's the best choice; they comply because they feel they have *no* choice.

Tolerating *"Good Enough"*: The *"I Can Live with It"* Attitude

As a fearless leader, you must examine where you and others are withholding emotional commitment. It is only then that you can apply the tools needed to achieve alignment.

Teams often align on a decision, but then circumstances change, and they do not revisit the decision to see whether their alignment has changed. For instance, a senior team agreed to adopt a new performance review system and begin implementation in the next six months. But a couple months later market conditions changed, a state of panic set in, and executives turned their attention to other matters. They did what was expedient: they postponed the decision to implement the new performance review system. But the problem was that no one communicated this change; it just happened by default. As a result, the organization went in different directions and people were frustrated and confused. There is no question that leaders must be able to change priorities and decisions whenever necessary; however, allowing decisions to slip out of alignment without formally realigning and communicating those changes to others is inefficient and ineffective.

Committed partners are rigorous in making sure alignment sticks. They do not allow alignment to lapse. The moment circumstances change that threaten the alignment of the group, committed partners reaffirm their alignment or alter it, and appropriately communicate to others.

How do committed partners prevent a breakdown in alignment from occurring? They hold each other accountable for maintaining or formally altering alignment when circumstances change. Their commitment is to sustain alignment and send a cohesive and consistent leadership message to the organization.

Without emotional commitment, complying (also called a pocket veto) is a temporary adhesive with no sticking power. When leaders use a pocket veto, saying what others want to hear and giving in to group pressure, their unspoken communication is, "I'll keep my true feelings in my pocket until the meeting is over. Then I'll conspire against the decision and say how I really feel."

When leaders tolerate "good enough," they withhold their ideas and contributions and accept things as they are. This disrupts the entire decision-making process from alignment to execution. Complying comes at a huge cost: the loss of future possibilities and opportunities.

Talking about Alignment as a Concept, and Not Defining It as a Behavior

When leaders are sloppy and undisciplined in translating words into explicit behavior, they get sloppy and undisciplined results. Leaders lose their edge every time they throw words into a cauldron and reduce them down to meaningless phrases. All too often leaders bandy about buzzwords such as *synergy, collective intelligence,* and *consensus decision making.* But without shared meaning and clear behaviors, new terminology is worthless.

How can you achieve and sustain alignment if you cannot define it in terms of behavior? The short answer is you can't. Without providing explicit behavioral standards and guidelines, people cannot learn and apply new skills and tools. In a high performance organization, people share a common language that is broadly understood and applied with shared skill sets. Because people understand the difference between complying versus aligning, they are able to hold one another accountable for consistent behavioral standards. Your stickability problem disappears.

Oppositional Speaking Escalates Conflict

"I disagree—now what do you have to say?" is the trademark of oppositional speakers. In meetings, oppositional speaking is typified with adversarial comments such as "I disagree," "No way this will work," or "I'm not on board." The reference point in oppositional speaking is "me"—how the individual feels about what he or she is saying. Because ideas are not treated with curiosity, a discussion can easily escalate into an argument.

When leaders engage in oppositional speaking, they have been snagged by victim or entitlement mentality. In some cases, opposing someone or something is the driving behavior. Everything is in the framework of us against them, or me against everyone else. In other cases, the only point of concern is how the decision would impact the individual.

Oppositional speaking focuses on finding the flaw and attacking what is wrong in an idea or person in order to be right. It starts by listening against a person or idea and is then followed by a positional statement, which can be as simple as "I disagree."

> **Oppositional Speaking**
> Finding the flaw and attacking what's wrong in order to be right.

Oppositional speaking is quite noticeable in meetings in which people defend, challenge, and argue with one another and do not seek to understand one another's views.

> **What Oppositional Speakers Do**
> - Make adversarial comments such as "I disagree," "No way," or "This will never work."
> - Make assumptions and challenge ideas without understanding them.
> - Invalidate and minimize others' points of view.
> - Polarize others with an either-or or black-or-white argument.
> - Act as if they are right and others are wrong.

In alignment dialogues, the framework of "I disagree" is replaced with listening for positive intention and focusing on how to build on ideas instead of tearing them down. It takes committed partners who can effectively intervene and coach one another when blind spots take over and the conversation becomes unproductive.

Forcing People to Comply versus Engaging Them to Align

"When our team was asked to support an enterprise initiative, I felt I had no choice. I thought I was being asked to rubber-stamp my approval," commented a frustrated leader. When people comply, they feel forced or pushed. You gain compliance, but you also get their resignation, resistance, and minimal investment of effort.

Jordan, the leader of a business unit, was described by his direct reports as "a bull in a china shop": *insensitive, clumsy, and bent on his decisions at the expense of others.* Jordan would run full steam ahead and tell others what he wanted from them. Asking questions was not his style. Why would it be, when he had all the answers? A peer commented: "He uses force and manipulation to get his way. If new data and information come in suggesting a midcourse correction, he will not revisit his initial decision. He is right, others are wrong, regardless of evidence to the contrary. This causes a lot of redundancy and rework."

In working with Jordan and his group, we saw the bull in the china shop firsthand. Jordan ran his agenda ruthlessly and was proud of the way his group could accomplish so much in such a short period of time. It was easy to see how he maintained such a fast pace: no one talked but him, and his opinion was final.

Jordan had no trouble making a decision or taking decisive action. But no one likes to be forced, and Jordan's team felt shut down. The quality of their work was low and their morale even lower. As one member said, "Jordan is controlling, and our team has been reduced to nothing but a pack of head-nodders." When you operate as a team of one, you get the corresponding result.

Most leaders do not realize the impact they have on others when it comes to decision making. The pendulum seems to swing from leaders who are slow to make decisions and rely on group consensus to leaders who impose their decisions and force the group to comply.

ACHIEVING AUTHENTIC ALIGNMENT

Real alignment requires committed partners who behave as owners and play big. From this perspective people do not work for a company, they *are* the company. Committed partners work together to achieve sustainable alignment because they know it is a key to superior execution.

New skill sets are needed for transforming automatic behaviors into an extraordinary way of working together. The prerequisites for achieving sustainable alignment are

- Taking 100%-zero accountability for business results and your impact on people
- Building and sustaining committed partnerships
- Talking straight responsibly
- Honoring and fulfilling commitments
- Holding each other accountable for high standards of behavior
- Constructively intervening whenever required to get the team back on track

The ability of committed partners to quickly align and ensure that the alignment is sustained or adjusted as needed is what distinguishes high performance teams. This beginning-to-end process, in which people act as owners, makes certain that two things are accomplished: (1) everyone supports the decision both emotionally and intellectually, and (2) everyone remains aligned throughout the implementation phase where most breakdowns take place.

Self-managing teams are, in practice, committed partners who work together as high performance teams. In business-as-usual teams, squabbling is an ongoing distraction, and team leaders must expend considerable energy managing others and refereeing conflict. Contrast this with high performance teams in which committed partners constructively intervene, coach each other in the moment, and quickly refocus the group on the business need.

But there is another element committed partners bring to alignment: caring for each other. Because they stand for the success of each other and intimately understand each other's blind spots, they turn the motto—when one succeeds, we all succeed, and when one fails, we all fail—into a daily practice. Their relentless commitment to greatness demands that everyone play big and surrender the right to dominate with personal agendas, preferences, and positions.

Declaring Decision Types: Providing Clarity *before* Asking for Alignment

People need to know where you stand on a decision before they engage in a conversation to align. There is nothing more frustrating or time-consuming to a group than spending time on an issue only to discover that the leader has already made a decision.

A key element in productive decision-making dialogues is declaring decision types—providing clarity on whether the decision has been made and if not, who will make it. Declaration of decision types is the accountability of the leader or decision owner.

The Consequences of Asking a Group to Make a Decision and Then Changing Your Mind

Talley, the senior vice president of customer relations, asked her team to "decide" on the strategy for a new and prestigious customer account. Talley's group spent a significant amount of time and effort on the project and took full ownership. They aligned on an approach, but that's when the problems began.

What Happened. When they presented their "decision" to Talley she said: *"I appreciate your input and ideas and I'll take them into consideration when I make my final decision."* The group was speechless. For the past several weeks they had engaged as decision owners, not as a recommending body. Talley, on the other hand, didn't think twice about changing her mind midstream and withdrawing the decision-making power from the group.

Needless to say, group members reacted with anger and disgust. This wasn't the first time they had wasted time on a decision that Talley either had already made or decided she was going to make on her own. One group member said, *"This is typical Talley. I could kick myself for falling for this again. She knew what she wanted before we started this discussion, and we never really had any authority to make the decision. What a waste of time."*

Lesson Learned. The quickest way to disempower a group is to ask them to make a decision that you have either already made or to give them decision-making authority and then withdraw it. There's nothing wrong with making the decision as the leader. However, it is critical that you provide the group with clarity with regard to their decision-making authority *prior* to asking them to engage in problem solving. If you want input from a group but do not want to taint their perspective with your own, be truthful and say, *"I have a preference, but I do not want it to influence your thinking. I want to hear what you think before I share my thoughts."* In this way, no one is blindsided.

I watch countless teams struggle for clarity when a leader starts a discussion without telling the group where he or she stands on the topic, and what type of decision-making authority he or she is giving the group. As a result, team members second-guess leaders, waste time, and throw their hands up in frustration. Our consulting organization developed two tools to address these problems: identifying decision types and identifying levels of alignment.

Let's start with decision types. Everyone needs to understand—*prior* to an alignment discussion—what type of decision they are being asked to make. Whether you are a team member or the team leader, clarity is essential for effective problem solving. Exhibit 9-1 outlines the three decision types. In this exhibit, the reference to "leader" refers to the decision owner: the person who has the authority to declare a Type 1, 2, or 3 decision.

Many of our clients use our decision types during meetings and for meeting agendas where each topic is identified as a Type 1, 2, or 3 decision. Group members always know what is being asked of them. This aids them in preparing for meetings and eliminates guesswork about where the leader stands and what is being requested of them. A group is much more efficient and focused when they know what is expected of them *prior* to the discussion. Let's walk through each decision type to understand how to use it and how alignment discussions differ with each.

If you are a group member, and not the team leader, you can take action and get the information you need for an effective group discussion. Make a request before the discussion begins so you and everyone else are clear on the decision type. Your request may be as simple as "Are we being asked to align on a Type 1, 2, or 3 decision?" Make sure you know what has or has not been decided, and who will make the final decision.

Decision Type	Decision Status	Accountability of Leader	Accountability of Group Members	Alignment Needed
Type 1	Decision *made* by the leader, alone.	Provides context and includes others in why he or she made the decision.	Clarify, and ask questions to authentically support the decision.	Leader requests emotional and intellectual alignment of group.
Type 2	Decision *to be made* by the leader, following group input.	Provides context, clarifies problem and opportunity, and requests and listens to input from the group.	Provide critical input, challenge thinking, generate ideas, and recommend solutions.	Leader provides closure on when he or she will make the final decision.
Type 3	Decision *to be made* by the group. The leader suspends veto power and supports the group's decision.	Provides context, clarifies problem and opportunity, and participates fully as an equal member of the group.	Dialogue, engage in healthy debate, and identify best solution.	Group members and team leader align emotionally and intellectually.

EXHIBIT 9-1: *Decision Types*

Type 1: A Decision Made by the Leader, Alone. Type 1 decisions are typically context decisions. They define direction and high-level objectives and establish expectations. In essence, Type 1 decisions provide the context for what you expect people to focus on and how you expect them to engage. This type of decision defines the parameters and focus of the game. For example, when you say, "We will be the best in customer service," you are making a Type 1 decision and taking a stand. Your decision is not open to debate; you have declared the context and framework in which the company will work and align. However, the implementation may require a Type 3 decision where your team develops and aligns on the plan.

CEOs and business leaders must make many Type 1 decisions. These decisions are legitimate and necessary and are also empowering and inspiring when handled effectively. Some leaders argue that decisions require group consensus and should include everyone to ensure buy-in. This is another area in which we operate backward. What these leaders are missing is that consensus building is the least effective method for moving a team or organization forward. The question is not one of inclusion; ultimately everyone needs to be included. The question is "Do you have the courage to take a bold stand and make a Type 1 decision to move your team or organization in a new direction?"

For example, establishing clear expectations for leadership behavior is a Type 1 decision. Of course, group buy-in is essential; however, the first step is for the leader to firmly declare his or her stand. Obtaining full alignment and support from others is the second step. Without a fearless leader who is willing to take a bold stand and make a Type 1 decision, teams and organizations flounder and stagnate as they become bogged down in trying to achieve the impossible: consensus.

The automatic pull of tolerating "good enough" will always result in a vocal faction arguing for maintaining the status quo or incremental improvements. When you make a Type 1 decision, you are saying that this is something you passionately believe in and you are asking others to partner with you. Your Type 1 decision turns your stand into action and makes your commitment entrenched and public so the alignment process can begin.

Consider when you have had a strong preference but did not declare a Type 1 decision. Perhaps you field-tested your idea with a group and waited to hear their reaction before making your decision. Or you made your decision, but doled it out in pieces to test the reaction and achieve buy-in one piece at a time. Chances are your behavior frustrated others. They did not know where you stood and were left to fill in the blanks.

Some leaders believe that a Type 1 decision will result in the group always expecting the leader to make decisions. This does not occur unless the leader arbitrarily makes Type 1 decisions. If used as a command and control tactic, they are ineffective. Appropriate Type 1 decisions are highly effective and allow you to bring urgency to a key area of the business.

The lack of Type 1 decisions is as problematic as making too many Type 1 decisions. If you are unwilling to take a stand and declare a Type 1 decision, you will lose credibility and support. Leaders who are indecisive or rely too heavily on consensus, stifle what teams and organizations can accomplish.

Once you make a Type 1 decision, you must learn how to gain emotional and intellectual alignment from others. Often this stage is skipped and leaders who make Type 1 decisions simply expect others to fall in line. Without giving others an opportunity to fully discuss and understand your decision, it will be viewed as an order to which they must comply.

Contrary to what most people believe, a Type 1 decision requires rigorous dialogue to gain the support of others. Just because you have made the decision, you cannot forgo the alignment discussion without serious consequences. In the alignment discussion, you must share what has led you to make this decision and why you are asking the group for their full support and alignment. How you talk to the group and disclose your personal passion for what you believe in and what you want to accomplish sets the stage. People need to understand what is personally behind the decision for you—why you are moved and inspired by this decision. Your role during the alignment discussion is to take accountability for the decision you have made and its impact on others. You must encourage others to ask any questions they have, raise all concerns, and express fully. The context for the conversation is this: everyone is accountable for fully understanding why you have made a Type 1 decision and discovering how they can emotionally and intellectually align with your decision as though they authored it themselves. This context keeps the conversation from becoming a debate or a rebuttal to dissuade you about your decision.

Do not leave decisions about the future of your team or organization to guesswork. Tell people exactly what your decision is and define the context and larger framework. With your committed partners, learn how to master Type 1 alignment conversations so when Type 1 decisions are essential, everyone has a method for moving beyond compliance to fully endorsing and supporting the decision.

Type 2: A Decision to Be Made by the Leader, Following Group Input.
Type 2 decisions are the most common type of decision. In a Type 2 decision, the leader gathers information, input, and feedback from the group but ultimately makes the final call. The team members' responsibility is to fully communicate their ideas, concerns, and considerations about the pending decision, recognizing that the leader will make the final decision.

Unfortunately, many leaders wait until they know which way the wind is blowing before they tell the group that this is a Type 2 decision. These leaders listen to group input, and if group sentiments line up with the leader's preference, the leader lets the group think that they are making the decision. But if the discussion reveals that the group does not agree, the leader uses a backdoor escape and says, "I'll take your input under consideration and get back to you later." This, of course, is not fearless leadership and defeats the purpose of being transparent and straightforward. People will be justifiably upset and exasperated with you because you were not direct and honest from the start.

When you declare that you are making a Type 2 decision, it opens up a dialogue for people to explore, debate, and question different approaches. If it is a legitimate Type 2 decision, you have not made up your mind and you are genuinely listening to group input and feedback. For this open forum to be effective, you must listen without judging or reacting. Then, after everyone feels that they have fully expressed, you can make your decision on the spot or reflect on their input and make your decision later. However, once you make your final decision, you must still include the group in an alignment conversation for buy-in. At this point, the conversation is the same as a Type 1 discussion. The decision has been made and now everyone needs to understand what drove you to make this decision, why you are passionate about it, and how they can support it as if they authored it themselves. This process is what makes your decision stick.

As with all decision types, inform the group *prior* to the discussion that this is a Type 2 decision. Then take accountability for making sure everyone has an opportunity to fully communicate and express his or her viewpoint.

Type 3: A Decision to Be Made by the Group, with the Leader Being an Equal and Participating Member. In a Type 3 decision, a leader is asking the team to make the decision and agrees to suspend his or her veto power. The leader engages as an equal team member and agrees to support the group decision even if it does not match his or her personal preference.

Be careful about Type 3 decisions: they can get you in trouble unless you are prepared to go the distance. Ron, an executive in a service company, told his group that he wanted a Type 3 decision about whether to move forward on a new product in the next quarter. He told the group that he trusted their judgment and would go along with whatever decision they made. The group participated in rigorous and heated discussions and finally reached a decision: "This is not the right time to introduce this product to the market." They unanimously vetoed introducing the new product in the next 12 months. Ron was miffed; he had not anticipated "group rejection" of the new product. He sulked for several days after the meeting, then at the next meeting he announced that he had decided to override the group decision and bring the product to market in the next quarter.

The group felt betrayed, not because Ron made the decision, but because he broke his commitment and reneged on the rules of engagement for a Type 3 decision. This is one of the worst mistakes a leader can make—telling a group that you will support their decision, and then changing your mind because their decision does not match your preference. Many months later, Ron's group was still stinging from the debacle and withheld their discretionary effort. Their reasoning: "Why should we give Ron our full effort when he so easily discards his commitments to the group?"

It is critically important to understand that if you endorse a Type 3 decision, you are not well served by invoking your veto power when you do not like the result. Make sure you are truly willing to suspend your veto power before you commit to a Type 3 decision. If you are not sure you can do this then make a Type 2 decision. A Type 3 decision must be strictly reserved for genuine group decisions.

If you are a group member, you have an accountability to make sure everyone is committed to a Type 3 decision, especially the team leader. This is where making a clear and direct request is essential. Before the discussion begins, ask, "Are you willing to suspend your veto power and go along with the group decision even if you don't agree with it?" Your question will help the team leader carefully consider his or her commitment and will reinforce the rules of engagement for a Type 3 decision.

The Five Levels of Alignment: Clearly Identifying Where Everyone Stands

The informal question "Do we all agree?" is often asked in meetings. Having no other option than to agree or disagree, many people nod and comply. The tragedy is that *complying* is often mistaken as *alignment*, until a breakdown occurs. At the time of a breakdown, the team becomes clear that they were not aligned in the first place and then must go through the exhausting process of rework and damage control.

Saying "Yes, I am aligned" is insufficient to determine if there is full emotional and intellectual commitment, and it is certainly inadequate for holding people accountable for their agreements. To avoid this pitfall, we developed the chart in the sidebar "The Five Levels of Alignment" to provide an efficient method for groups to talk about where they are in the alignment process.

The Five Levels of Alignment: Where Are You?

Level 1: Resigned (not aligned). "I am resigned about . . ."

Level 2: Concerned (not aligned). "I am concerned about . . ."

Level 3: Complying (not aligned). "I am going along with the decision because . . ."

Level 4: Intellectually committed (partially aligned). "I am only intellectually committed because . . ."

Level 5: Emotionally and intellectually committed (fully aligned). "I am fully on board and I am not holding anything back."

The Five Levels of Alignment are designed to help individuals and teams identify what prevents them from fully aligning (Level 5) and help them talk about their concerns. As a result, people are able to engage in an open and honest dialogue where they can easily pinpoint key areas of concern and resolve issues preventing alignment. The five levels of alignment are not only valuable in stimulating an open dialogue and engaging people who would otherwise not speak up, but they are also a barometer for measuring if the group is united at Level 5, or if individuals are at different levels.

An important factor to note is that the levels of alignment are not a sequential progression. In other words, an individual or team does not need to move through each level in order to reach Level 5. Further, an individual may be both resigned and complying at the same time (Level 1 and Level 3). The only level that is discrete and does not overlap with other levels is Level 5—emotional and intellectual alignment. This level is reserved for full emotional and intellectual commitment. When an individual says he or she is aligned at Level 5, it means, "I am committing to support the decision, both emotionally and intellectually, without any reservations or conditions. I am not resigned, concerned, complying, or withholding emotional commitment." Level 5 is a statement of commitment to set aside one's personal agenda or preference and support the decision both publicly and privately as if you authored it yourself.

There are many ways in which you can use the levels of alignment in a group discussion. You can use them at the beginning of a discussion to find out where people stand before the alignment dialogue begins, as a checkpoint during the discussion, or at the end of the discussion to determine if group alignment has been achieved.

Level 1: Resigned. In a decision-making conversation, Level 1 refers to being actively disengaged and believing that nothing will change. Carolyn was resigned during a group discussion on what was needed to create what the company called a WOW customer experience. Since this was a hot topic for the CEO, she felt it would be politically incorrect to do anything but comply and agree. But after participating in a team learning session, she learned how to communicate about her resignation using the five levels of alignment. When the group asked her where she was with regard to the levels of alignment she was straightforward and said, "I'm at Level 1 — resigned. We've had this discussion many times without any action. I'm resigned that two months from now we'll be revisiting this same topic again."

Carolyn's comment prompted others to express their concerns and soon the team was able to identify the bottleneck that kept progress from occurring. Because Carolyn and others now had a way to express their concerns without being judged, the group was able to have a productive dialogue.

People who are resigned may ultimately go along with a decision, but their resignation will contaminate support from others and undermine the decision. It is important to address resignation openly. Only when people have an opportunity to express their concerns and work through them with the group can they become fully aligned.

Resignation can manifest in any or all of the following ways:

- Behaviors that reveal a belief that something or someone is unchangeable

- Weariness and apathy from dealing with the same unresolved issue
- Giving up and believing that one's opinion does not matter
- Feeling that the decision will fail to produce the results needed

Level 2: Concerned. People will agree to decisions in spite of serious concerns, doubts, or skepticism. If it is politically correct not to speak up, they won't. Or if they feel their concerns will not be listened to, people will withhold them, and along with them, their support. Often people are uneasy but unaware of what specifically is bothering them. Without sufficient dialogue and a way to help people express their concerns, many people sit on the sidelines and do not speak up in meetings.

Don had many concerns about the customer experience strategy but he was quiet and did not express them. A committed partner noticed Don's lack of participation in the meeting and asked him, "Where are you with regard to the levels of alignment?" When asked the question directly, Don responded, "I'm concerned. I guess that puts me at Level 2. I don't see how this will work." Don went on and explained his concerns to the group, and in the discussion several others expressed similar concerns as well as alternative approaches that would address them. Don became engaged in the conversation and contributed to the final decision, making him an owner in what the group decided to do.

As a group member or team leader, you can use the levels of alignment to support people in articulating what they are thinking and feeling. The entire group will benefit as the efficiency and quality of decision making improves.

Common concerns that people feel but may not express include these:

- A concern that the decision will negatively impact a third party—an individual, group, business unit, or the organization.
- A concern that there are unintended consequences—collateral damage—that have not been fully considered.
- A concern that there are insufficient resources (people, time, money) to support the decision and its implementation.
- A concern that the decision will derail other important commitments.

Level 3: Complying. As we discussed earlier, people comply for a variety of reasons. When people comply, they abdicate their accountability to the group or leader. You can identify complying behavior by the flatness of energy in the room. People do not pay attention or listen to one another, and there is a feeling of sluggishness or even boredom, as the group deals with agenda items.

Shawn was tired of listening to the same few people talk. All he wanted was for the meeting to end so he could get back to work. But a committed partner asked him, "What's going on for you? Where are you at with regard to the levels of alignment?" The specific nature of the question and the fact that a scale is provided makes it easy for people to articulate their response. Shawn replied, "I suppose I'm complying and resigned at the same time. That puts me at Level 1 and Level 3. Only a few people are talking and I don't feel that my input is valued by others."

When an individual is asked to talk about his or her level of alignment, it often opens up a new way of thinking for everyone. The group talked about what Shawn said and how a handful of people were dominating the meeting. This new awareness coupled with a commitment to high performance resulted in a positive change in group behavior. The vocal participants took accountability for their impact and made room for others to contribute. The dynamic of the meeting changed and the group was able to reach a decision in which they had full support.

Complying behavior is a form of resignation. The signs include these:

- Disengaging from the conversation
- Superficially engaging in the conversation and going along with the group
- Being politically correct and noncommittal and letting the group take accountability for the decision
- Demonstrating restlessness or disinterest
- Pushing for closure in order to move on to another topic or bring the meeting to a close

Level 4: Intellectually Committed. Most groups mistake Level 4 alignment for being fully aligned. It is not. Intellectual alignment works fine until something happens and circumstances change. It is only then that group members recognize that they were only *intellectually committed and not emotionally aligned.* Intellectual commitment is a positive sign and indicates that the group is moving toward full alignment; however, it is insufficient for sustainable alignment. When something happens to test the strength of the decision, intellectual alignment folds under pressure and people go off in different directions.

Ursula was a strong proponent for creating an exceptional customer experience. When it came time to commit to a plan of action she threw her hat in the ring and wholeheartedly aligned. But a few months later, when it was time to implement changes in her area, she felt differently. She was unprepared for the impact the new plan was having on her people, and when she saw their response, she withdrew her support for the decision.

When an individual or group is not *emotionally and intellectually committed*, alignment is unsustainable. Something will invariably happen that will cause the group to splinter and execute a decision inconsistently, or not execute it at all.

Signs of intellectual alignment include these:

- Supporting the decision, but lacking full commitment for executing the decision from beginning to end
- Understanding the decision intellectually but failing to consider the impact on others
- Believing it is the right thing to do but lacking personal conviction to champion the decision
- Thinking you are intellectually and emotionally committed, when there is still something holding you back

Level 5: Emotionally and Intellectually Committed. Leaders spend most of their time analyzing, evaluating, and assessing, but they spend little time considering the emotional domain of commitment. Alignment is both intellectual and emotional, and most breakdowns occur because there is insufficient commitment in both areas. Intellectual commitment is comfortable and familiar: it includes a checklist of such key business factors as financial, legal, resource, and personnel considerations that must be satisfactorily met before a decision is made. In contrast, the landscape of emotional commitment is less familiar and less comfortable.

Emotional commitment requires a personal investigation of two elements:

1. How you personally feel about the decision—your level of commitment, passion, and enthusiasm.
2. How the decision lines up with your personal core values.

When we ask leaders if they are emotionally committed, they answer, "Yes, I think we should move ahead." However, "*I think*" is not a feeling. Therefore, the questions you must ask and answer to gauge emotional commitment are different from those used to assess intellectual commitment:

- Are you willing to stand for this decision, publicly and privately, even when you are uncomfortable and challenges occur?
- Are you enthusiastic, energized, and passionate about this decision?
- Are you motivated by what can be achieved?
- Are you willing to actively enlist others?

Emil did not respond immediately when he was asked about his level of alignment on a decision. Instead, he reflected about whether he was willing to go the distance and actively support the decision at every level in the organization. He knew there would be difficulties and challenges, and he wanted to make sure he was willing to remain aligned through thick and thin. After resolving that he was committed at Level 5, he shared his stand with the group and said, "You can count on my full alignment and support."

Emotional commitment answers the question, "How will people support this decision in practice—will they be indifferent, neutral, and unmoved or inspired, enthusiastic, and passionate?

How a CEO Achieved Authentic Alignment with Successor Candidates

In a horse race for the CEO position in a manufacturing company, the incumbent CEO asked the two internal candidates to align on how they would work together if one of them became the next CEO. Both candidates said they would stay with the organization and support each other fully regardless of who became the heir apparent.

What Happened. The incumbent CEO felt there were issues that needed to be resolved between the two candidates. In private sessions with each candidate followed by a combined session with both, we discovered they were aligned in principle but not in practice. One candidate, Sid, was merely complying (in other words, he was at Level 3) with what he thought the CEO wanted to hear. The other candidate, Bruce, said he was on board but was not sold on whether the goodwill would last with Sid when the decision was ultimately made (in other words, he was at Level 4, intellectually aligned).

We met with the CEO and the two candidates to uncover what it would take to reach Level 5 alignment: emotional and intellectual commitment. The conversation started with Sid saying, *"It's easy to agree now, but how can we trust each other to keep our agreements when one of us will win and the other will lose?"* I answered his concern with, *"First, you have to trust each other's integrity and word. Second, the traditional view of winner and loser is not a useful construct. As committed partners, it's your accountability to decide how you want to engage throughout this transition and then align on your commitment."* *"Yeah, but we still have to deal with the reactions of others,"* said Bruce. *"That's true, and again, you have a choice. You can either allow automatic behavior to take over and people will build camps and line up behind the candidate of their choice, or you can decide together to demonstrate what it means to be committed partners. How you behave will tell others if your culture is real and here to stay,"* I concluded.

By the end of the two-day discussion, Sid and Bruce were emotionally and intellectually committed to support each other regardless of who was selected as the next CEO.

The Result. Bruce became the new CEO. Within the first few days of the announcement, Sid and Bruce went on the road and spoke to groups together to demonstrate their partnership.

Lesson Learned. By not accepting intellectual alignment and insisting on authentic alignment between the CEO candidates, the incumbent CEO successfully provided continuity in leadership. Four years later, Bruce and Sid are viewed by the organization as the premiere example of committed partnerships.

Rules of Engagement for High Performance Meetings

The rules of engagement are different in a high performance organization when compared to its traditional counterpart. They are explicit behaviors that group members apply in meetings at all levels in the organization.

Together with the levels of alignment and decision types, the rules of engagement provide the guidelines for how people are expected to behave. Understanding them is one thing; applying them requires practice, rigor, and discipline.

Only the elite master how to conduct meetings that consistently deliver high performance results. In the sidebar, a list is provided of the rules of engagement used by high performance teams. The team must align on each behavior and give explicit permission to hold one another accountable for consistently applying the rules of engagement.

The Rules of Engagement

1. **Be 100% accountable for results and your impact on others.** Participate fully, and hold one another accountable for the rules of engagement.

2. **Check your ego at the door.** Contribute as a full team member, not as an individual, your role, or your title.

3. **Be willing to be uncomfortable.** Be emotionally honest, surface and confront the real issues.

4. **Listen for positive intention.** Listen for the commitment and contribution of others.

5. **Speak only when it forwards the action.** Make sure what you say advances the conversation, or don't say it.

6. **Check your assumptions instead of reacting.** Clarify what you "think" you heard, before responding or reacting.

7. **Talk straight responsibly.** Be direct without blaming or judging.

8. **Eliminate all side conversations and distractions.** Be respectful and pay attention, one person speaks at a time.

9. **Be willing to be rigorously coached.** Generously listen to coaching, apply it immediately, and actively coach others.

10. **Eliminate oppositional speaking.** Build on one another's ideas, and do not invalidate the viewpoints of others.

THRIVING ON ENERGY

While it is a dramatic example, Napoleon described the emotional investment individuals must make before giving themselves fully: "*A man does not have himself killed for a half-pence a day or for a petty distinction; you must speak to the soul in order to electrify him.*"

Achieving the alignment required to be a world-class organization is not possible without a battle cry that inspires and electrifies people. People must be moved to learn and grow personally and see the benefits from this, so they are on fire to apply their new capabilities and skills to organizational goals.

High performance teams thrive on energy because of the exceptional way in which committed partners work together. They stand for the success of each other, honor and fulfill commitments, talk straight responsibly, settle for nothing less than emotional and intellectual alignment, and hold each other accountable. For committed partners, these practices are a way of life.

The unbridled passion of high performance teams is plain to see, and it is not unusual to hear one team member say to another, "Are we having a bad day?" Then you hear chuckling, along with the response, "Thanks for pointing out my blind spot. I was whining like a victim, wasn't I?" The conversation is fast and to the point, and automatic behavior is instantly replaced with extraordinary behavior. People do not walk on eggshells or take offense at the slightest remark.

High performance teams learn how to constructively intervene and keep the group on track while simultaneously strengthening relationships. They are imperfect, but committed, teams who never stop learning and practicing.

LEADERSHIP EXPLORATION

1. **Where are you not aligned—emotionally and intellectually—with people, initiatives, and/or strategy?** Use the alignment levels to pinpoint where you are: Level 1, resigned; Level 2, concerned; Level 3, complying; Level 4, intellectually aligned; or Level 5, emotionally and intellectually aligned. Consider where you are not aligned with your boss, direct

reports, coworkers, the next level up, and stakeholders. The easiest way to assess where alignment is missing is to ask, *"Where am I frustrated, tolerating people or situations, withholding commitment, or lacking passion and enthusiasm?"*

If you waffle in answering the question *"Am I emotionally and intellectually aligned?"* then your answer is no. The absence of a clear and resounding, *"Yes, I am fully aligned"* informs you that something is missing or preventing you from giving your all.

Not being aligned at Level 5 does not mean you are not committed or engaged. Quite the contrary: chances are that you have a frustrated commitment or an unmet expectation that requires further exploration with the appropriate person.

2. **What stops you from being fully aligned?** Explore what prevents you from emotionally and intellectually committing. Often the lack of alignment can be traced to not feeling listened to or understood, or not making a clear and direct request to the appropriate person. Start by identifying where you feel that your commitment has been thwarted. Allow room for the likely possibility that you may be sabotaging yourself; focus on your behavior and what you can do to alter the situation.

A reminder about requests: many times we fail to make requests because we think we will not receive a positive response. Set aside your resignation and play big: identify the request you want to make and do not skimp on what you need to communicate. Breakthroughs are produced by taking bold stands and making clear and direct requests, and then committing to action.

LEADERSHIP ACTION

Discover What Blocks Your Team from Aligning— Emotionally and Intellectually

With your team, identify critical areas in which group members are not aligned. Use the five levels of alignment and dialogue to discover what is preventing Level 5 alignment by asking:

1. Do you feel you have not been understood or that your ideas have not been listened to?
2. What have you not fully communicated? What have you withheld?
3. Are you trapped in the need to be right or the victim mindset? Where do you need to take accountability?
4. Are your personal preferences getting in the way of supporting enterprise objectives and aligning with the group?
5. Are you willing to suspend your preference or agenda to support the group decision?
6. What request do you have of the team or individual members?

Call for Level 5 Alignment

You do not need to settle for anything less than Level 5 alignment; however, it must be real and not another form of compliance. Support one another in working through concerns and issues that prevent the group from aligning. Remind one another of the choice each person must make: to play small where the focus is on individual needs and preferences, or to play big where the focus is on achieving the enterprise mission—a purpose that is much greater than the needs of any single individual.

If you or the group have not reached Level 5 alignment, you have two choices. The first choice is to reexamine the issue under discussion to determine if the group is on the right track. You must allow for the possibility that Level 5 alignment cannot be achieved if you are not solving the right problem or if there is a value-based conflict. The second choice is to pursue Level 5 alignment by exploring what has not yet been addressed or resolved. Keep the conversation open until all issues have been surfaced. Learn and practice what it means to work together as committed partners. Your goal is to make sure that everyone is fully heard so you can achieve lasting alignment.

> *Courage is not simply one of the virtues,*
> *but the form of every virtue at its testing point.*
>
> —C. S. Lewis (1898–1963)

Chapter
10
Holding Each Other
Accountable

In the right key, one can say anything, in the wrong key, nothing.
The only delicate part is the establishment of the key.

—George Bernard Shaw (1856–1950)

CEOs and executives often ask us "We have a leader in jeopardy. Can this leader be salvaged?" With rare exception, the answer is yes. Given the right tools and environment, leaders can transform their behavior and sustain this change over time. What is required is the willingness of the leader in question to honestly confront his or her blind spots and take 100% accountability for business results and his or her impact on people. The leader must learn new skills for how to engage with others. But equally as important, the work environment must support the practices of committed partners: standing for the success of each other, honoring and fulfilling commitments, talking straight responsibly, aligning emotionally and intellectually, and *holding each other accountable*.

Leaders are often frustrated when their message about behavior does not get through, and the same undesirable behavior continues. Simply telling an individual that he or she needs to "get on board" or work more effectively with others is pointless. Let's go back to basics: words alone do not alter behavior. They click in at an intellectual level, and while people may understand the logic of what you are saying, they will not recognize the emotional impact their behavior has on others. Further, even if they do understand the impact of their behavior, most do not have the skills to correct it and sustain new behaviors over time. Even with the best intention, a leader will default to old and unproductive behaviors without a structure of support.

In our work with leaders and executives, we consistently find them to be highly committed and accountable. It is rare to encounter a leader who does not have an overriding commitment to do his or her best. But this is often accompanied by the frustration of feeling hampered, misunderstood, and alone. Combine this feeling of separation with a low level of awareness about the impact on others, and you have the formula for good leaders behaving in unproductive ways.

A predictable blueprint emerges in working with leaders and teams: people do not change their behavior unless they experience a shocking comprehension about how their behavior is inconsistent with their fundamental beliefs and values. For a leader to choose to alter his or her behavior, something—such as a constructive intervention—must happen to create a profound and heightened sense of self-awareness.

What is needed is a way of cracking the code for dramatically transforming leadership effectiveness. This chapter examines the all-important question: "How do you hold others accountable in a way that is both supportive and produces the result needed?" In answering this question we examine another one: "Who has the accountability?" Above all, you must understand where you are placing accountability so you can balance supporting people to do their best while holding them accountable. This chapter will also teach you how to dismantle the automatic behaviors that prevent people from holding each other accountable and constructively intervene in an unproductive situation.

THE KEY TO GREATNESS: HOLDING EACH OTHER ACCOUNTABLE

A culture of 100% accountability is a self-correcting environment in which leaders at all levels actively coach one another and intervene in unproductive behavior. They accept nothing less than what an individual or team is capable of achieving. They hold people up to high standards of behavior instead of focusing on their limitations.

> **Holding Each Other Accountable**
> Holding people up to their greatness not down to their limitations.

When you hear the words "holding each other accountable," what comes to mind? Do you think of a punitive action such as punishing someone for making a mistake? If you do, you are in the mainstream. Holding people accountable is commonly perceived as something that is negative and disciplinary. As a result, it is not leveraged as a crucial skill because people are uncomfortable with both holding others accountable and being held to account.

Without committed partnerships, holding to account does revert to its reputation of being punitive. In the absence of a commitment to stand for the success of each other, people do not have a framework for how to address problems in a supportive manner. Committed partners are aware that they have blind spots and give each other explicit permission to coach and hold each other accountable.

In a high performance culture, holding one another accountable is an essential behavior to help others excel. By calling for the best in performance, committed partners transcend perceived limitations and go beyond past successes. When people are motivated by this greater purpose of being the best, barriers dissolve quickly and they energetically push one another to achieve more.

If you are the leader of a team, you will no longer need to referee conflict or cajole people to align when you have committed partners who hold each other accountable. They will demand this of each other. But be prepared because they will also demand this of you. As a new team and environment emerges, people will confidently speak up and coach you. You will find yourself the recipient of requests, coaching, and being held to account for your leadership impact.

If you are a member of a team, you will have the freedom and power to shape the future and hold others accountable as your partner, including the team leader. You play a critical role in helping people work effectively together so the organization can achieve its objectives.

A CEO who had successfully led his organization through a transformational process disclosed to me: "The reversal in management direction took me by surprise. I was accustomed to a hierarchical company in which senior leaders made decisions and communicated them downward. Now we have informal leaders emerging at all levels who are holding our senior leaders accountable. My advice to leaders who take on high performance: be prepared for your people to hold you and other senior leaders accountable for your behavior."

Holding each other accountable requires the willingness to constructively intervene and take a stand that says "We're going to handle this breakdown or issue right now." Where coaching enlightens someone to the existence of a problem and raises his or her level of awareness, constructive intervention is the *insistence* that the problematic behavior be handled *in the moment*. Committed partners draw a line in the sand and address the issue immediately. This is what happened in our story below.

The Great Rant: Holding Leaders Accountable for Their Commitment to Play Big

What Happened. There was a general atmosphere of whining, complaining, and taking shots at one another, and there was collective denial that they were doing this. The leadership group of a major business operation was behaving in a way that was inconsistent with what *they* said they were committed to: building a high performance culture. They had their feet nailed to the floor and were arguing about being right. The team leader, Pierre, attempted to handle the situation, but rather than taking a strong stand, he simply said, *"Let's get back to our agenda."*

Neither group members nor the team leader stopped the unproductive behavior. What was needed was for someone to take a strong stand and say, *"Our behavior is not demonstrating our commitment to work in partnership. We need to stop attacking and blaming one another and take accountability for how we are derailing this conversation."*

But no one spoke up. My group and I were working with the team and finally I couldn't take it anymore. I intervened and said, *"This pettiness is unacceptable. I know each of you personally and you are all so much bigger than this. You have led this business to greatness and have succeeded in engaging everyone in building a high perfor-*

mance culture, yet in this meeting you are not behaving as committed partners. You have forgotten your commitment to stand for the success of one another and are engaging in old, automatic behaviors."

The group was stunned into silence. I said much more, and it was far more colorful and impassioned than what I've described here; in fact, the people present at this meeting refer to it as "The Great Rant." They were stunned because, in that moment, they saw how they were sabotaging their mission by their behavior. From that point forward, the meeting snapped into place and there was a clear and undivided focus on business matters.

The Result. The leadership team was remarkable in their ability and willingness to respond quickly to coaching. As soon as they recognized they were playing small, they changed their behavior. Their commitment to being effective was much stronger than their commitment to being right.

Lesson Learned. High performance teams, like any other teams, become trapped in automatic behaviors. The difference is the speed at which they recover. The question you may be asking is, *"Would this team have self-corrected their behavior without outside intervention?"* My answer is yes. At the time of this meeting, the team was in the early stages of learning how to hold one another accountable. They may have taken longer to get to the point where they stopped the unproductive behavior, but they would have succeeded.

Holding each other accountable is a high-level skill that committed partners master through practice. It is the final agreement of committed partners and is by far the most challenging because of our fear that we will make things worse instead of better.

LOCATING ACCOUNTABILITY IN THE PROPER PLACE

Any discussion of accountability must start with this question: Who has the accountability? Above all, you must understand where accountability is located. You must clearly understand if you are fostering an environment in which "good reasons" are tolerated over results as previously discussed.

The point often missed? Without explicit behavioral standards, leaders have no foundation for holding people accountable. They are left with a fragmented approach to leadership behavior that results in inconsistent standards.

Let's reinforce what should now be set in stone: Fearless leaders are not perfect. But they are *committed to following an explicit rule set* that gives them the ability to work effectively together to generate opportunities and the resilience to overcome challenges.

Unspoken Truces: Covering Up for Each Other

In addition to our list of blind spots, there is another automatic behavior that prevents people from holding each other accountable: engaging in unspoken truces and covering up for each other.

"I'll scratch your back if you scratch mine" is an example of a pact or truce. It implies that the parties are covering up and protecting each other from blame or harm. Although truces are not formally declared, they exist just the same. They are an underhanded deal in which people go to bat for one another and conceal the real issue. For example, "I'll ignore your blind spots if you ignore mine. I will not hold you accountable for your behavior if you do the same for me. I'll pretend that everything is copacetic if others challenge our performance."

Truces commonly exist between leaders as a hands-off agreement to avoid interfering in each other's areas. In an unspoken contract, leaders agree not to talk about anything that makes each other uneasy. They do not interfere with each other's areas even when someone is in trouble. Sadly, these unspoken agreements hurt the organization and are seldom confronted.

Eliminating Reasons and Holding People Accountable for Results

"Why aren't you accessible to your people? They tell me you're never around when you're needed," asked the irritated executive of his direct report who had relocated her family to Indonesia 18 months prior. "I've had a lot of things to deal with," responded the direct report. "But why are you not managing your time more effectively?" asked the executive. "Well, I'm still learning about the business, and as you know, we're struggling with the economic downturn." And so the conversation went, in circles. The executive wanted to understand why and the direct report provided "good reasons."

The discussion of accepting reasons in place of results deserves further exploration. In Chapter 7 we discussed how a good reason is not a result. Let's build on this and add how holding people accountable requires that we eliminate reasons and replace them with results.

As we discussed, many leaders rely on "why" questions when they are dealing with performance or behavioral issues. They believe that if all parties understand *why* the behavior is occurring, it can somehow be resolved. This is based on the presumption that by uncovering the reason for the dilemma, the problem can be logically addressed and rectified. Unfortunately, "why" questions elicit "good reasons" that bring us back to the business-as-usual formula: no result plus a "good reason" equals the result.

When reasons and results are treated as interchangeable, nothing is accomplished. The conversation focuses on why things did not happen, and the results become lost. For example, the question "Why didn't the technology group advise us of this problem sooner?" puts the focus on *who* or *what* caused the problem. But no matter how much time you spend analyzing and rehashing what happened, the bottom line is you still do not have a result.

In order to deal effectively with behavior, you must separate the *result* from the *reason*. It cannot be said enough: the result is the result, not the reason.

This brings us to the all-important agreement of committed partners: holding themselves and others accountable. Let's start with the question "Where are you placing accountability?" Do you accept accountability for solving problems by pleading with others to change their behavior, or do you place accountability on others to change their behavior and deliver the results?

You may be unknowingly contributing to a "good reason–no result" environment by not consistently holding others accountable. Are you asking such questions as "Why did this happen?" or "Why wasn't action taken to prevent this from happening?" These questions are useful in analyzing a breakdown, but they are not useful in holding people personally accountable for performance and results. You must refocus the conversation on *their* accountability and *their* commitment to change their behavior.

Putting Accountability Where It Belongs

Let's revisit a fundamental principle: *you cannot change the behavior of anyone but yourself.* It does not matter how great your skills of persuasion are. Changing behavior is a personal choice and does not happen by mandate. Holding others accountable for their behavior and impact requires understanding where accountability is at all times. Is it on your back as you bargain for the change you want, or do you place the burden squarely on the other person's back so he or she is accountable for making the choice to change?

As with all automatic behavior, avoiding discomfort is a major factor that keeps us from holding others accountable. No one wants to deal with conflict or engage in a conversation that could result in discord. Instead, we avoid handling issues directly and pass the problem on to others. The result is poor or unproductive behavior that is tolerated for years, costing companies time, money, and results.

In working with CEOs and leaders, our group has observed two common approaches that leaders take to change the behavior of others: (1) they take accountability for how others behave and try to persuade them to change, or (2) they hold others accountable for changing their behavior and provide them with both support and consequences.

The first approach—taking accountability for how others behave—is based on the flawed belief that you have the power to change the behavior of others. This belief is played out in conversations where leaders use a variety of techniques:

Pleading. *"Please stop doing this,"* or *"I know you want to do better, don't you?"*
Lecturing. *"You should know better,"* or *"Let me explain what you need to do."*
Berating. *"How could you be so stupid?"* or *"You're irresponsible."*
Intimidating. *"One more time and you're through,"* or *"If you can't figure this out, I'll find someone who will."*

In these approaches, accountability rests with you and your ability to persuade others to change. Leaders tell people "Don't do this," and then people engage in the same behavior again. Then leaders say "I'm serious.

Don't do this." But the behavior migrates and shows up in a different way, and the problem persists. The monkey remains on your back, and the individual does not have an opportunity to make corrective changes. By maintaining accountability for the problem, you become mired in managing people problems with unsuccessful results.

Fortunately, there is a second approach: you can help people become personally accountable for their behavior and the choices they make. This approach is based on transferring accountability to the appropriate person, so you can stop engaging in the futile endeavor of trying to change another person's behavior. Exhibit 10-1 summarizes the difference between these two approaches.

The Approach	The Message	The Measurement	The Accountability
Approach 1: **Taking accountability for the behavior of others**	*"I want you to change your behavior."*	Results are measured by your ability to persuade others to change their behavior.	On You: You own the problem and must now convince others to change their behavior.
Approach 2: **Transferring accountability to the appropriate party**	*"Your behavior will tell me what choice you have made."*	Results are measured by the individual's choice to change his or her own behavior.	On Others: You hold others accountable for changing their behavior.

EXHIBIT 10-1: *Putting Accountability Where It Belongs*

As a committed partner, it is your job to support others in taking personal accountability. You must do everything possible short of enabling the person. Always keep in mind that your job is to help people feel powerful, not powerless. Be their partner, but do not take accountability for the choices they make. Set clear limits and boundaries, articulate the behaviors you expect, provide them with support and resources to learn new skills, and establish unambiguous consequences. Let behavior and results be the determining factors in performance, not effort and reasons.

This does not mean leaving people alone to solve problems. In a committed partnership, you are accountable for helping others be more effective by demonstrating your commitment to their success. Unless you have made a decision to fire an individual, you must keep your feet solidly planted in helping him or her succeed.

> **Let Behavior Be the Determining Factor, Not Words**
> Set limits, provide support, establish consequences, and pay attention to how people behave.

CONSTRUCTIVELY INTERVENING AND HOLDING EACH OTHER ACCOUNTABLE

Holding each other accountable is a purposeful action to address unproductive behavior and quickly correct it. Committed partners coach each other and constructively intervene to support each other and drive results. They are tough on commitments, easy on people.

Actually, *coaching* is a mild word when used to describe how committed partners engage; *constructive intervention* is a more apt description because it connotes the rigor and discipline required. However, for the purpose of this discussion, I am using the phrases "constructive intervention" and "coaching" interchangeably.

Holding each other accountable is not limited to leaders holding their teams accountable. In a high performance environment, it happens in all directions—upward, downward, and horizontal. Let's take an example of how team members held their team leader accountable for his impact. When a major breakdown occurred between a chemical supplier and the business unit, the leader reacted and said he would not use this supplier again. But team members were unwilling to react to a breakdown. Instead they held the team leader accountable for behaving consistently with his commitment to work in partnership.

In a meeting of the team, one member said to the team leader, "I want to coach you on a blind spot. Are you open to this?" The team leader, who was used to being coached, agreed. The direct report continued, "I feel that you're reacting instead of working this through. I share your frustration, but I also share your commitment to work in partnership with our suppliers. I request that we have a conversation with the supplier about our expectations and our mutual accountability instead of blaming them. Would you be willing to do this?" Having learned that being right and dogmatic was a sure formula for shooting himself in the foot, the team leader responded without hesitation. He agreed to join team members in meeting with the supplier for the purpose of resolving the breakdown and restoring the partnership.

Committed partners give each other permission to hold each other accountable. But they do not use this as a license to criticize, devalue, or attack each other.

Giving Coaching

Ask for permission to coach every time you provide input; once is not enough. Simply say, "I have some coaching for you. Are you open to listening?" This allows the individual to shift gears and listen to what you have to say. The rule is, never coach someone who has not given you explicit and recent permission.

Once permission is granted, begin by establishing the context. Authentically communicate your commitment to the success of the individual, to your relationship, and to mutual business outcomes. Stating the context and commitment out loud reminds all parties of the purpose of coaching: to support each other in reaching a higher level of excellence.

Be direct and emotionally honest when you provide coaching, and ask questions to understand the experience of the other person. Focus on the unproductive behavior by separating the behavior from the commitment of the individual so you are not indicting the person. For example, "It's not like you to break a commitment. When you tell me you're going to do something, you do it. This situation was the exception. When you did not deliver on your commitment it had a negative impact on my group and I need to communicate this to you." With this statement, the person is not "bad"; their *behavior* is unproductive and limiting. Further, the coaching treats the behavior as the exception and does not generalize to "all the time" or "in every situation." In this way, people can listen to what is being said without becoming defensive. On the other hand, if the behavior of an individual is consistently unproductive, then examine what you have been doing (or not doing) to allow this behavior to continue.

Receiving Coaching

Start by explicitly granting permission for others to coach you and hold you accountable. If you are a leader with a formal title and position, people will not trust your permission until you demonstrate, over and over again, that it is safe to coach you and that there are no negative consequences. It is up to you to demonstrate that you seek and welcome coaching from others.

Listen without defending, arguing, or explaining. This is not easy, especially given how awkward and imperfect most of us are in delivering coaching. You will need to consciously shift gears and listen with positive intention. Remember at all times that your committed partners are a stand for your success and want to support you in living up to your greatness.

When you have a reaction to feedback, take accountability in the moment and say "I'm reacting, but I do not want my reaction to stop what you have to say. Let's talk this through so you can help me overcome my reaction. I want your coaching and input."

You can also self-intervene and ask yourself questions when you notice that you are reacting. Ask: "What assumptions am I making? Am I taking this personally instead of hearing the contribution the individual is trying to make?" Reactions such as arguing or explaining why you did something simply reveal that you are human and have automatic behaviors like everyone else.

Coaching is not useful unless committed partners are willing to apply the coaching they receive. Before you categorically reject coaching by saying "I've tried that before and it doesn't work," replace your judgment with curiosity. Consider the coaching carefully, and try it on as if you were trying on a new jacket. Check it out from many different angles to discover something new about how you can be more effective. Then, let others know that you have applied their coaching. Your partners need to know that you listen and that their coaching makes a difference.

GETTING ALL ISSUES ON THE TABLE WHERE THEY CAN BE RESOLVED

You can handle anything that is out in the open. When you are transparent, authentic, and straightforward, people feel safe to speak up and issues are quickly resolved.

Start by asking the right questions. For example, the CEO and senior group were frustrated with production delays. The CEO asked, "What are we going to do about this?" A team member jumped in and said, "Let's ask a different question: How are we—the senior team—accountable for contributing to these delays?" Accountability and ownership of the problem is the precursor for discovering effective solutions.

When others see leaders publicly asking the question "How are we accountable for this problem?" or "How did our behavior contribute to this breakdown?" the work environment starts to shift. When leaders examine their own behavior instead of pointing the finger at others, they set a positive example for the organization. People model the behavior of leaders and start asking the question "How am I personally accountable for this problem or breakdown?" Imagine the velocity with which people make things happen when you have an entire team or organization asking "How am I personally accountable and what can I do to resolve this issue?"

One of the most effective ways to encourage others to speak up and put issues on the table is to start the conversation with something you can genuinely own up to and take accountability for. A senior vice president did this with his group when he said, "I owe you an apology. I haven't been accountable for the problems we keep encountering with delivering to the customer on time. Instead I've been refereeing conflict between two departments hoping they would resolve this issue. Well, that strategy hasn't worked so it's time for me to change my behavior and I'm asking you to do the same. I want us to have an open and honest conversation today—not a free-for-all discussion where we attack one another—so we resolve this issue once and for all." When the senior vice president "walked the talk" and put his behavior in the spotlight, he raised the behavioral standards for others.

HOW COMMITTED PARTNERS HOLD EACH OTHER ACCOUNTABLE

In a high performance organization, leaders expect and anticipate breakdowns. They do not indulge in the illusion that holding each other accountable creates a utopian environment. They know that automatic behaviors will continually resurface. They recognize that they will make mistakes, violate their agreements with committed partners, and undermine relationships and results. But they prepare for the inevitable breakdowns by switching their attention from "How can we avoid breakdowns?" to "How fast can we recover when breakdowns occur?"

Committed partnerships are the foundation for producing exceptional business results. Therefore, you must hold others accountable for both business results and building and sustaining committed partnerships. Only in this way can you build a high performance team and keep it going.

Committed partners look far beyond their immediate team or area and accept accountability for their relationships across all groups in the organization. They do not indulge in the luxury of selecting who they want to be committed partners with; they build committed partnerships everywhere.

Let's bring our focus back to you. As a committed partner, you are accountable for repairing damaged relationships, cleaning up the past, and building and sustaining the partnership. You are also accountable for immediately addressing and resolving any breakdowns. How do you hold yourself and others accountable?

- Do you take accountability and ownership when a breakdown occurs?
- Do you hold others accountable in a positive and supportive manner?
- Are you inconsistent in holding others accountable?
- Do you give others explicit permission to coach you?
- Do you listen to coaching and apply it?

As a committed partner, your job is to foster extraordinary relationships with others and build an environment where people care for each other and the organization. It is also your accountability to hold people up to their greatness and make sure that no one feels isolated or alone.

How Committed Partners Support a Leader in Trouble

Geoff, a highly competent leader of a business operation, was defensive and resistant when others tried to reach out to him during a difficult situation. His group was in trouble and business results were suffering. But instead of listening to input from others, Geoff withdrew and handled things alone.

What Happened. Several colleagues got together and "conspired for" Geoff. Then they met with him and said, *"We know you're having a difficult time. But shutting us out and not letting us support you is not what we committed to. We're your partners and we're not going to allow you to fail, be tough, or act like you can handle this alone."* Geoff was moved by the caring and concern of his peers, and for the first time he stopped covering up and began opening up.

The Breakthrough. Geoff was unaware of the extent to which he had withdrawn and excluded others. After the conversation with his peers, Geoff no longer felt alone and he was able to confidently resolve a situation that had been causing serious problems. Geoff summarized it best when he said, *"I never really understood what holding each other accountable meant until now. It means standing for the success of each other in good times and bad, and not allowing anyone to fail. I was trapped in trying to prove that I could handle this situation by myself and I was wrong. Without my colleagues holding me accountable and supporting me, I would have failed."*

Lesson Learned. Leaders in trouble are leaders in isolation. At the first sign that a leader is going it alone, committed partners pull together and hold the individual accountable for recognizing and correcting his or her course of action. Committed partners shrug off conventional judgments of the individual in trouble and do not label him or her as weak, inadequate, or incapable. Instead they operate with a resounding motto, "Failure is not an option," and stand shoulder to shoulder and face the challenge together.

Committed partners place accountability in the appropriate place. In the situation with Geoff, his peers supported him so Geoff could feel confident and make course corrections. They did not leave him alone to handle the situation. At the same time, they did not rescue or enable Geoff by solving the problem for him. They held Geoff accountable for rising above the circumstances and provided him with unfaltering support.

Leaders in trouble are leaders in isolation.

Do you hold yourself and others accountable for working effectively together? When you see a leader in trouble do you support the leader in turning the situation around? If you have truces or a hands-off arrangement not to interfere with others' areas, then it is impossible to build a high performance team. You must decide if you are committed to the success of others and to living the true meaning of the phrase, "all for one and one for all."

Stop Playing Referee

In a business-as-usual environment, the team leader is often the discussion facilitator, final decision maker, and the "parent" who feels he or she must manage unruly "children." Not so with high performing teams. Team leaders place accountability where it belongs—on people changing their own behavior—and hold them accountable for behaving in a way that advances the group objectives.

How a Team Held Two Adversaries Accountable for Their Behavior

A leadership team was dealing with a conflict between two influential members—Prem and Arty—which was costing the group time and energy. Both individuals had a powerful need to be right and had no qualms about verbally sparring in meetings. It reached a point where the team was spending considerable nonproductive time putting out fires created by the two warring team members.

What Happened. In a team-building session, the conflict between the two sparring members became readily apparent. What also became apparent was how frustrated the team was with how Colleen, the team leader, was handling the situation.

When we asked Colleen why she was allowing this behavior to continue, she responded, *"I've talked to both Prem and Arty and things have improved somewhat."* A team member spoke up and said: *"Nothing has improved for us as a team and we're still wasting time."*

Up until this point Colleen had been able to ignore the impact of Prem and Arty on the group. But when group members began sharing their pent-up frustrations, she listened. They told her that they had calculated time lost in nonproductive conversations over the course of a year, which they estimated at over $300,000. Colleen took accountability and said: *"I've dropped the ball. I haven't held myself accountable and I've tolerated this war between Prem and Arty."* Then Colleen turned to Prem and Arty and said: *"I will not choose between the two of you. I expect you to resolve your differences immediately. I'll support you in any way possible but be clear: I am holding you accountable for resolving this conflict and demonstrating appropriate behavior both in meetings and outside of meetings."*

Lesson Learned. If you are a team leader, you must "walk your talk" if you expect others to follow the same behavioral standards. As you build a high performance culture, people will hold you accountable for higher standards. If you are a team member, you can take action and hold yourself and others accountable for the agreements of your committed partnership. It often takes a member of the group to remind others of their commitment to play big.

DECIDING THAT ANYTHING IS POSSIBLE

Being a fearless leader means giving yourself and each other permission to constructively intervene and hold each other accountable for greatness. Every time you hold each other accountable, you up the ante and make it possible for everyone to reach a higher level of success. You must draw on your inner strength to stand for the success of others while simultaneously placing accountability where it belongs.

The simple fact is that we don't hold people accountable when we don't care. The energy you put into someone is in direct proportion to your depth of caring and partnership. When you hold people accountable for their behavior and results, you are asking them to be an owner and live up to their highest capabilities. Your courage to hold others accountable, confront issues, and be emotionally honest demonstrates your confidence in their ability.

The very act of being a fearless leader alters the context and redefines what is possible. When you change your behavior, everything changes: the dynamic of the relationship, the environment, your partnership with others, and what you can achieve. You are powerful beyond belief when you recognize that you can influence change without expecting others to change.

Your fearless leadership is tested with every decision you make. It is as simple as criticizing or blaming others versus *taking decisive action and holding people accountable as your committed partners*. The rule in high performance is: if something occurs in your head more than once, there is an action you need to take. And that action is not to think more. Nothing happens until you are willing to stand for your commitment to people and the organization and demonstrate it in your behavior.

You must decide that anything is possible. Move beyond any resignation you may have that a conversation will not alter anything; one conversation can alter everything. It can instantly change the context, the relationship, and the future.

LEADERSHIP EXPLORATION

1. **How do you respond to being held accountable?** When others hold you accountable, do you feel criticized or judged? Or do you experience being supported by your committed partners? Ask others how you respond to being held accountable and listen to their feedback.
2. **Do you consistently hold others accountable?** Or do you take a hands-off approach and have unspoken truces not to interfere in another's area? Be honest about whether you hold others accountable or let them off the hook. Whom do you hold accountable? Whom do you not hold accountable?
3. **Do you try to change the behavior of others by pleading, lecturing, berating, or intimidating?** Does it work? Do you believe you can change another's behavior? Do you believe others can change your behavior?
4. **Are you willing to place accountability where it belongs?** If you have been unsuccessful in changing the behavior of others, then it's time to learn how to place accountability where it belongs. To hold others accountable, you must be willing to stand for their success. Most significantly, you must place the locus of control for changing the behavior of others

on them, in the same way you must place the locus of control for changing your behavior on you.

LEADERSHIP ACTION

Take Decisive Action and Stand for the Greatness of Others

Identify an individual or group that you have not held accountable. Follow the steps below:

1. **Start the conversation by establishing the context.** Share your commitment to the success of the person or group, reaffirm your committed partnership or the desire to build one, and commit to mutual business results. The context you establish is crucial in setting the right tone and mood for the conversation.

2. **Take accountability for where you have not fully communicated and held others accountable.** A cautionary note: If you are frustrated and want to take a person to task, hold yourself to account first before having the conversation. Attacking, accusing, or criticizing others achieves nothing. Until you can authentically take accountability for how your behavior has contributed to the problem, you are not ready to hold others to account.

3. **Learn from the breakdown.** Ask, "What have we learned that will help us prevent the same problem from occurring again?" "How can we become more effective in anticipating breakdowns?" "How can we ensure that we hold each other accountable the moment we notice something is off?" "How can we be supportive and constructive when we hold each other accountable?"

Hold Yourself and Others 100% Accountable for Business Results and Impact on People

100% accountability is not a slogan; it is a way of life. There will be times when you fall into the victim mindset, engage in conspiracies against others, and withhold your emotional commitment and enthusiasm. This is normal behavior. *When* it occurs—not *if* it occurs—remember your commitment to playing big and being 100% accountable. You will make mistakes and become frustrated and, perhaps, even resigned. But this is to be expected. Instead of judging yourself or others when a breakdown occurs, simply recover quickly and get back on track.

Here is the secret to playing big and succeeding: Your commitment must be greater than your need to be right. When you commit to being 100% accountable, you are making a life choice that will be tested daily. At all times, stand steadfast in your commitment to this high standard of behavior and you will have the power and freedom to alter what is possible for you and others.

1. **Take action and hold yourself accountable.** Whenever your blind spots and automatic behaviors surface, make a deliberate choice to play big. At that moment you can choose to indulge in your automatic behaviors or take 100% accountability and engage with others in an extraordinary way. Whenever you are faced with this choice, take decisive action, adjust your behavior, and stand steadfast in your commitment to play big.

2. **Take action and hold others accountable.** Stand for the success of others and hold them accountable out of your commitment *to* them, not your judgment *of* them. Hold others up to the greatness they are capable of achieving and do not settle for anything less. Take decisive action the moment you see the need to hold others accountable; do not let your discomfort stop you. Instead, use your discomfort as an indicator that there is something you need to responsibly communicate.

> *Only those who will risk going too far*
> *can possibly find out how far one can go.*
>
> —T.S. Eliot (1888–1965)

Chapter
11

100% Accountability: A New Canvas on Which to Paint the Future

Destiny is no matter of chance, it is a matter of choice;
it is not a thing to be waited for, it is a thing to be achieved.

—WILLIAM JENNINGS BRYAN (1860–1925)

According to legend, in ancient Rome, engineers were compelled to take full accountability for what they built. As the scaffolding was removed from a new Roman arch, the lead engineer who built the structure was required to stand beneath it. If the capstone came crashing down, he would be the first to know (this story illustrates an important point even though tenements in ancient Rome collapsed frequently). The point is that the Roman engineer knew he was 100% accountable for business results and his personal impact on at least *one* person. Millennia before President Truman popularized his famous leadership stand about where the buck stops, Roman engineers firmly grasped, *"The capstone stops here."*

Are you willing to stand under the arch you build and live up to your highest ideals? As a fearless leader you must "break the mold" on old thinking and automatic behavior and propel the organization into a new game with new rules.

This chapter brings together what you can do *right now* to transform yourself, your team, and your organization. The following actions do not require the approval or agreement of others. They are within your power and sphere of influence:

1. Make a purposeful choice to play big.
2. Elevate the context and engage others at the highest level.
3. Learn together and step into greatness.
4. Build networks of committed partnerships everywhere.
5. Measure your success.

MAKE A PURPOSEFUL CHOICE TO PLAY BIG

You would not have invested your time and energy to learn about fearless leadership if it did not resonate with something deep inside of you. I wrote this book for you. As I composed each chapter, I envisioned a world full of fearless leaders, each with an unyielding sense of purpose, a steadfast inner strength, and a bold commitment to triumph over any challenge.

It is likely that you already possess the inner qualities and values needed to be a fearless leader. But do you have the courage to live by these high standards daily and unleash your greatness and the greatness of others? You have two choices in front of you: you can choose to play big and expand your purpose so you can *be* more, which is the key to achieving more, or you can choose to play small and sacrifice the ability to shape the future. It is as simple as that.

When you act as an owner and take a bold stand and decisive action, the future alters. You behave differently, you make different choices, and your actions create a ripple effect in the organization. Your behavior alters everything.

When you choose to play big, the behaviors with which you meet your challenges are

1. Taking 100% accountability regardless of what others choose
2. Working together as committed partners
3. Taking a bold stand and acting decisively

Being a fearless leader releases you from the bondage of false expectations: what others should do, how the world should be different, and how you must shoulder the burden alone. The victim mindset is not for you. You have the power to transform how you relate to any challenge or circumstance. You have infinite capacity to invent and reinvent; with a new canvas in front of you, you can create a masterpiece.

Hope Is Not a Strategy

The thesis of this chapter can be summed up in a Chinese proverb: "Starving man wait long time for roast duck to fly into mouth." Fearless leaders do not wait for anything. They are the authors of the future, the pioneers, and the risk takers who lead others in a purposeful march toward greatness. They create a new leadership context for how people work together. They build a culture of accountability where people are inspired to grow and excel, and they stay the course.

This does not mean that as a fearless leader, you will have a life unencumbered by challenges or breakdowns. There will always be difficulties and complications in business and in life. The world will always test your mettle through new battles, struggles, and obstacles. If your hope is for a perfect world, you will live in a permanent state of dissatisfaction. The world is not perfect and never will be. You have far too much talent, passion, and commitment to let your future ride on the mercurial wings of hope—wishing that things or people were different.

> **Hope Is Not a Strategy**
> Stop wishing for others to change, and transform yourself.

You have a much greater purpose. You cannot afford to squander your energy and vitality on things that are not worthy of you. I am asking you to rise above your automatic behavior and stop wasting your time in the futile effort of trying to change people and circumstances. I am not suggesting that you settle for things as they are. You must never, never settle for anything less than your highest ideals and convictions. I am asking you to direct your full force of will on transforming yourself and engaging with others in an extraordinary way.

Becoming resigned, getting stuck in victim mentality, and playing small is natural and normal. This will happen over and over again. Learn from your mistakes and with your committed partners, and acknowledge that you are perfect in your imperfection. Blind spots are of no consequence when you have the courage to confront and own them and recover quickly.

There will be times when you will be petty and small-minded. This is normal behavior. You will react, and you will believe that you are completely right and everyone else is totally wrong. But you cannot indulge in your need to be right. At these times, you must remember your resolve is to be effective, not be right. Catch yourself when you react and alter your behavior in the moment. Hold yourself and others accountable to a higher standard of behavior and performance.

Do not be enslaved by a mindset that diminishes and weakens your call to expand what you and your organization can achieve. When you become resigned again—and you will—remember you have committed partners who will stand beside you to face any challenge. Together, you will scale the mountain that not long ago appeared impossible to climb.

Use Your New Road Map

I am asking you to take on the challenge of continual transformation. Transform who you are, and do not allow anything or anyone to stop you, including your "smaller" self. There is much more for you to do. As a fearless leader, you must persistently demonstrate your conviction of purpose, particularly when you are caught in a vortex of confusion and upheaval. It is here you must ask "Where am I playing small?"

You now have a new and powerful road map for self-intervention and being a committed partner to others. Let's bring together the questions I have been asking you throughout the book. These questions focus your attention on what you *can* do and stop the automatic behavior of fixating on what others *should* do. Every time you hit an impasse ask

1. **Where am I not taking 100% accountability?** How is my action—or lack of action—contributing to this situation or breakdown?
2. **What am I withholding from others?** Where am I withholding my partnership, straight talk, commitment, enthusiasm, or support?

3. **What decisive actions do I need to take?** Where do I need to take a bold stand, commit to the success of others, clean up a relationship, talk straight responsibly, authentically align, or hold myself and others accountable?
4. **What requests do I need to make of others?** Where am I complaining or conspiring with others instead of making a clear and direct request to the appropriate person? Where am I holding back and not being direct? What request do I need to make now?

You must be willing to take pure, in the moment action to fearlessly lead others. If you vacillate with the winds of change, it will keep everyone off balance. When you provide people with a uniform set of behaviors and the tools to learn and practice new skills, they will raise the standard of behavior for everyone and you will see leaders emerge at all levels.

Fearless leadership is a transformational methodology for excelling and achieving results. You can apply it to a team, business group, or the entire organization. You can transform corporate values into enduring and consistent behaviors of 100% accountability and committed partnerships.

ELEVATE THE CONTEXT AND ENGAGE OTHERS AT THE HIGHEST LEVEL

One of your most powerful tools for engaging people is a compelling context that captures both hearts and minds. Every time you speak to a group or an individual, you have an opportunity to provide them with a framework that powerfully connects them to the larger purpose.

Let's revisit how context determines how people perceive reality. Context defines focus, meaning, purpose, and direction; and it defines what people observe, act upon, and produce.

When you provide only an intellectual context, you will engage some people but you lose the majority. However, when you provide an emotional and intellectual context, people are inspired to act. The question is "Do you want people to merely understand your message, or do you want them to take action and help you achieve your goals?"

A marketing vice president known for his penchant for details, said to his group: "Our market share has dropped 21 percent in the past two years. I am going to review the specific changes we are making to address this issue." Leaders often become mired in the details of a challenge or problem and forget the larger purpose. But it is purpose that drives people to do something differently, not information alone. In this example, the vice president provided information. But this is useful only if the context has already been established. By themselves information-only messages do not inspire people to take up arms and fight the battle. Context is not something you can communicate once and then forget. You must continually communicate the context at every opportunity so people remain connected to the larger mission.

Most leaders have been taught the conventional and often tedious approach of presenting their message by stating: "Here's the problem, here's what we've done in the past, and here's what we're going to do in the future." But *the message is not compelling*. People are not inspired by information alone. They are inspired by your courage, your stand, and your willingness to be authentic and real.

A CEO faced with an aggressive competitor who was encroaching on the company's market share said to her leadership group: "I didn't see the urgency of a problem that many of you have been talking about. Our competitors are breathing down our necks and whittling away at our market share. I now clearly see what is happening and what we need to do, and we are going to act quickly. This is my stand: We will outsmart our competitors, we will outmaneuver them, and we will take back what we have lost, plus more. I don't have all the answers, but I know I have your partnership and you have my commitment. We will be the market leaders and be known as the best in our industry. Now let's talk about how we will do this."

The CEO's message was authentic and powerful because she connected with her leaders on an emotional level. She rallied them by taking accountability for not acting quickly and by taking a bold stand that was both decisive and inspiring. Finally, she elevated the context and reconnected leaders to the larger mission: being the best. Her message is an example of a context that instills urgency and galvanizes people to fight the foe together.

The Critical Path from Concept to Content to Context

Leaders often miss the distinctions between concept, content, and context. Here's a simple quiz: are the phrases "high performance," "fearless leadership," "100% accountability," and "committed partnerships" concepts, content, or context? The answer is: they are all of the above depending upon how leaders communicate them to others.

Using the term *high performance* as an example, let's examine how you can transform it from a concept to a compelling context. As you read each approach below, identify your natural inclination. Do you attempt to engage others by discussing theoretical concepts, delving into detailed content, or by providing an inspiring context?

High Performance as a Concept. A *concept* is a thought, idea, or notion conceived in the mind. As a concept, high performance is an intellectual abstraction. For example: "High performance is a model for achieving optimal effectiveness and maximum profitability." Leaders who are stimulated by intellectual abstraction and thought-provoking theories are frequently intrigued with new concepts or ideas.

High Performance as Content. *Content* refers to the composition, texture, and configuration of an idea. When referring to high performance as content, it takes on substance as details are presented. For example: "High performing teams yield 10 times the productivity of business-as-usual teams." Content focuses on fine points, facts, and information.

High Performance as Context. *Context* provides people with a larger frame of reference, a compelling mission, and personal meaning. It provides the emotional framework that generates personal commitment. For example: "Every day we must each make the personal choice to work together as a high performance team. There are days when I forget to apply the behaviors we have learned. Then one of you reminds me that I need to take accountability for my impact. At that moment, I remember our larger mission and forget my own pettiness. This is what I am asking of you: keep our purpose in front of you at all times. For us, high performance is not some lofty concept; it is a way of life. We are learning and growing together and as committed partners, we are unbeatable."

This message calls for people to take personal accountability for how they choose to behave every day. The message emotionally connects people to the larger mission. No longer is the goal an abstraction; it is something that every person can influence and contribute to.

How do you communicate to others? Do you talk about a concept, content, or context? If you are a *concept* person who finds ideas, intellectual abstractions, theories, and high-level thinking fascinating, you will most likely use this approach to engage others. You probably talk about lofty ideas and high-level strategies. Unfortunately, concepts by themselves lack practical, on-the-ground action to make them useful. Even though you may clearly see how the concept applies, others may not see it without a powerful context.

If you are a *content* person—someone who loves details and facts and figuring out the process from A to Z—you will use this approach to persuade others. The problem is that not everyone shares your love of details. Although it may surprise you, your facts are not compelling to everyone. Leaders often tell us that they must overcome years of technical thinking in order to learn a new way to engage and motivate people.

If you are a *context* person, your natural proclivity is to inspire people with a visionary message and a compelling purpose. What you must ask yourself is "Am I providing a compelling *personal* mission for people to engage at a higher level of performance?" Although you may be providing an organizational or business context, by itself this is not sufficient to gain the discretionary effort and commitment you will need from people to achieve your business mission.

To provide a personal context, you must raise the standard of behavior and help people learn and grow. You must put yourself and your behavior on the line and lead by example. People need to see how you struggle, recover, and overcome blind spots so they have a new model for winning together.

To create a credible personal context, do the following:

1. **Articulate the new behavior that is needed.** Highlight the new action, thinking, and speaking needed. For example: *"We are going to do something that our competitors aren't doing—build committed partnerships with our customers.*

We must think and behave differently so we can discover new ways to forge our relationship with our customers."

2. **Tap the inherent desire and capacity of people to learn and grow.** For example: *"I want each of us to learn together and fully tap our potential. We'll learn how to build committed partnerships with each other and with our customers. I will be learning right along with you. With these new skills, we will accomplish our business objectives."*

3. **Invite others to make a personal choice and partner with you.** For example: *"I need your partnership—I can't do this alone. And, I don't want your compliance; I want your alignment. The power to shape our future is in your hands. Will you join me in building committed partnerships with our customers?"*

4. **Connect to a compelling business objective.** For example: *"Our mission is clear—we will deliver a world-class customer experience. We will achieve this because of your commitment to engage with our customers in an extraordinary way."*

You do not need to be the CEO to establish a powerful context. Every project, endeavor, and relationship requires a context. Regardless of title or position, it is within your power to expand the context and emotionally engage others every time you speak. It requires only a sentence or two to reconnect people to their personal commitment and the organization's larger mission.

LEARN TOGETHER AND STEP INTO GREATNESS

When people learn how to be committed partners, they discover a new way to communicate with one another that they did not have access to before. This is far more impactful than leaders realize. When people discover that they have the power to influence others and shape the future, they apply new skills and behavior to all areas of their life—at work and at home. The positive results they produce drive them to learn and achieve more. The new behaviors become embedded because people make a *life choice* to change their behavior. This crossover between work life and personal life is powerful testimony to what people want and need: a way to be more effective in all areas of their life. Corporate values become much more than words; they become powerful behavioral practices that are integrated into the fabric of your organization.

You now have a methodology for discussing blind spots without offending, talking straight about breakdowns without blaming, and holding each other accountable without reprimanding. You can build a learning organization where people are excited about learning and growing together.

BUILD NETWORKS OF COMMITTED PARTNERSHIPS EVERYWHERE

A leader asked me, "If I can't change the behavior of others, what can I do?" My answer: "The real work. You can transform yourself, be a committed partner, and ask others to join you." Transforming your behavior and building a culture of accountability demonstrates that you are serious about your commitment to organizational change. You will no longer need to referee conflict or be the only person who is holding people accountable. With uniform behavioral standards and shared skill sets, each individual will take 100% accountability for raising the level of performance of the organization.

Let's underscore the point of building committed partnerships: to produce consistent, superior business results. Committed partnerships are a competitive advantage as the example below demonstrates.

Leaders Build a Profitable Committed Partnership with a Strategic Customer

The senior team of a major business unit in a worldwide chemical company asked our organization to help them build a committed partnership with a strategic customer. There were significant challenges with the customer, and the chemical company had been unsuccessful in resolving them.

What Happened. In meeting with the senior team from the chemical company, we saw that although they wanted an effective relationship with the customer, their fixed views and opinions were preventing this from happening. It took focused and rigorous discussions to help the group alter their fixed judgments about the customer and overcome entrenched behaviors of blaming the customer for breakdowns.

A combined meeting was set up for the chemical company's senior team and the customer's senior team. In this joint meeting, several members from the senior team of the chemical company spoke up and took accountability for recent breakdowns and genuinely apologized for their impact. The customer was stunned, in a good way. Unsolicited, customer team members stepped up and took accountability for how they had reacted and contributed to the problem. By the end of an intensive two-day meeting, both teams came together and formed a committed partnership. The energy and excitement was palpable, and the combined team was buzzing with innovative ideas.

The New Canvas. Both teams reported that their committed partnership not only changed how they worked together, it allowed them to bring a new technology to market in record time. Historically, it had taken two years from concept to commercialization, but this new team successfully brought the new technology to market in less than 12 months. A customer team member stated, *"We broke the mold on the traditional supplier-customer model. Instead of two adversarial teams protecting our individual interests, we now operate as one team. We work better, faster, smarter, and revenues for both companies reflect this."*

Lesson Learned. A single team can build a committed partnership with another group if they are willing to take 100% accountability. When one group acts as the owner of the relationship for both groups and takes accountability (not blame) for the problems and breakdowns, the dynamic instantly changes and new possibilities emerge.

Does your group or business unit have committed partnerships with both your internal and external customers? If this is something you believe will add value to the bottom line, then start by building committed partnerships within your group. Everyone must operate with the same methodology and skill sets. When your group genuinely accepts ownership of the problem or breakdown, you are ready to engage with the customer group. Being a fearless leader lets you think big and build committed partnerships with customers, the community, and other stakeholders.

MEASURE YOUR SUCCESS

Teams and individuals often lose sight of how radically they have changed their behavior unless they measure their progress and record their breakthroughs. The assessment in the sidebar "Are We Playing Big?" can be used by individuals or teams to reinforce the new leadership context of 100% accountability and committed partnerships. Monitor the results so

---

Are We Playing Big?

Directions: Use the following scale to rate yourself or the team:

1. Seldom if at all   4. Often
2. Occasionally   5. Consistently
3. Sometimes

100% Accountability

- I take 100% accountability for business results and my impact on others.
- I do not use excuses or reasons to justify the lack of results.
- When there is a breakdown, I take accountability and do not blame others.
- I own my blind spots and do not justify or defend them.
- I actively seek coaching and apply it.
- I take a bold stand and decisive action.
- I do not engage in conspiracies against individuals or groups.
- I respect cultural differences and build understanding and partnership across cultural lines.

Committed Partnerships

- I stand for the success of others both privately and publicly.
- I honor and fulfill commitments.
- I talk straight responsibly.
- I align emotionally and intellectually as if I authored the decision myself; I suspend my personal agenda and support the enterprise mission.
- I consistently hold myself and others accountable for playing big at all times.

you can compare how people view their progress and their team. Record team breakthroughs so everyone can see how their behavior directly impacts business results.

A NEW CANVAS ON WHICH TO PAINT THE FUTURE

To paraphrase Vitruvius's seminal work De Architectura, let's recall the story of Archimedes. He decided to take a bath, and while getting into the water, he noticed something for the first time. Archimedes became consciously aware that the level of the water in the tub rose as he got in, and at that moment he had a breakthrough of epic proportions: "Wow. I just invented how to measure material density. The King is going to pay me some major drachmas for this. Eureka!" Archimedes screamed and took to the streets naked, having forgotten to dress.

How many times do you miss what is right in front of you? How many times do your preconceived judgments prevent you from noticing something new? How many possibilities do you shut down? How many opportunities elude you? As a fearless leader, you must be proactive and continually ask questions that expand your scope of vision:

1. **What am I not seeing?** What is right in front of me that I am missing? What am I avoiding? How can my committed partners help me view this situation differently?
2. **What opportunities and possibilities are right in front of me?** What assumptions or judgments are getting in my way? How is my need to be right getting in my way? Where do I need to take accountability for my blind spots and genuinely listen to others?
3. **What can I learn from this breakdown or situation?** Why is this challenge in front of me at this time? How did my behavior contribute to this breakdown? What is preventing me from acting quickly to resolve this issue? What can I do differently so I will not repeat this breakdown again?

What is right in front of you, which is often missed, is the fact that you have the choice and capacity to play big at any time. You have the ability to transform yourself and move people and the organization to a higher level of effectiveness. You must decide that anything is possible and inspire this same level of confidence in others. Your willingness to be relentless in changing *your* behavior and modeling how leaders are expected to behave is your ticket to success.

I am making a clear and direct request of you to express your fearless leadership each day in how you engage with others. We need fearless leaders everywhere. Your courage and passion are needed to build a future that liberates people from the shackles of blind spots, so they can contribute to their fullest potential. You have the power to shape the future by putting a space between stimulus and response, as Viktor Frankl described it, and make a purposeful choice to engage with others in an extraordinary way.

I am asking you to be fearless and lead the way for others. Guide them through challenges by working together as committed partners to achieve the common good. Your actions will transform not only you; they will transform what is possible for everyone.

> **The Path of Fearless Leaders**
> When you feel alone, reach out for your committed partners.
> When you stumble and fall, recover quickly.
> When you succeed beyond your expectations, acknowledge everyone's contribution and climb higher.

Thank you for the privilege of allowing me to be your partner in this important exploration. Intellectually understanding the concepts we have discussed is one thing, but applying them is fearless leadership in action. In writing this book, I have encountered my own blind spots and challenges. Each time I hit a barrier, I remembered my larger mission: to drive your leadership effectiveness to new heights where the impossible becomes possible. Without knowing it, you have inspired me. I acknowledge you for your commitment to play big and be big. And I thank you for the significant difference you will make in the lives of many, many others. The footstep of one person creates a path for everyone.

The die is cast.

—GAIUS JULIUS CAESAR (100–44 BC)

About the Author and Malandro Communication

A s president and CEO of Malandro Communication since its inception in 1980, Loretta Malandro has built a leading business consulting firm that specializes in leadership and organizational transformation.

Delivering its proven technology—100% Accountability™—the Malandro organization works worldwide with CEOs, executives, and leaders to take their corporations to new levels of performance by skillfully aligning and mobilizing people to drive enterprise objectives. The 100% accountability methodology is a beginning-to-end process for achieving leadership alignment, building a culture of accountability, and producing lasting behavioral change to ensure sustainability.

A key differentiator of the Malandro group is the ability to combine a strong business and organizational perspective with expert intervention. The Malandro behavioral experts relentlessly uncover and permanently resolve the root cause of leadership and organizational ineffectiveness. Their services include executive consulting and coaching, breakthrough project consulting, high performance leadership sessions, high performance team sessions, and turnkey communication tools for rapidly diffusing cultural change throughout an organization.

Delivering consulting services globally and at its corporate headquarters in Scottsdale, Arizona, USA, the Malandro organization develops and customizes the approach best suited to address the unique needs of each client. Providing full support for leadership and organizational transformation, Malandro certifies client candidates in the 100% accountability process to deliver the methodology throughout their organizations.

Selected clients include AngloGold Ashanti, CNA, De Beers, DuPont, Farm Credit Canada, Finning International, IBM, Idaho Power, Intel,

Nexen, Placer Dome Inc., Rabo AgriFinance, Rohm and Haas, Xerox, Vale Inco, and Zurich Financial Services.

Dr. Malandro is the author of the international book *Say It Right the First Time* and other landmark books, including *Courtroom Communication Strategies* and *Nonverbal Communication*. She is a former professor at Florida State and Arizona State universities. She received her Ph.D. in communication theory and research from Florida State University and her undergraduate degree from Kent State University. The recipient of many academic awards, Malandro was on the first international debate team cosponsored by the U.S. government and the National Speech Association, where she and teammates debated in the Russian language throughout the former Soviet Union.

Malandro Communication
Scottsdale, Arizona, USA
Telephone: 480-970-3200
Web site: www.malandro.com
E-mail: partners@malandro.com

Acknowledgments

This book is dedicated to two groups of fearless leaders: (1) the CEOs and executives who have inspired me to reach higher, go further, and be more, and (2) my exceptional consulting partners who deliver our work worldwide and consistently demonstrate their commitment to excellence.

The first group—leaders who take a bold stand, act decisively, and engage with others in an extraordinary way—is responsible for indelibly shaping my lifelong path and work in organizations worldwide. Each leader has contributed to the methodology presented in this book and has been a teacher in my life. I am indebted to them for the level of trust they have placed in my organization over the years.

> Chip U'ren, Dan Minor, David M.Thomas, Dennis Chookaszian, Don Budinger, Don Hurzeler, Frank Patalano, Frank Proto, Dr. George Buckley, Gian Fulgoni, Greg Honey, Greg Stewart, Hal Logan, Jack Mulroney, Janet Plaut Giesselman, Jeremy Wyeth, Jim Gowans, John Pemberton, John J. Ryan, John Talucci, John Van Brunt, John Willson, Joy Serne, Dr. Kevin Toomb, J. LaMont Keen, Dr. Larry Barker, Larry Biederman, Mark Cutifani, Dr. Mark Daniel, Marvin Romanow, Dr. Michael Fitzpatrick, Michael A. Friedman MD, Michael Winship, Mike Waites, Phil du Toit, Phil Engel, Raj Gupta, Robert Van Gieson, Stephen Hamlin, Steve Thomas, and Tapani Jarvinen.

The fearless leaders in the second group are my consulting partners who passionately deliver our work worldwide. They are the real authors for they deliver our metholodgy, shape it to address our clients' needs, and consistently produce exceptional results. They actively research, develop, test, expand, and refine our methodology. Each consulting partner has made a unique contribution to this book and our organization, but it is the collective power of this extraordinary group of people that is responsible for our success today. I am fortunate to be surrounded by a world-class consulting team, and I thank all the members for their heartfelt dedication and commitment.

I extend my deep gratitude to Jim Poole, the strategic and transformational leader of our business and writing team. He was unrelenting in providing our team with a clear direction and vision for what this book could be, and he personally held me accountable for producing the best result possible. My deep appreciation and thanks go to Ron Bynum, my personal coach and friend, who contributed significantly by generating ideas, pushing me to consider different perspectives, and encouraging me every step of the way. Sharon Ellis, my longtime friend and business associate, has read the material for this book more than anyone else; she has provided not only valuable input, but she also has inspired me during both the highs and lows of the arduous process of writing a book. I also thank Frank Picarello for his insightful review of the manuscript in its early stages.

Special thanks go to Carolyn Gill for her tireless editorial input and artistic contributions. Thanks also go to Valerie Demetros for her valuable editorial guidance and content contributions, and to Ruth Mills for her input and direction. For their expertise and enthusiastic support, I am deeply appreciative of the McGraw-Hill team headed by Mary Glenn.

For her generosity of spirit and love of life, I thank my mother, Josephine. Although now deceased, she has shaped who I am today and lives on in my life. And to my father, Rudy, who always reminds me that he is the first "Dr. Malandro": thank you for your steadfast love and support.

Finally, to the thousands of leaders I have traveled with on this path of transformation over the years: I thank each of you for your commitment to playing big. You are my heroes and my inspiration.

Index

Accountability:
  abdication of, need to be right and,
    82–83
  50/50, 105–106
  100% (*see* 100% accountability)
  100%-zero, 150–151, 159, 162–163
  resolving past issues and, 165–168
  taking, 126
  talking straight and, 213–214
  (*See also* Holding each other
    accountable)
Action:
  decisive, taking despite discomfort,
    125–127
  future, aligning on, 215–216
  turning insight into, 84–85
  (*See also* Leadership action)
Adversaries, holding accountable, 262–263
Agreements of committed partners,
    157–164
Alignment, 219–246
  authentic (*see* Authentic alignment)
  as concept versus behavior, 225–226
  emotional commitment and, 222–224
  energy and, 244
  forcing compliance versus engaging
    alignment and, 227
  as learned behavior, 220
  oppositional speaking that escalates
    conflict and, 226–227
  tolerating "good enough" and,
    224–225

Alternatives, failure to investigate,
    73–74
Ambiguity (*see* Uncertainty)
Apologizing, 126
Assumptions, automatic listening and,
    76–79
Authentic alignment, 228–243
  clarity in decision making and,
    229–235
  factors deterring, 221–227,
    245–246
  levels of, 235–242, 246
  meaning of, 220–221
  rules of engagement in high perfor-
    mance meetings and, 242–243
Authentic commitments, 184, 189–190
  guidelines for, 192–193
Automatic listening, 75–81
  assumptions and, 76–79
  exceptions and, 79–80
  victim mentality and, 102
Avoiding difficult conversations/
    situations:
  as blind spot, 44–46
  moving toward situations versus,
    119–127
  price of, 200–205

Barriers to change, 6–16
  behavioral blind spots as, 11–16
  ignoring unproductive behavior as,
    14–16

Behavior:
  alignment as concept versus behavior
      and, 225–226
  blind spots and (*see* Blind spots,
      behavioral)
  as determining factor in accountability,
      256
  discomfort with discussing, 15
  identifying, 31–32
  need for change in, 7–8
  need for explicit standards for,
      18–20
Beliefs, 108–109
Berating, 254, 255
Blaming others or circumstances as
      blind spot, 46–48
Blind spots, behavioral, 11–16, 33–62
  avoiding difficult conversations as,
      44–46
  blaming others or circumstances as,
      46–48
  confronting, 57–60
  conspiring against others as, 50–52
  definition, 11
  discussing openly, 130–131, 136,
      138
  going it alone as, 38–40
  "I know" attitude as, 4–44
  insensitivity to one's impact on
      others as, 40–42
  need to be right and (*see* Need to be
      right)
  not taking a stand as, 54–56
  tolerating "good enough" as, 56–57
  treating commitments casually as,
      48–50
  unidentified, 34–38
  vehicular blind spots compared, 11
  withholding emotional commitment
      as, 52–53

Breakdowns:
  aligning on recovery from, 169
  committed partnerships and,
      146–148
  talking straight and, 214–215
  (*See also* Conflict; Problem resolution)
Breakthroughs, 28–29
Building a case to prove you are right,
      73
Business success, committed partner-
      ships for, 146–148

Casual promises, 184–185
Change:
  factors impeding, 6–16
  100% accountability and, 25
  organizational transformation and,
      17–22
  transformation versus, 120–133
Clean up, 165–168
Coaching, 256–258
  giving, 257
  receiving, 258
Co-conspirator role, 99
Commitment(s), 173–197
  authentic, 184, 192–193
  avoidance of, 126
  clarity about making, 190–194
  committed partners' relationship to,
      174–183
  credibility, trust, and confidence
      and, 175–176
  emotional (*see* Emotional commitment)
  emotionally and intellectually com-
      mitted level of alignment and,
      236–237, 240–241, 246
  excuses for failing to fulfill, 177–180
  gaining versus unleashing, 20–22
  holding leaders accountable for,
      250–251

Commitment(s) *(Cont.)*:
  honoring, 189
  intellectually committed level of
    alignment and, 236, 239–240
  language of, 182–183, 191–192
  making requests for, 194–195
  managing, 189–190
  managing requests for, 195
  to one another's success, 164
  promises compared with, 183–190
  revoking, 193–194
  talking straight and, 213–214
  team reaction to leader's lack of,
    176–177
  treating casually, as blind spot,
    48–50
  your word as your bond and,
    180–182
Committed partnerships, 23–24,
    145–172
  agreements of partners and, 157–164
  becoming a committed partner and,
    137, 139
  building, 131–132, 164–169
  building networks of, 276–277
  business success related to, 146–148
  calling for, 136, 138
  committing to one another's success
    and, 164
  communicating expectations and,
    169
  focusing on mission-critical objectives,
    136, 138
  holding each other accountable and,
    259–263
  long-term advantage of, 169
  ownership and, 151–157
  resolving past issues and, 165–168
  trust and, 151–157
  working together and, 148–151

Communication, 169
  oppositional speaking and, 226–227
  precision of, 208–209
  (*See also* Language; Talking straight)
Compliance:
  as barrier to authentic alignment,
    222–224
  complying level of alignment and,
    236, 238–239
  forcing, engaging alignment versus, 227
Complying level of alignment, 236,
    238–239
Concerned level of alignment, 236,
    238
Conditional circle of trust, 155
Confidence, commitments and, 175–176
Conflict:
  holding each other accountable and,
    262–263
  oppositional speaking and, 226–227
Conspiring against others:
  as blind spot, 50–52
  cleaning the slate, 168
  examples of, 100
Conspiring for one another, committed
    partnerships and, 158–161
Constructive intervention, 256–258
Context:
  engaging people and, 271–275
  personal, expanding, 90–96
Conversations:
  difficult, avoiding (*see* Avoiding
    difficult conversations/situations)
  private, making public, 209
Counterintuitive thinking, for transfor-
    mation, 123–127
Courage:
  to confront blind spots, 60
  to take 100% accountability, 127–128
  for taking a stand, 129

Covering up, accountability and, 252
Credibility, commitments and, 175–176
Cultural differences, talking straight
  and, 210–211

Decision making, declaring decision
  types and, 229–235
Decisive action, taking despite discomfort,
  125–127
Denial, moving beyond, 90
Difficult conversations/situations,
  avoiding (*see* Avoiding difficult
  conversations/situations)
Discomfort:
  gaining comfort with, 207
  moving toward versus avoiding
    uncomfortable situations and,
    119–127
  taking decisive action in spite of,
    125–127
  (*See also* Avoiding difficult conversa-
    tions/situations)

Effectiveness, trading for being right,
  68–70
Either-or thinking, 74
Emotional commitment:
  convincing versus enlisting and,
    134–135
  emotionally and intellectually
    committed level of alignment
    and, 236–237, 240–241, 246
  transformation and, 120–133
  withholding, as barrier to authentic
    alignment, 222–224
  withholding, as blind spot, 52–53
  (*See also* Taking a stand)
Emotional honesty, 207–208
Emotionally and intellectually committed
  level of alignment, 236–237, 240–241

Energy, high performance teams and, 244
Engaging people, 136, 138
  context and, 271–275
Evidence, gathering to prove you are
  right, 73
Exceptions, automatic listening and,
  81–84
Excuses for failing to fulfill commitments, 177–180

Fear, moving toward versus avoiding
  uncomfortable situations and,
  119–127
Fearless leadership, 3–32
  acting as owner and, 127–128
  behavioral change needed for, 7–8
  being unreasonable and, 132
  building committed partnerships
    and, 131–132
  characteristics of, 22–25
  confronting blind spots and, 57–60
  decision to become a fearless leader,
    25–27
  definition of, 4
  five requirements for, 127–132
  getting outside victim triangle and, 99
  invitation to become a fearless
    leader and, 28–29
  moving toward versus avoiding issues
    and, 119–127
  need for, 18
  openly discussing blind spots and,
    130–131
  promise and results of, 5–6
  purposeful choice to play big and,
    268–271
  taking a bold stand and, 129–130
  taking 100% accountability and,
    127–128
  what it is and is not, 110–111

Flexibility, loss of, need to be right and, 83–84

Future:
new path for, 279–280
vision of, inspiring people and, 137, 139

Future action, aligning on, 215–216

Going it alone as blind spot, 38–40

"Good enough" (*see* Tolerating "good enough")

Groups:
conflict between, victim mentality and, 103
teams contrasted with, 22–23

Holding each other accountable, 247–266
adversaries and, 262–263
by committed partners, 259–263
constructive intervention and, 256–258
covering up for each other and, 252
eliminating reasons and holding people accountable for results and, 252–253
getting all the issues on the table and, 258–259
locating accountability in the proper place and, 251–256
openness to possibilities and, 263–264
supporting a leader in trouble and, 260–262

Honesty, emotional, 207–208

"I know" attitude as blind spot, 4–44

Indecision as blind spot, 54–56

Inner circle of trust, 154–155

Insensitivity to one's impact on others as blind spot, 40–42

Insight, turning into action, 84–85

Inspiring people, 140–141
vision of future and, 137, 139

Intellectually committed level of alignment, 236, 239–240

Intention:
expecting others to judge you by, 71–73
positive, listening for, 161–164

Intimidating, 254, 255

Issues, putting on the table (*see* Putting all issues on the table)

Language:
of commitment, 182–183
igniting victim mentality, 101–102
owner, 101–102
(*See also* Talking straight)

Leadership:
committed partners' support of leader in trouble and, 260–262
fearless (*see* Fearless leadership)
inaccurate assumptions of, 19–20

Leadership action:
accountability and, 265–266
alignment and, 245–246
asking team to coach you on your blind spots and, 61–62
commitments and, 196–197
committed partnerships and, 171–172
identifying how you relate to organization and others and, 31–32
initiating clean ups, 171–172
need to be right and, 86–87
taking a stand and, 142–143
talking straight and, 217–218
victim mentality and, 113–114

Leadership exploration:
accountability and, 264–265
alignment and, 244–245
avoiding critical conversations and, 217
behaviors tolerated and endorsed and, 30–31
cleaning up and taking accountability, 170
commitments and, 195–196
committed partnerships and, 170–171
identifying blind spots and, 60–61
need to be right and, 85–86
taking a stand and, 141–142
victim mentality and, 111–113
Leadership transformation, organizational transformation and, 17–22
Lecturing, 254, 255
Listening:
automatic, 75–81, 102
for emotional meaning, 126
for positive intention, 161–164

Need to be right, 63–87
automatic listening and, 75–81
blind spots combined with, 66–68
consequences of, 81–84
factors creating fixation on, 70–74
letting go of, 84–85
reasons for, 64–66
strength of, 63
trading relationships and effectiveness for being right and, 68–70

100% accountability, 106–108, 267–280
acceptance by committed partners, 149–151
building networks of committed partners and, 276–277
choosing purposefully, 268–271

100% accountability (*Cont.*):
courage to take, 127–128
critical path from concept to content to context and, 273–275
engaging others and, 271–275
future path and, 279–280
holding each other accountable and (*see* Holding each other accountable)
learning together and, 275–276
measuring success and, 278–279
responsibility compared with, 106
100%-zero accountability, 150–151, 162–163
Oppositional speaking, 226–227
Organization, reconnecting people to (*see* Reconnecting people to organization)
Organizational transformation:
leadership transformation and, 17–22
unleashing commitment and, 20–22
Outer circle of trust, 155
Owner language, 101–102
Owner mentality, 106–107
Ownership:
acting as owner and, 127–130
committed partnerships and, 151–157

Partnerships, committed (*see* Committed partnerships)
Persecutor role, 98–99
Personal context, expanding, 90–96
Pie-in-the-sky promises, 184, 187–189
Playing big versus playing small, 89–114
creating what you believe and, 108–111
50/50 accountability and, 105–106
100% accountability and, 106–108

Playing big versus playing small *(Cont.)*:
  personal context and, 90–92
  purposeful choice to play big and,
    268–271
  resignation and, 93–96
  victim mentality and (*see* Victim
    mentality)
Pleading, 254, 255
Problem resolution:
  ineffective, need to be right and, 83
  (*See also* Breakdowns; Conflict)
Promises, commitment compared with,
    183–190
Putting all issues on the table:
  holding each other accountable and,
    258–259
  talking straight and, 209

Reasons, results and, 252–253
Reconnecting people to organization,
    132–140
  convincing versus enlisting and,
    134–135
  taking a stand and, 132–140
Referee, avoiding playing role of,
    262–263
Relationships, trading for being right,
    68–70
Requests for commitments, making and
    managing, 194–195
Resignation:
  playing big versus playing small and,
    93–96
  victim mentality and, 96
Resigned level of alignment, 236,
    237–238
Results, reasons and, 252–253
Results orientation, 22, 24–25
Revoking commitments, 193–194
Rigidity as blind spot, 42–44

Rules of engagement, in high perfor-
    mance organizations, 242–243

Secrets, 203–205
Self-sufficiency as blind spot, 38–40
Situations, difficult, avoiding
    (*see* Avoiding difficult conversa-
    tions/situations)
Slippery promises, 184, 186–187
Straight talk (*see* Talking straight)
Success:
  committed partnerships for, 146–148
  measuring, 278–279

Taking a stand, 23, 115–143
  courage for, 129
  elements of, 135–140
  failure to take a stand and
    (*see* Indecision)
  moving toward versus avoiding issues
    and, 119–127
  reconnecting people to organization
    and, 132–140
Talking straight, 199–218
  accountability and, 213–214
  aligning on future action and, 215–216
  asking permission for, 214–215
  being willing to be uncomfortable
    and, 207
  cultural sensitivity and, 210–211
  emotional honesty and, 207–208
  precision and, 208–209
  price of avoiding difficult conversa-
    tions and, 200–205
  putting all issues on the table and,
    209
  requiring straight talk from your
    group and, 210
  speaking responsibly and, 208–209
  as a team, 216–217

Teams:
asking to coach you on your blind
spots, 61–62
groups contrasted with, 22–23
lack of leader's commitment and,
176–177
talking straight and, 216–217
Thoughts, identifying, 31–32
Tolerating "good enough":
as barrier to authentic alignment,
224–225
as blind spot, 56–57
Transformation:
change versus, 120–133
counterintuitive thinking for,
123–127
leadership and organizational, 17–22
ongoing nature of, 109–110
unleashing commitment and, 20–22
Treating commitments casually as blind
spot, 48–50
Truces, unspoken, 252
Trust:
building, breaking up victim triangle
and, 103–105
commitments and, 175–176
committed partnerships and,
151–157
purposefully expanding circle of,
152–157

Trust *(Cont.)*:
resolving issues concerning,
165–168
treating commitments casually and,
48–50
Truth, seeing your own perceptions as,
71

Uncertainty:
keeping level low, 202–203
moving toward versus avoiding issues
and, 119–127
Unidentified blind spots, 34–38
Unreasonableness, value of, 132
Us-versus-them mentality, 74
victim triangle and, 102–105

Victim mentality, 96–105
bases of, 97–100
language igniting, 101–102
resignation and, 96
silos and divisiveness and, 102–105
Victim role, 97–98
Vision of future, leaving people with,
137, 139

Withholding emotional commitment
as blind spot, 52–53
World-class organizations, characteristics
of, 9–10